Praise for

THE KOREAN WAR

"Mr. Cumings's book is a squirm-inducing assault on America's moral behavior during the Korean War.... He mows down a host of myths.... His book is a bitter pill, a sobering corrective."   —*The New York Times*

"With a directness that's disarming for the field—which is riddled with writers who approach their subjects in slow and circling accretion of detail—Cumings wastes no time limning many long-ignored facts and striking down sheaves of clichés and shibboleths of received learning about this "forgotten" war. It's an insurrectionary work of history that leaves few preconceptions intact."   —*PopMatters*

"Cumings has done a lot of research over the years, has a superb grasp of his material and is never less than stimulating."   —*The New York Times Book Review*

"Well-sourced [and] elegantly presented. Mr. Cumings invokes Nietzsche, Brecht and Sophocles in thoughtful riffs on human memory and the 'need to forget.'"   —*The Wall Street Journal*

"A career study of this pivotal twentieth-century episode."   —Associated Press

"Cumings has written a powerful book which serves to refute many historical myths and distortions in the United States about the Korean War."   —History News Network

MODERN LIBRARY CHRONICLES

Currently Available

KAREN ARMSTRONG on Islam

DAVID BERLINSKI on mathematics

RICHARD BESSEL on Nazi Germany

TIM BLANNING on Romanticism

IAN BURUMA on modern Japan

PATRICK COLLINSON on the Reformation

BRUCE CUMINGS on the Korean War

FELIPE FERNÁNDEZ-ARMESTO on the Americas

LAWRENCE M. FRIEDMAN on law in America

PAUL FUSSELL on World War II in Europe

F. GONZÁLEZ-CRUSSI on the history of medicine

PETER GREEN on the Hellenistic Age

ALISTAIR HORNE on the age of Napoleon

PAUL JOHNSON on the Renaissance

FRANK KERMODE on the age of Shakespeare

JOEL KOTKIN on the city

STEPHEN KOTKIN on the fall of Communism

HANS KÜNG on the Catholic Church

MARK KURLANSKY on nonviolence

EDWARD J. LARSON on the theory of evolution

MARGARET MACMILLAN on the uses and abuses of history

MARTIN MARTY on the history of Christianity

MARK MAZOWER on the Balkans

JOHN MICKLETHWAIT AND ADRIAN WOOLDRIDGE on the company

ANTHONY PAGDEN on peoples and empires

RICHARD PIPES on Communism

COLIN RENFREW on prehistory

KEVIN STARR on California

MICHAEL STÜRMER on the German Empire

GEORGE VECSEY on baseball

MILTON VIORST on the Middle East

A. N. WILSON on London

ROBERT S. WISTRICH on the Holocaust

GORDON S. WOOD on the American Revolution

Forthcoming

ALAN BRINKLEY on the Great Depression

JASON GOODWIN on the Ottoman Empire

BERNARD LEWIS on the Holy Land

ORVILLE SCHELL on modern China

ALSO BY BRUCE CUMINGS

The Origins of the Korean War, Volume I:
Liberation and the Emergence of Separate Regimes, 1945–1947

The Origins of the Korean War, Volume II:
The Roaring of the Cataract, 1947–1950

Korea's Place in the Sun: A Modern History

Parallax Visions: Making Sense of American–East Asian Relations

Dominion from Sea to Sea: Pacific Ascendancy and American Power

THE KOREAN WAR

BRUCE CUMINGS

THE KOREAN WAR

A HISTORY

A MODERN LIBRARY CHRONICLES BOOK
THE MODERN LIBRARY
NEW YORK

2011 Modern Library Paperback Edition

Published in the United States by Modern Library, an imprint of The Random House
Publishing Group, a division of Random House, Inc., New York.

MODERN LIBRARY and the TORCHBEARER Design are registered trademarks of
Random House, Inc.

Originally published in hardcover in the United States by Modern Library,
an imprint of The Random House Publishing Group, a division of
Random House, Inc., in 2010.

LIBRARY OF CONGRESS CATALOGING-IN-PUBLICATION DATA

Cumings, Bruce
The Korean War/Bruce Cumings.
p. cm.—(A modern library chronicles book)
Includes bibliographical references and index.
ISBN 978-0-8129-7896-4
1. Korean War, 1950–1953. 2. Korean War, 1950–1953—United States.
3. Korean War, 1950–1953—Social aspects—United States. I. Title.
DS918.C75 2010   951.904'2—dc22   2010005629

Printed in the United States of America

www.modernlibrary.com

4   6   8   9   7   5

DEDICATED TO PRESIDENT KIM DAE JUNG
(1925–2009):

dissident, politician, statesman, conciliator, peacemaker

CONTENTS

CHRONOLOGY

1904–1905   Japan wins Russo-Japanese War; Korea becomes a Japanese protectorate.

1910   Japan annexes Korea as its colony and abolishes the Choson dynasty.

1919   Independence movement against Japanese rule begins on March 1, and after many months of nationwide protest is crushed.

1932   Japanese establish the puppet state of Manchukuo on March 1, comprising three northeastern provinces of China.

1937   Japan provokes Sino-Japanese War.

1941   Japan attacks the United States at Pearl Harbor.

1945   Korea liberated following the surrender of Japanese forces to the Allies.

1945–1948   U.S. Army Military Government in Korea.

1948   Republic of Korea and Democratic People's Republic of Korea established.

1950–1953   Korean War.

1961   General Park Chung Hee leads the first military coup.

1980   General Chun Doo Hwan crushes the Kwangju rebellion and leads the second military coup.

1987   Nationwide protests force the military dictatorship to hold presidential elections.

1992   Kim Young Sam elected president and ushers in a more democratic political era.

1994   Kim Il Sung dies and his son, Kim Jong Il, becomes top leader in the North.

1997   Kim Dae Jung becomes the first member of the opposition to win the presidency in the South.

2000   First summit between Korean heads of state held in Pyongyang; Kim Dae Jung awarded the Nobel Peace Prize.

2002   Roh Moo Hyun elected.

2007   Lee Myung Bak elected.

GLOSSARY

AMG	U.S. Army Military Government
CIC	Counter-Intelligence Corps (American)
DPRK	Democratic People's Republic of Korea (North)
G-2	U.S. Military Intelligence
JCS	Joint Chiefs of Staff (American)
KCIA	Korean Central Intelligence Agency
KMAG	Korean Military Advisory Group (American)
KNP	Korean National Police (South)
KPA	Korean People's Army (North)
KTRC	Korean Truth and Reconciliation Commission (South)
KWP	Korean Workers' Party (North)
NSC	National Security Council
NWY	Northwest Youth Corps (South)
OSS	Office of Strategic Services
PLA	People's Liberation Army (China)
PRC	People's Republic of China
RAF	Royal Air Force (British)
ROK	Republic of Korea (South)

ROKA   Republic of Korea Army

SCAP   Supreme Command, Allied Powers

SKWP   South Korean Workers' Party

UNC   United Nations Command (1950–present)

UNCOK   UN Commission on Korea

UNCURK   UN Commission on the Unification and Reconstruction of Korea

USAF   U.S. Air Force

USAMGIK   U.S. Army Military Government in Korea (1945–48)

INTRODUCTION

This is a book about the Korean War, written for Americans and by an American about a conflict that is fundamentally Korean, but one construed in the United States to have been a discrete, encapsulated story beginning in June 1950 and ending in July 1953, in which Americans are the major actors. They intervene on the side of the good, they appear to win quickly only to lose suddenly, finally they eke out a stalemated ending that was prelude to a forgetting. Forgotten, never known, abandoned: Americans sought to grab hold of this war and win it, only to see victory slip from their hands and the war sink into oblivion. A primary reason is that they never knew their enemy—and they still don't. So this is also a book seeking to uncover truths that most Americans do not know and perhaps don't want to know, truths sometimes as shocking as they are unpalatable to American self-esteem. But today they have become commonplace knowledge in a democratized and historically aware South Korea.

The year 2010 marks the sixtieth anniversary of the Korean War's conventional start, but also the centennial of Japan's colonization of Korea. This war had its distant gestation in that imperial history, and especially in northeast China (or Manchuria as it was called) at the dawn of Japan's aggression in 1931. Japan's ambitions to colonize

Korea coincided with Japan's rise as the first modern great power in Asia. Seizing on a major peasant rebellion in Korea, Japan instigated war with China in 1894 and defeated it a year later. After another decade of imperial rivalry over Korea, Japan smashed tsarist Russia in lightning naval and land attacks, stunning the world because a "yellow" country had defeated a "white" power. Korea became a Japanese protectorate in 1905 and a colony in 1910, with the blessing of all the great powers and especially the United States (President Theodore Roosevelt admired the skills and "virility" of Japan's leaders, and thought they would lead Korea into modernity.)

It was a strange colony, coming "late" in world time, after most of the world had been divided up and after progressive calls had emerged to dismantle the entire colonial system. Furthermore, Korea had most of the prerequisites for nationhood long before most other countries: common ethnicity, language, and culture, and well-recognized national boundaries since the tenth century. So the Japanese engaged in substitutions after 1910: exchanging a Japanese ruling elite for aristocratic Korean scholar-officials, most of whom were either co-opted or dismissed; instituting a strong central state in place of the old government administration; exchanging Japanese modern education for the Confucian classics; eventually they even replaced the Korean language with Japanese. Koreans never thanked the Japanese for these substitutions, did not credit Japan with creations, and instead saw Japan as snatching away their ancien régime, Korea's sovereignty and independence, its indigenous if incipient modernization, and above all its national dignity.

Unlike some other colonized peoples, therefore, most Koreans never saw imperial rule as anything but illegitimate and humiliating. Furthermore, the very closeness of the two nations—in geography, in common Chinese civilizational influences, indeed in levels of development until the mid-nineteenth century—made Japanese dominance all the more galling to Koreans, and gave a peculiar intensity to the relationship, a hate/respect dynamic that suggested to Koreans, "there but for accidents of history go we."

The result: neither Korea nor Japan has ever gotten over it. In North Korea countless films and TV dramas still focus on atrocities committed by the Japanese during their rule, propaganda banners exhort people to "live like the anti-Japanese guerrillas," and for decades the descendants of Koreans deemed by the government to have collaborated with the Japanese were subject to severe discrimination. South Korea, however, punished very few collaborators, partly because the U.S. occupation (1945–48) reemployed so many of them, and partly because they were needed in the fight against communism.

The Korean conflict thus inherited a Japanese-Korean enmity that broke into a decade of warfare in Manchuria in the 1930s, and in that sense is almost eighty years old—and no one can say when it will finally end. The grandsons of the aggressors and the victims in the Pacific War retain power in Tokyo and Pyongyang and have never reconciled. If the conventionally defined Korean War is obscure to most Americans, this older clash is even more murky, played out in a distant and alien realm, one apparently marginal to the main contours of World War II. Our old enemy in Pyongyang, meanwhile, grabbed hold of this eighty years' war as they see it and perceive it, held on with white knuckles, and have never let go; they structured their entire society as a fighting machine determined, sooner or later, to win a victory that was palpable for a moment in 1950 but has exceeded their grasp ever since.

So this book is about a forgotten or never-known war and therefore, ipso facto, is also about history and memory. Its major themes are the Korean origins of the war, the cultural contradictions of the early 1950s in America, which buried this conflict almost before it could be known, the harrowing brutality in the air and on the ground of a supposedly limited war, the recovery of this history in South Korea, and the way in which this unknown war transformed the American position in the world—and history and memory.

The basic military history of the 1950–53 phase of this war can be presented quickly, because the conflict divides neatly into three parts: the war for the South in the summer of 1950, the war for the North in the fall and winter of 1950, and China's intervention, which soon brought about a stabilization of the fighting along what is now the demilitarized zone, or DMZ, even though a form of trench warfare went on for another two years. If there is anything that has been well covered in the American literature, it is this military history—including volumes of official history from Roy Appleman, Clay Blair's excellent *The Forgotten War*, and many other books. There are also various oral histories and memoirs that give insight into American servicemen in a war and a land that most of them thought to be godforsaken.

Least known to Americans is how appallingly dirty this war was, with a sordid history of civilian slaughters amid which our ostensibly democratic ally was the worst offender, contrary to the American image of the North Koreans as fiendish terrorists. The British author Max Hastings wrote that Communist atrocities gave to the United Nations cause in Korea "a moral legitimacy that has survived to this day."[1] What then of South Korean atrocities, which historians now know were far more common? Ironically, this disturbing experience was featured in popular magazines of the time such as *Life*, *The Saturday Evening Post*, and *Collier's*, before MacArthur's censorship descended. Then it was suppressed, buried and forgotten for half a century; still today, even to talk about it thus seems biased and unbalanced. Yet by now it is one of the best-documented aspects of the war.

I have written much about the Korean War in the past, and this book both distills that knowledge for the general reader and invokes new themes, ideas, and issues. I wish I could write with the serene confidence that other historians do in similarly short books, offering their settled interpretations unencumbered by footnotes and sources. So many things about this war are still so controversial, however, vehemently debated and hotly affirmed or denied (or simply unknown), and my head is so drilled with obligations owed to fellow scholars, that I have added unobtrusive endnotes that cite important documents or make quick reference to books in the bibliography. (If I name an author of one of these books in the text, I dispense with notes.) Those books, in turn, offer a wealth of insight and argument for readers who want to learn more about the unknown war. For the ever-dwindling number of American veterans of this war, I offer salutations for shouldering a thankless task and fervent hope that this war will soon come to an end, so that they can again encounter their North Korean counterparts before it is too late—this time in peace, to share indelible memories and rediscover each other's humanity.

Another comment about the evidentiary basis of this book: How do we evaluate sources? If formerly secret American documents reveal that South Korean jails held tens of thousands of political prisoners, or that the police worked hand in glove with fascist youth groups, or that these same forces massacred their own citizens on mere suspicion of leftist tendencies, this is crucial evidence because one assumes that Americans on the scene would prefer not to report these things about their close ally. If during decades of military dictatorships no one dares speak of mass political murders, and then after an equally long struggle from below to oust these dictators, a new generation growing up in a democracy carries out careful, painstaking investigations of these murders, that evidence is far more important than government statements to the effect that none of it happened, or if it happened, no orders from higher-ups could be located (unfortunately this has been the Pentagon's typical response to recent South Korean revelations). If historical evidence from the time contradicts the contemporary image of North Korea as the most reprehensible and intolerable dictatorship on the planet, perhaps that can help Americans understand why no military victory was possible in Korea.

All Asian names except those of famous people (like Syngman Rhee) are given last name first; for widely known individuals or for those who have published in the West, I use the name as they write it (for example Kim Dae Jung, or Dae-sook Suh).

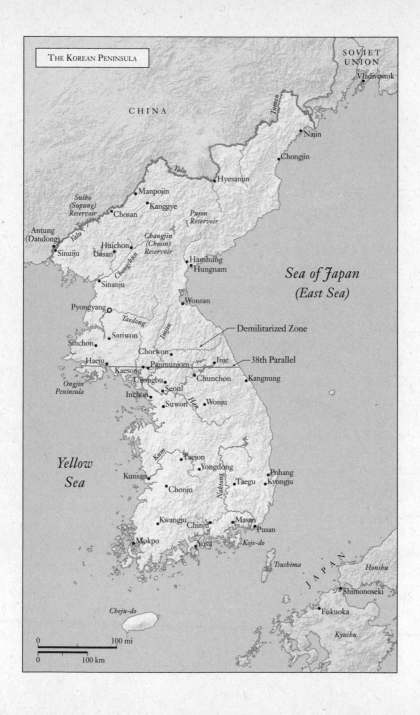

THE KOREAN PENINSULA

SOVIET UNION

Vladivostok

CHINA

Tumen

Najin

Chongjin

Yalu

Hyesanjin

Manpojin

Suibo (Supung) Reservoir

Kanggye

Chosan

Pujon Reservoir

Antung (Dandong)

Yalu

Huichon

Unsan

Changjin (Chosin) Reservoir

Sinuiju

Chongchon

Hamhung

Hungnam

Sinanju

Pyongyang

Wonsan

Taedong

Sariwon

Sinchon

Imjin

Chorwon

Demilitarized Zone

Haeju

Kaesong

Panmunjom

Inje

38th Parallel

Ongjin Peninsula

Uijongbu

Chunchon

Kangnung

Inchon

Seoul

Suwon

Han

Wonju

Yellow Sea

Sea of Japan (East Sea)

Kum

Taejon

Yongdong

Pohang

Kunsan

Chonju

Taegu

Kyongju

Naktong

Kwangju

Chinju

Masan

Mokpo

Yosu

Pusan

Koje-do

Tsushima

Honshu

JAPAN

Shimonoseki

Cheju-do

Fukuoka

Kyushu

0   100 mi

0   100 km

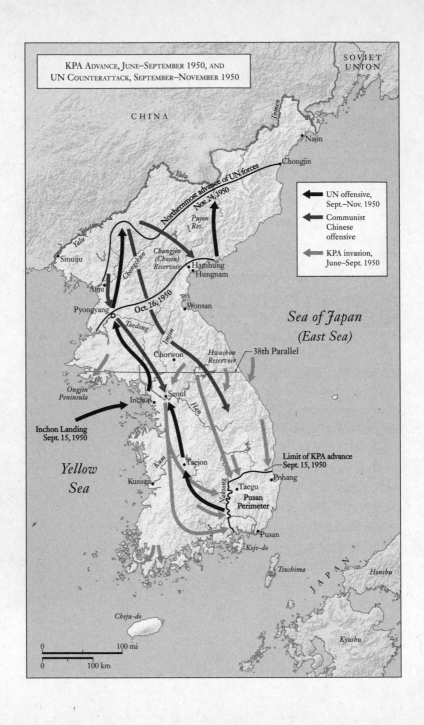

KPA Advance, June–September 1950, and
UN Counterattack, September–November 1950

SOVIET UNION

CHINA

Najin

Chongjin

Yalu

Northernmost advance of UN forces
Nov. 24, 1950

Pujon Res.

Yalu

Sinuiju

Changjun (Chosn) Reservoir

Hamhung
Hungnam

Anju

Chongjun

Pyongyang

Oct. 26, 1950

Wonsan

Taedong

Imjin

Sea of Japan
(East Sea)

Chorwon

Hwachon Reservoir

38th Parallel

Ongjin Peninsula

Seoul

Inchon

Han

Inchon Landing
Sept. 15, 1950

Yellow
Sea

Kum

Taejon

Kunsan

Limit of KPA advance
Sept. 15, 1950

Pohang

Taegu

Naktong

Pusan Perimeter

Pusan

Koje-do

Tsushima

JAPAN

Honshu

Cheju-do

Kyushu

UN offensive,
Sept.–Nov. 1950

Communist
Chinese
offensive

KPA invasion,
June–Sept. 1950

0   100 mi

0   100 km

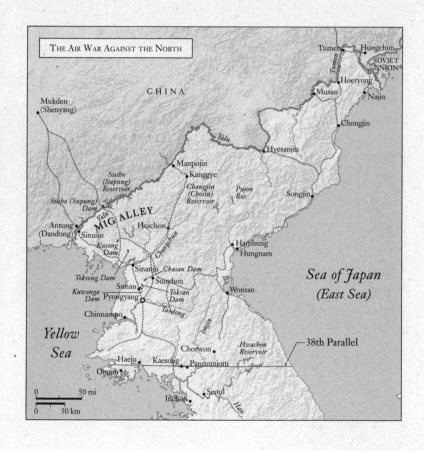

THE AIR WAR AGAINST THE NORTH

Tumen
Hungchun
SOVIET
UNION
Hoeryong
Najin
Musan
CHINA
Chongjin
Mukden
(Shenyang)
Yalu
Hyesanjin
Manpojin
Kanggye
Suiho
(Supung)
Reservoir
Changjin
(Chosin)
Reservoir
Pujon
Res.
Songjin
Suiho (Supung)
Dam
Yalu
MIG ALLEY
Antung
(Dandong)
Sinuiju
Huichon
Kusong
Dam
Hamhung
Hungnam
Chongchon
Toksong Dam
Sinanju
Chasan Dam
Kuwonga
Dam
Sunan
Sunchon
Toksan
Dam
Wonsan
Pyongyang
Chinnampo
Taedong
Yellow
Sea
Imjin
Chorwon
Hwachon
Reservoir
38th Parallel

Sea of Japan
(East Sea)

Haeju
Kaesong
Panmunjom
Ongjin
0   50 mi
Inchon
Seoul
0   50 km
Han

CHAPTER ONE

THE COURSE
OF THE WAR

On the very day that President Barack Obama fielded a student's question in Moscow about whether a new Korean War was in the offing (July 7, 2009), the papers were filled with commentary on the death of Robert Strange McNamara. The editors of *The New York Times* and one of its best columnists, Bob Herbert, condemned McNamara for knowing the Vietnam War was unwinnable yet sending tens of thousands of young Americans to their deaths anyway: "How in God's name did he ever look at himself in the mirror?" Herbert wrote. They all assumed that the war itself was a colossal error. But if McNamara had been able to stabilize South Vietnam and divide the country permanently (say with his "electronic fence"), thousands of our troops would still be there along a DMZ and evil would still reside in Hanoi. McNamara also had a minor planning role in the firebombing of Japanese cities in World War II: "What makes it immoral if you lose and not immoral if you win?" he asked; people like himself and Curtis LeMay, the commander of the air attacks, "were behaving as war criminals." McNamara derived these lessons from losing the Vietnam War: we did not know the enemy, we lacked "empathy" (we should have "put ourselves inside their skin and look[ed] at us through their eyes," but we did not); we were blind prisoners of our own assumptions.[1] In Korea we still are.

Korea is an ancient nation, and one of the very few places in the world where territorial boundaries, ethnicity, and language have been consistent for well over a millennium. It sits next to China and was deeply influenced by the Middle Kingdom, but it has always had an independent civilization. Few understand this, but the most observant journalist in the war, Reginald Thompson, put the point exactly: "the thought and law of China is woven into the very texture of Korea ... as the law of Rome is woven into Britain." The distinction is between the stereotypical judgment that Korea is just "Little China," or nothing more than a transmission belt for Buddhist and Confucian culture flowing into Japan, and a nation and culture as different from Japan or China as Italy or France is from Germany.

Korea also had a social structure that persisted for centuries: during the five hundred years of the last dynasty the vast majority of Koreans were peasants, most of them tenants working land held by one of the world's most tenacious aristocracies. Many were also slaves, a hereditary status from generation to generation. The state squelched merchant activity, so that commerce, and anything resembling the green shoots of a middle class, barely developed. This fundamental condition—a privileged landed class, a mass of peasants, and little leavening in between—lasted through twentieth-century colonialism, too, because after their rule began in 1910 the Japanese found it useful to operate through local landed power. So, amid the crisis of national division, upheaval, and war, Koreans also sought to rectify these ancient inequities. But this aristocracy, known as *yangban,* did not last so long and survive one crisis after another by being purely exploitative; it fostered a scholar-official elite, a civil service, venerable statecraft, splendid works of art, and a national pastime of educating the young. In the relative openness of the 1920s, young scions proliferated in one profession after another—commerce, industry, publishing, academia, films, literary pursuits, urban consumption—a budding elite that could readily have led an independent Korea.[2] But global depression, war, and ever-increasing Japanese repression in the 1930s destroyed much of this progress, turned many elite Koreans into collaborators, and left few options for patriots besides armed resistance.

Korea was at its modern nadir during the war, yet this is where most of the millions of Americans who served in Korea got their impressions—ones that often depended on where the eye chose to fall. Foreigners and GIs saw dirt and mud and squalor, but Thompson saw villages "of pure enchantment, the tiles of the roofs upcurled at eaves and corners...the women [in] bright colours, crimson and the pale pink of watermelon flesh, and vivid emerald green, their bodies wrapped tightly to give them a tubular appearance." Reginald Thompson had been all over the world; most GIs had never been out of their country, or perhaps their hometowns. What his vantage point in 1950 told him, in effect, was this: here was the Vietnam War we came to know before Vietnam—gooks, napalm, rapes, whores, an unreliable ally, a cunning enemy, fundamentally untrained GIs fighting a war their top generals barely understood, fragging of officers,[3] contempt for the know-nothing civilians back home, devilish battles indescribable even to loved ones, press handouts from Gen. Douglas MacArthur's headquarters apparently scripted by comedians or lunatics, an ostensible vision of bringing freedom and liberty to a sordid dictatorship run by servants of Japanese imperialism. "What a Quixotic business," Thompson wrote, trying to impose democracy—to try to achieve "an evolutionary result without evolution." The only outcome of fending off the North, he thought, would be a long occupation if not "conquest and colonization."

THE CONVENTIONAL WAR BEGINS

The war Americans know began on the remote, inaccessible Ongjin Peninsula, northwest of Seoul, on the night of June 24–25, 1950, Korean time; this was also the point at which border fighting began in May 1949, and the absence of independent observers has meant that both Korean sides have claimed ever since that they were attacked first. During the long, hot summer of 1949, one pregnant with impending conflict, the ROK had expanded its army to about 100,000 troops, a strength the North did not match until early 1950. American order-of-battle data showed the two armies at about equal strength by June 1950. Early that month, MacArthur's intelligence apparatus identified a total of 74,370 Korean People's Army (KPA) soldiers, with another 20,000 or so in the Border Constabulary. The Republic of Korea Army (ROKA) order of battle showed a total of 87,500 soldiers, with 32,500 soldiers at the border, 35,000 within thirty-five miles, or a day's march, of the 38th parallel. This data did not account for the superior battle experience of the northern army, however, especially among the large contingents that had returned from the Chinese civil war. The North also had about 150 Soviet T-34 tanks and a small but useful air force of 70 fighters and 62 light bombers—either left behind when Soviet troops evacuated in December 1948, or purchased from Moscow and Beijing in 1949–50 (when war bond drives ensued for months in the North). Only about 20,000 South Korean troops remained in the more distant interior. This was the result of a significant redeployment northward toward the parallel in the early months of 1950, after the southern guerrillas appeared to have been crushed. The northern army had also redeployed southward in May and June 1950, but many KPA units—at least one third—were not aware of the impending invasion and thus were not mobilized to fight on June 25. Furthermore, thousands of Korean troops were still fighting in China at this time.

Just one week before the invasion John Foster Dulles visited Seoul and the 38th parallel. By then he was a roving ambassador and, as the odds-on Republican choice for secretary of state, a symbol of Harry Truman's attempt at bipartisanship after Republicans opened up on him with the "who lost China?" campaign. In meetings with Syngman Rhee the latter not only pushed for a direct American defense of the ROK, but advocated an attack on the North. One of Dulles's favorite reporters, William Mathews, was there and wrote just after Dulles's meeting that Rhee was "militantly for the unification of Korea. Openly says it must be brought about soon…Rhee pleads justice of going into North country. Thinks it could succeed in a few days…if he can do it with our

John Foster Dulles peering across the 38th parallel, June 19, 1950. To his left, in the pith helmet, is Defense Minister Shin Sung-mo; behind him, in the porkpie hat, is Foreign Minister Ben Limb. *U.S. National Archives*

help, he will do it." Mathews noted that Rhee said he would attack even if "it brought on a general war." All this is yet more proof of Rhee's provocative behavior, but it is no different from his threats to march north made many times before. The Dulles visit was merely vintage Rhee: there is no evidence that Dulles was in collusion with him.[4] But what might the North Koreans have thought?

That is the question a historian put to Dean Acheson, Truman's secretary of state, in a seminar after the Korean War: "Are you sure his presence didn't provoke the attack, Dean? There has been comment about that—I don't think it did. You have no views on the subject?" Acheson's deadpan response: "No, I have no views on the subject." George Kennan then interjected, "There is a comical aspect to this, because the visits of these people over there, and their peering over outposts with binoculars at the Soviet people, I think must have led the Soviets to think that we were on to their plan and caused them considerable perturbation."

"Yes," Acheson said. "Foster up in a bunker with a homburg on— it was a very amusing picture."[5] Pyongyang has never tired of waving that photo around.

At the same time, the veteran industrialist Pak Hung-sik showed up in Tokyo and gave an interview to *The Oriental Economist*, published on June 24, 1950—the day before the war started. Described as an adviser to the Korean Economic Mission (that is, the Marshall Plan), he was also said to have "a circle of friends and acquaintances among the Japanese" (a bit of an understatement; Pak was widely thought in South and North to have been the most notorious collaborator with Japanese imperialism). In the years after liberation in 1945 a lot of anti-Japanese feeling had welled up in Korea, Pak said, owing to the return of "numerous revolutionists and nationalists." By 1950, however, there was "hardly any trace of it." Instead, the ROK was "acting as a bulwark of peace" at the 38th parallel, and "the central figures in charge of national defense are mostly graduates of the former Military College of Japan." Korea and Japan were "destined to go hand in hand, to live and let live," and thus bad feelings should be "cast overboard."

The current problem, Pak said, was the unfortunate one that "an economic unity is lacking whereas in prewar days Japan, Manchuria, Korea, and Formosa economically combined to make an organic whole." Pak Hung-sik was the embodiment of the Japanese colonial idea—having been born a Korean his only unfortunate, but not insurmountable, fate. For Pak and Kim Il Sung, the 1930s were *the beginning:* hugely expanded business opportunities for Pak (the founder of Seoul's Hwashin department store, its first on the American model), a decade of unimaginably harsh struggle for Kim. After this beginning, a civil war between the young leaders of Korea who chose to collaborate with or to resist Japan in the 1930s was entirely conceivable, and probably inevitable.

War came on the last weekend in June 1950, a weekend about

which much still remains to be learned. It is now clear from Soviet documents that Pyongyang had made a decision to escalate the civil conflict to the level of conventional warfare many months before June 1950, having tired of the inconclusive guerrilla struggle in the south, and perhaps hoping to seize on a southern provocation like many that occurred in 1949, thus to settle the hash of the Rhee regime. Maturing clandestine American plans to launch a coup d'état against Chiang Kai-shek on Taiwan complicated this same weekend; Dean Rusk met with several Chinese at the Plaza hotel in New York on the evening of June 23, 1950, hoping that they would form a government to replace Chiang's regime, which was threatened by an impending invasion from the Chinese Communists. He and Acheson wanted a reliable leader in Taipei, so that their secret desire to keep the island separate from mainland control would field a government that Truman could justify supporting.[6]

The fighting on Ongjin began around 3 or 4 A.M. on June 25; initial intelligence reports were inconclusive as to who started it. Later on, attacking elements were said to be from the 3rd Brigade of the Democratic People's Republic of Korea (DPRK) Border Constabulary, joined at 5:30 A.M. by the formidable 6th Division. At about the same time, according to the American official history, KPA forces at the parallel south of Chorwon assaulted the 1st Regiment of the ROKA 7th Division, dealing it heavy casualties; it gave way and the 3rd and 4th KPA divisions, with an armored brigade, crashed through and began a daunting march toward Seoul. South Korean sources asserted, however, that elements of the 17th Regiment had counterattacked on the Ongjin Peninsula and were in possession of Haeju city, the only important point north of the 38th parallel claimed to have been taken by ROK forces.

Roy Appleman, America's official historian of the war, relied on James Hausman's heavily sanitized account of the war's start on the Ongjin Peninsula. Hausman later told a Thames Television documentary crew that his good friend Paek In-yop (brother to Paek Son-yop) was the commander on Ongjin, "and when the war broke

out as you know he was there not only defending his line but coun-
terattacking" (that is, across the parallel). As for "those who think
that the South may have started this war," Hausman went on, "I
think...I think they're wrong." Another Thames interviewee, Col.
James Peach, an Australian who was with the UN observer group,
reported that the Ongjin commander, Paek, was "a get-going sort of
chap" who led the "twin-tiger" 17th Regimental Combat Team: "I,
I never quite knew what went on. There's a bit of a mystery still
about Haeju, I think it might have been Paek and his merry men,
the 17th Regiment, attacking it...We didn't hear anything about it
until the war had been going for a while, and I never quite knew
what went on. It's been said that they attacked there and that the
North Koreans responded." Peach went on to say that he didn't
think this version held much water. (Note also that if the South Koreans attack, it is "Paek and his merry men"; when the North Koreans do the same, it is heinous aggression.)[7]

Whether 17th Regiment soldiers may have occupied Haeju on
June 25, or even initiated the fighting on Ongjin, is still inconclusive, with the existing evidence pointing both ways. There is no evidence, however, to back up the North's claim that the South
launched a general invasion; at worst there may have been a small
assault across the parallel, as happened many times in 1949. Whatever transpired, the North met it with a full invasion.

South of the attacking KPA units was the ROK 7th Division,
headquartered at the critical invasion-route town of Uijongbu; it
had not committed its forces to battle even by the morning of June
26, probably because it was waiting to be reinforced by the 2nd Division, which had entrained northward from Taejon. When the 2nd
Division arrived later that day, it collapsed and the troops panicked.
It was through this gaping hole in the Uijongbu corridor that North
Korean troops poured on the afternoon and evening of June 26, thus
jeopardizing the capital. An American official on the scene later
wrote that "the failure of the 2nd Division to fight" was the main
reason for the quick loss of Seoul. South Korean units mutinied or

fled before the oncoming Northern troops for many reasons, including their relative lack of firepower, their poor training, their officers who had served Japan, and ultimately the unpopularity of the Rhee government—which had nearly been voted out by a moderate coalition in reasonably free elections held on May 30, 1950.

President Rhee tried to leave the city with his top officials as early as Sunday evening, and on June 27 the entire ROK Army headquarters relocated south of Seoul, without telling their American allies. That left troops engaging the enemy north of Seoul without communications, and panicked both the troops and the civilian population. The next day most ROK divisions followed suit, withdrawing to the south of the capital, and Gen. "Fatty" Chae famously and egregiously blew the major Han River bridge without warning, killing hundreds who were crossing it. Later that day President Rhee took off southward in his special train. During the battle for Taejon he vowed to stay there and fight to the death, but soon he was back on his train, headed for the southwestern port of Mokpo, thence by naval launch to Pusan, where he would remain inside the defensive perimeter.[8] Military morale evaporated and civilians panicked. Seoul fell to a Northern invasion force of about 37,000 troops. By month's end fully half of the ROKA soldiers were dead, captured, or missing. Only two divisions had their equipment and weapons, all the rest (about 70 percent of the total) having been left in place or lost on the battlefield.

The quick and virtually complete collapse of resistance in the South energized the United States to enter the war in force. Secretary of State Dean Acheson dominated the decision making, which soon committed American air and ground forces to the fight. On the night of June 24 (Washington time), Acheson decided to take the Korean question to the UN, before he had notified President Truman of the fighting; he then told Truman there was no need to have him back in Washington until the next day. At emergency White House meetings on the evening of June 25, Acheson argued for increased military aid to the ROK, U.S. Air Force cover for the evacuation of Americans, and the interposition of the Seventh Fleet between Taiwan and the China mainland—thus obviating a Communist invasion of the island, dividing China and leaving Taiwan governed by the Republic of China even today. On the afternoon of June 26 Acheson labored alone on the fundamental decisions committing American air and naval power to the Korean War, which were approved by the White House that evening.

Thus the decision to intervene in force was Acheson's decision, supported by the president but taken before United Nations, Pentagon, or congressional approval. His reasoning had little to do with Korea's strategic value, and everything to do with American prestige and political economy: "prestige is the shadow cast by power," he once said, and the North Koreans had challenged it; American credibility was therefore at stake. South Korea was also essential to Japan's industrial revival, Acheson thought, as part of his "great crescent" strategy linking northeast Asia with the Middle East (and which we discuss later on).

George Kennan, who supported the June decisions, recalled from notes taken at the time that Acheson broke off collegial discussions on the afternoon of June 26:

> He wanted time to be alone and to dictate. We were called in [three hours later] and he read to us a paper he had produced, which was the first draft of the statement finally issued by the President, and which was not significantly changed by the time it finally appeared, the following day ... the course actually taken by this Government was not something pressed upon [Acheson] by the military leaders, but rather something arrived at by himself, in solitary deliberation.

Acheson later concurred with Kennan, saying, "that's as I recall it." Kennan noted that the decisions of June 26 were the key ones; Acheson agreed that they were taken before congressional or UN consultations ("it wasn't until 3:00 in the afternoon [on June 27] that the U.N. asked us to do what we said we were going to ... in the morning").[9]

On this same summer Saturday evening the Soviet ambassador to the UN, Adam Malik, was taking his ease on Long Island rather than wielding his much used and abused veto on the Security Council, a boycott conducted ostensibly because the UN had refused to admit China. He was planning to return to Moscow for consultations on July 6.[10] The longtime Soviet foreign minister, Andrei Gromyko, later told Dean Rusk that on Saturday night Malik instantly wired Moscow for instructions, and for the first time ever in its experience got back a message direct from Generalissimo Stalin: *nyet*, do not attend.[11] Stalin's reasons are not known, but he may have hoped to facilitate the entry of U.S. forces into a peripheral area, thus to waste blood and treasure, or perhaps he hoped that American dominance of the UN would destroy the perceived universality of the international body.

Acheson's June 25–26 decisions prefigured the commitment of American ground forces, which came in the early hours of June 30. The Joint Chiefs of Staff remained "extremely reluctant" to commit infantry troops to the fighting right up to June 30, and were not consulted when Truman made his decision. They were reticent both because Korea was a strategic cul-de-sac and perhaps a trap in the global struggle with Moscow, and because the total armed strength of the U.S. Army was 593,167, with an additional 75,370 in the Marines. North Korea alone was capable of mobilizing upward of 200,000 combat soldiers in the summer of 1950, quite apart from the immense manpower reserve of China's People's Liberation Army (PLA).

The immediate precipitating factor for the decision to dispatch U.S. ground forces was MacArthur's conclusion, after visiting the front lines, that the ROK Army had mostly ceased to fight. From the start of the war and throughout the summer and fall of 1950, Korean units ceased to exist, lacked equipment to fight the North

Koreans, or proved unable to hold the lines in their sectors. Most veterans of the first two years of the war thought South Koreans "did no fighting worthy of the name," they just broke and ran. (By the summer of 1951 the ROKA had lost enough matériel to outfit ten divisions, according to Gen. Matthew B. Ridgway, and still needed "thorough training and equipment and instruction on all levels.") An American colonel told the British journalist Philip Knightly, "South Koreans and North Koreans are identical. Why then do North Koreans fight like tigers and South Koreans run like sheep?" The Morse code "HA" was used all over the front to signal that South Korean forces were "hauling ass." ROKA officers exploited their own men, and beat them mercilessly for infractions. One GI observed an officer execute a man for going AWOL, shooting him in the back of the head and kicking him into a grave. The man had a wife and three children. But racism also infected GI views of their Korean enemy and ally. Most Americans, a veteran remembered, "had an ingrained prejudice against Koreans" that made any kind of empathy or understanding difficult. "They hated Koreans by reflex action." It was only after truce talks began in 1951 that the ROKA had the time to develop, however slowly, its fighting temper.[12]

But the Americans also had no idea that they would be fighting against truly effective troops, a disastrous misjudgment of the Korean enemy that began right at the top, on the day the war began. "I can handle it with one arm tied behind my back," MacArthur said; the next day he remarked to John Foster Dulles that if he could only put the 1st Cavalry Division into Korea, "why, heavens, you'd see these fellows scuttle up to the Manchurian border so quick, you would see no more of them." At first MacArthur wanted an American regimental combat team, then two divisions. Within a week, however, he cabled Washington that only a quarter of the ROKA troops could even be located, and that the KPA was "operating under excellent top level guidance and had demonstrated superior command of strategic and tactical principles." By the beginning of July he wanted a minimum of 30,000 American combat soldiers, meaning more than four infantry divisions, three tank battalions, and assorted artillery; a week later he asked for eight divisions.[13]

Misjudgments also grew out of the ubiquitous racism of whites coming from a segregated American society, where Koreans were "people of color" subjected to apartheid-like restrictions (they drank from "colored" fountains in Virginia, could not marry Caucasians in other southern states, and could not own property in many western states). Consider the judgment of the respected military editor of *The New York Times*, Hanson Baldwin, three weeks after the war began:

> We are facing an army of barbarians in Korea, but they are barbarians as trained, as relentless, as reckless of life, and as skilled in the tactics of the kind of war they fight as the hordes of Genghis Khan.... They have taken a leaf from the Nazi book of blitzkrieg and are employing all the weapons of fear and terror.

Chinese Communists were reported to have joined the fighting, he erred in saying, and not far behind might be "Mongolians, Soviet Asiatics and a variety of races"—some of "the most primitive of peoples." Elsewhere Baldwin likened the Koreans to invading locusts; he ended by recommending that Americans be given "more realistic training to meet the barbarian discipline of the armored horde."[14]

A few days later Baldwin remarked that to the Korean, life is cheap: "behind him stand the hordes of Asia. Ahead of him lies the hope of loot." What else "brings him shrieking on," what else explains his "fanatical determination"?[15] Mongolians, Asiatics, Nazis, locusts, primitives, hordes, thieves—one would think Baldwin had exhausted his bag of bigotry to capture a people invading their homeland and defending it against the world's most powerful army. But he came up with another way to deal with "the problem of the convinced fanatic":

> In their extensive war against Russian partisans, the Germans found that the only answer to guerrillas... was "to win friends and influence people" among the civilian population. The actual pacification of the country means just that.

(A pacification, perhaps, like that in the Ukraine.)

Somewhat uncomfortable with North Korean indignation about "women and children slain by American bombs," Baldwin went on to say that Koreans must understand that "we do not come merely to bring devastation." Americans must convince "these simple, primitive, and barbaric peoples... that we—not the Communists— are their friends."[16] Now hear the chief counsel for war crimes at the Nuremberg Trials, Telford Taylor:

> The traditions and practices of warfare in the Orient are not identical with those that have developed in the Occident... individual lives are not valued so highly in Eastern mores. And it is totally unrealistic of us to expect the individual Korean soldier... to follow our most elevated precepts of warfare.[17]

In the summer months of 1950 the Korean People's Army pushed southward with dramatic success, with one humiliating defeat after another for American forces. An army that had bested Germany and Japan found its back pressed to the wall by what it thought was a hastily assembled peasant military, ill-equipped and, worse, said to be doing the bidding of a foreign imperial power. By the end of July, American and ROK forces outnumbered the KPA along the front, 92,000 to 70,000 (47,000 were Americans), but in spite of this, the retreat continued. In early August, however, the 1st Marine

Brigade went into action and finally halted the KPA advance. The front did not change much from then until the end of August. The fighting stabilized at what came to be called the Pusan Perimeter, an eighty-by-fifty-mile right-angled front. Kim Il Sung later said that the plan was to win the war for the South in one month, and by the end of July he had nearly done so.

This perimeter had its northern anchor on the coast around Pohang, its southeastern anchor in the coastal Chinju-Masan region, and its center just above the major city of Taegu. The latter became a symbol of the American determination to stanch the KPA's advance; but it was Pohang in the northeast that was probably the key to stopping the KPA from occupying Pusan and unifying the peninsula. Roy Appleman wrote that the "major tactical mistake" of the North Koreans was not to press their advantage on the northeast coastal road. The KPA 5th Division worried too much about covering its flanks, instead of moving quickly on Pohang and thence combining with the 6th Division marching from the southeast to menace Pusan.

Northern forces had paused south of the capital for nearly a week before restarting a dual-pincer, tank-led blitzkrieg to the southwest and southeast. This pause has caused some historians to wonder if the initial thrust was aimed mainly at Seoul, the nerve center of the South, hoping to hold it and watch the Rhee regime collapse; in any case the pause gave vital time to MacArthur to organize a defensive line in the southeast. This perimeter became the place where American power finally stiffened. North Korea had brought its forces along the perimeter to 98,000, and thousands of guerrillas, including many women, were active in the fighting. In August Gen. John H. Church, commander of the 24th Infantry Division and a veteran of the Anzio campaign, concluded that Korea was not like the European battles of World War II: "It's an entirely different kind of warfare, this is really guerrilla warfare." It was "essentially a guerrilla war over rugged territory," according to British sources; American troops were "constantly exposed to the threat of infiltration by guerrillas sweeping down from the hills into and behind its positions."[18]

Virtually any village suspected of harboring or supporting guerrillas was burned to the ground, usually from the air. Furthermore, cities and towns thought to be leftist in inclination were simply emptied of their population through forced evacuations. All but 10 percent of civilians were moved out of Sunchon, Masan was emptied of tens of thousands of citizens, "all civilians" were moved out of Yechon. Amid a threat that "the leftists and Fifth column, living in Taegu, are conspiring to create a big disturbance," and with the perimeter under great strain, vast numbers of Taegu citizens were evacuated for fear of "an uprising." By mid-August, many of these removed citizens were concentrated on islands near Pusan, forbidden to leave.[19]

Still, by this time the North Koreans were badly outnumbered. MacArthur had succeeded in committing most of the battle-ready divisions in the entire American armed forces to the Korean fighting; by September 8 all available combat-trained army units had been dispatched to Korea except for the 82nd Airborne Division. Although many of these units were with the impending Inchon amphibious operation, some 83,000 American soldiers and another 57,000 South Korean and British faced the North Koreans along the front. By this time the Americans had five times as many tanks as the KPA, their artillery was vastly superior, and they had complete control of the air since the early days of the war.

At the end of August North Korean forces launched their last major offensive along the perimeter, making "startling gains" over the next two weeks, which severely strained the UN lines. On August 28, Gen. Pang Ho-san ordered his troops to take Masan and Pusan in the next few days; three KPA battalions succeeded in crossing the Naktong River in the central sector, Pohang and Chinju were lost, and the perimeter was "near the breaking point" with KPA forces pressing on Kyongju, Masan, and Taegu. U.S. commanders relocated Eighth Army headquarters from Taegu to

Pusan, and prominent South Koreans began leaving Pusan for Tsushima. On September 9, Kim Il Sung said the war had reached an "extremely harsh, decisive stage," with the enemy being pressed on three fronts; two days later U.S. commanders reported that the frontline situation was the most dangerous since the perimeter had been established. "After two weeks of the heaviest fighting of the war," Appleman wrote, UN forces "had just barely turned back the great North Korean offensive." American casualties were the highest of the war to date, totaling 20,000, with 4,280 dead, by September 15.

In mid-September 1950, General MacArthur masterminded his last hurrah, a tactically brilliant amphibious landing at Inchon that brought American armed forces back to Seoul five years after they first set foot on Korean soil. Inchon Harbor has treacherous tides that can easily ground a flotilla of ships if they choose the wrong time, but the American passage through the shifting bays and flats was flawless. Adm. Arthur Dewey Struble, the navy's crack amphibious expert who led the World War II landing operations at Leyte in the Philippines and who directed the naval operations off Omaha Beach during the Normandy invasion, commanded an enormous fleet of 270 ships in the Inchon operations, depositing eighty thousand marines with hardly a loss. The marines landed mostly unopposed, but then slogged through a deadly gauntlet before Seoul finally fell at the end of September. Against this the North Koreans could do nothing; Kim Il Sung placed about two thousand poorly trained troops to defend the harbor, and for unknown reasons, failed to mine the port. They were not surprised by the invasion, as the American mythology has it, but could not resist it and so began what their historians call euphemistically "the great strategic retreat."

Regular North Korean forces continued pulling back in the face of the American decision to launch attacks across the parallel in early October, luring the enemy in deep, influencing MacArthur to split his forces into two huge columns against much contrary advice, and imploring their Chinese allies to come to their aid. Captured documents show that the North made a critical decision to fight the Americans at key points to cover a general withdrawal of their forces; a captured notebook quoted Pak Ki-song, chief of political intelligence in the KPA 8th Division:

> The main force of the enemy still remained intact, not having been fully damaged. When they were not fully aware of the power of our forces, they pushed their infantry far forward ... to the Yalu River. This indicated that they underestimated us. All these conditions were favorable to lure them near.

Another KPA officer captured at the time of the joint Sino-Korean offensive said that until late November, the KPA had been "continuously withdrawing":

> One may think that going down all the way to the Pusan perimeter and then withdrawing all the way to the Yalu River was a complete defeat. But that is not so. That was a planned withdrawal. We withdrew because we knew that UN troops would follow us up here, and that they would spread their troops thinly all over the vast area. Now, the time has come for us to envelop these troops and annihilate them.

He said that combined KPA and Chinese forces striking from the front would be aided by "eight strong corps which will harass and attack the enemy from the rear."[20] Although large numbers of foot-soldiers were captured in MacArthur's trap, most officers escaped and led large units back through the mountains and into the North. Many guerrillas also escaped into mountainous areas of the South, and became a major problem for American forces in the winter of 1950–51. (In early 1951 KPA forces had moved back as far south as

Andong and Sangju in North Kyongsang province to envelop UN troops.)

Shortly after the Inchon landing, a document was retrieved giving Kim Il Sung's epitaph on the southern fighting: "The original plan was to end the war in a month," he said, but "we could not stamp out four American divisions." The units that had captured Seoul disobeyed orders by not marching southward promptly, thereby giving "a breathing spell" to the Americans. From the beginning, "our primary enemy was the American soldiers," but he acknowledged that "we were taken by surprise when United Nations troops and the American Air Force and Navy moved in." This suggests that Kim anticipated the involvement of American ground forces (probably drawn from U.S. troops stationed in Japan), but not in such size, and not with air and naval units—a curious oversight, unless the Koreans thought that Soviet air and naval power would either deter or confront their American counterparts. It would have been hard for anyone, including the Joint Chiefs of Staff, to imagine that the vast majority of American battle-ready infantry would be transferred around the globe to this small peninsula, of seeming marginal import to U.S. global strategy.

The war for the South left 111,000 South Koreans killed, 106,000 wounded, and 57,000 missing; 314,000 homes had been destroyed, 244,000 damaged. American casualties totaled 6,954 dead, 13,659 wounded, and 3,877 missing in action. North Korean military casualties are not known with any certainty, but probably totaled at least 50,000.

"A GLUT OF CHINAMEN": THE MARCH NORTH

The American-led forces might have reestablished the 38th parallel and called the war a success for the containment doctrine. It would have been a surgically precise intervention, short but arduous, a sweet and telling defeat for the Communists and clear evidence of American credibility. No one could ever have taken this victory away from Harry Truman. But as the war proceeded during the summer, nearly all of Truman's high advisers decided that the chance had come not only to contain Communist aggression, but to roll it back. Truman approved a march north toward the end of August; the evidence is clear that the decision to invade the North was made in Washington, not in Tokyo. The historian D. Clayton James remarked that this decision "must rank in quixotism with the Bay of Pigs invasion in 1961," but he thinks it resulted from "groupthink" in Washington. Not so: it was the logical follow-on to the debate over containment and rollback bubbling along in the Truman administration for more than a year. But James is right that civilian centrality—Acheson's centrality—in the key decisions, first to defend the South and then to invade the North, separated Korea dramatically from the shared and collegial civil-military decision making of World War II.[21]

The decision was embodied in NSC document number 81, written mostly by Dean Rusk, which authorized MacArthur to move into North Korea if there were no Soviet or Chinese threats to intervene. It explicitly called for "a roll-back" of the North Korean regime; war dispatches routinely referred to the "liberated areas" in the North. At first he was told to use only Korean units in operations near the Chinese border, but soon the JCS told MacArthur to feel unhindered. MacArthur was correct in telling senators in 1951 that the crossing of the parallel "had the most complete and absolute approval of every section of the American government," if we grant him the license of mild exaggeration owed to a person who had been badly blindsided by Truman-aligned reconstructions of history.

Kim Il Sung crossed the five-year-old 38th parallel, not an international boundary like that between Iraq and Kuwait, or Germany and Poland; instead it bisected a nation that had a rare and well-recognized unitary existence going back to antiquity. The counter-logic implied by saying "Koreans invade Korea" disrupts the received wisdom or renders a logical reconstruction of the official American position impossible. In the most influential American book on justice in war, Michael Walzer defends the Truman administration's initial intervention with the following argument: the U.S. response to North Korean aggression was correct because Truman took the problem to the United Nations, which was the legitimate organ of world decision and opinion, and thus global justice ("it was the crime of the aggressor to challenge individual and communal rights"). In justifying the American invasion of North Korea, however, the U.S. ambassador to the UN called the 38th parallel "an imaginary line." Walzer then comments, "I will leave aside the odd notion that the 38th parallel was an imaginary line (how then did we recognize the initial aggression?)." Walzer bypasses this mouthful without further thought, because it is the essence of his argument that Truman was right to defend the 38th parallel as an international boundary—that was "the initial aggression."[22] Why is it aggression when Koreans cross the 38th parallel, but imaginary when Americans do the same thing?

China Is Near

In September and October the general conclusion of all American intelligence agencies was that China would not come into the war. On September 20 the CIA envisioned the possibility that Chinese "volunteers" might enter the fighting, and a month later it noted "a number of reports" that Manchurian units might be sent to Korea. However, "the odds are that Communist China, like the USSR, will not openly intervene in North Korea." On November 1, Gen. Walter Bedell Smith, director of the CIA, accurately wrote that the Chinese "probably genuinely fear an invasion of Manchuria," and that they would seek to establish a cordon sanitaire for border security "regardless of the increased risk of general war." But on November 24 as MacArthur lunged toward the Yalu River border, the

CIA still found insufficient evidence to suggest a Chinese plan for "major offensive operations." Intelligence agencies did not lack information; instead the problem resided at the level of assumptions and presuppositions: Moscow wouldn't intervene because it would fear global war; Beijing wouldn't either, because Moscow dictated to its leaders.

The Russians and the Chinese had a division of labor before the war started: Russian military advisers were in North Korea and Chinese military advisers were in North Vietnam in 1950. Both worked with the respective armies on strategic planning, logistics, army organization, and political controls. While the Koreans prepared their invasion, the Vietnamese "were planning a full-scale assault on the French forces along the Sino-Vietnamese border."[23] This was less a conscious or planned division of labor than a result of Soviet occupation of North Korea and Chinese occupation of northern Vietnam after World War II, and connections between Mao and Ho Chi Minh during the Yanan period.

A Chinese military intelligence group arrived in Pyongyang within three weeks of the war's start, and as early as August 4 Mao considered intervening in Korea: if the Americans were to invade the North "we must therefore come to [North] Korea's aid and intervene in the name of a volunteer army." Around the time of the Inchon landing a high North Korean officer, Pak Il-yu, requested Chinese military assistance, and then on October 1 Kim Il Sung held an emergency meeting with the Chinese ambassador to plead that the PLA 13th Army Corps quickly cross the Yalu River. By then Chinese intervention was certain, the only question was the timing: on September 30 Mao told Stalin "we have decided" to send as many as twelve infantry divisions. The Kremlin, however, fretted that a big Chinese offensive against the Americans might precipitate a world war, and backed off from a previous commitment to provide airpower to protect China's coasts. China went ahead regardless, which apparently surprised Stalin.[24]

North Korean and Chinese documents make clear that China

did not enter the war purely as a defensive measure to protect its border, as has long been known, but also because Mao determined early in the war that should the North Koreans falter, China had an obligation to come to their aid because of the sacrifice of so many Koreans in the Chinese revolution, the anti-Japanese resistance, and the Chinese civil war. The PRC's Foreign Affairs Ministry referred to China's obligations to "the Korean people who have stood on our side during the past decades." The October 1 crossing of the 38th parallel caused Mao a sleepless night, but he made the lone decision to intervene, and informed Stalin of his decision the next day. As if some telepathy were at work, MacArthur told the Department of the Army on the same day that "the field of our military operations is limited only by military exigencies and the international boundaries of Korea. The so-called 38th Parallel, accordingly, is not a factor."[25] In other words, NSC 81, the rollback strategy itself, caused the Chinese intervention, and not the subsequent arrival of American troops at the Yalu River.

Chinese forces attacked in late October, bloodied many American troops, and then disappeared. It is likely that the Chinese hoped this would suffice to stop the American march to the Yalu, perhaps at the narrow neck of the peninsula above Pyongyang. But this also would leave the DPRK as a small, rump regime. Around this time Kim Il Sung arrived in Beijing on an armored train, moving under cover of darkness and blanketed security. He was accompanied by three other uniformed Koreans, and China's northeast leader, Kao Kang. High PRC leaders, including Chou En-lai and Nieh Jung-chen (the two besides Mao most closely linked to the Korean decision), were not seen in Beijing in the same period, reappearing for the funeral of Jen Pi-shih on October 27.[26] But the Americans resumed their advance, as did the North Korean–Chinese strategy of luring them deep into the interior of North Korea, thus to stretch their supply lines, wait for winter, and gain time for a dramatic reversal on the battlefield.

MacArthur and his G-2 chief, Charles Willoughby, trusted only themselves, and had an intuitive approach to intelligence that mingled the hard facts of enemy capability with hunches about the enemy's presumed ethnic and racial qualities ("Chinamen can't fight"). This combined with MacArthur's "personal infallibility theory of intelligence," in which he "created his own intelligence organization, interpreted its results and acted upon his own analysis."[27] When the CIA was formed it threatened MacArthur's exclusive intelligence theater in the Pacific and J. Edgar Hoover's in Latin America. MacArthur and Willoughby thus continued the "interdiction" that they practiced against the Office of Strategic Services (OSS) in the Pacific War. Although the CIA did function in Japan and Korea before June 1950, operatives had to either get permission from Willoughby or hide themselves from MacArthur's G-2 (as well as the enemy target). Effective liaison in the handling of information barely existed. At the late date of March 1950 some minimal cooperation ensued when Gen. J. Lawton Collins of the JCS asked that MacArthur share with them Willoughby's reports on China and areas near to it.

On Thanksgiving Day (November 23) the troops in the field had turkey dinners with all the trimmings—shrimp cocktail, mashed potatoes, dressing, cranberry sauce, pumpkin pie. They did not know that thousands of Chinese soldiers surrounded them, carrying "a bag of millet meal" and wearing tennis shoes at 30°F below zero. (The North Koreans and Chinese had "one man back to support one man forward," Thompson wrote; the Americans had nine back and one forward—and "scores of tins, of candy, Coca-cola, and toilet supplies.")[28] The next day MacArthur launched his euphemistically titled "reconnaissance in force," a general offensive all along the battle line. He described it as a "massive compression and envelopment," a "pincer" movement to trap remaining KPA forces. Once again American and South Korean forces were able to run north unimpeded. The offensive rolled forward for three days against little or no resistance, with ROK units succeeding in entering the northeastern industrial city of Chongjin. MacArthur

Gen. Douglas MacArthur surveys Korea from *The Bataan* on the eve of the "reconnaissance in force." *U.S. National Archives*

launched the marines toward the Changjin Reservoir (known by its Japanese name, Chosin, in the American literature) and sent the 7th Division north of the Unggi River, in spite of temperatures as low as 22 degrees below zero. Within a week the 7th Division had secured Kim Il Sung's heartland of Kapsan, and reached Hyesan on the Yalu River against no resistance.

Finally CIA daily reports caught the pattern of enemy rearward displacement, arguing that such withdrawals had in the past preceded offensive action, and noting warily that there were "large, coordinated and well-organized guerrilla forces in the rear area" behind the Allied forces, along with guerrilla occupation of "substantial areas in southwest Korea." But as late as November 20 the estimates were still mixed, with some arguing that the Communists were simply withdrawing to better defensive points, and others that the pattern of "giving ground invariably in face of UN units mov-

American soldiers enjoy Thanksgiving dinner on the banks of the Yalu, November 23, 1950. *U.S. National Archives*

ing northward" merely meant "a delaying action," not preparation for all-out assault. Lost amid the hoopla of victory by Christmas were reports from reconnaissance pilots that long columns of enemy troops were "swarming all over the countryside"—not to mention the retrieval of Chinese POWs from six different armies.

Strong enemy attacks began on November 27, through a "deep envelopment" that chopped allied troops to pieces. The 1st Marine Division was pinned down at the Changjin Reservoir, the ROK II Corps collapsed again, and within two days a general withdrawal ensued. On December 4 the JCS cabled MacArthur that "the preservation of your forces is now the primary consideration"— that is, the utterly overexposed core of the entire American expeditionary force, now battered and surrounded. Two days later Communist forces occupied Pyongyang, and the day after that the allied front was only twenty miles north of the parallel at its northernmost point. The combined Sino-Korean offensive cleared North Korea of enemy troops in little more than two weeks from its inception. Gen. Edward Almond wrote that "we are having a glut of Chinamen"; he hoped he would have the chance later "to give these yellow bastards what is coming to them." By the end of December, Seoul was about to fall once again, to a Sino-Korean offensive launched on New Year's Eve.[29]

MacArthur had described the first Sino-Korean feint as "one of the most offensive acts of international lawlessness of historic record"; the KPA, he told Washington, was completely defeated, having suffered 335,000 casualties with no forces left. Thus, "a new and fresh [Chinese] army now faces us." (In fact, KPA forces far outnumbered Chinese at this point.) Then, when large Chinese units entered the fighting at the end of November, he radioed back that he faced "the entire Chinese nation in an undeclared war." All the Chinese? Did he mean those famous "Chinese hordes"? There weren't any, Reginald Thompson rightly said; in late 1950 the total of enemy forces in the North never outnumbered those of the UN, even though MacArthur's headquarters counted eighteen Chinese divisions (somehow a few hundred POWs had fortuitously managed to come from each and every one of them).[30] The Chinese just exploited night maneuvers, deft feints, unnerving bugles and whistles, to make UN soldiers think they were surrounded.

As soon as Chinese troops intervened in force, MacArthur ordered that a wasteland be created between the war front and the Yalu River border, destroying from the air every "installation, factory, city, and village" over thousands of square miles of North Korean territory. As a British air attaché at MacArthur's headquarters put it, except for the city of Najin near the Soviet border and the Yalu River dams, MacArthur's orders were "to destroy every means of communication and every installation and factories and cities and villages. This destruction is to start at the Manchurian border and to progress south."[31] This terrible swath of destruction, targeting every village in its path, followed Chinese forces right into

South Korea. Soon George Barrett of *The New York Times* found "a macabre tribute to the totality of modern war" in a village north of Anyang:

> The inhabitants throughout the village and in the fields were caught and killed and kept the exact postures they held when the napalm struck—a man about to get on his bicycle, fifty boys and girls playing in an orphanage, a housewife strangely unmarked, holding in her hand a page torn from a Sears-Roebuck catalogue crayoned at Mail Order No. 3,811,294 for a $2.98 "bewitching bed jacket—coral."

Secretary of State Dean Acheson wanted censorship authorities notified about this kind of "sensationalized reporting," so it could be stopped.[32]

On November 30 Truman also rattled the atomic bomb at a news conference, saying the United States might use any weapon in its arsenal to hold back the Chinese; this got even Stalin worried. According to a high official in the KGB at the time, Stalin expected global war as a result of the American defeat in northern Korea; fearing the consequences, he favored allowing the United States to occupy all of Korea: "So what?" Stalin said. "Let the United States of America be our neighbors in the Far East.... We are not ready to fight." Unlike Stalin the Chinese were ready—but only to fight back down to the middle of the peninsula, rather than to start World War III.

Gen. Matthew Ridgway's astute battlefield generalship eventually stiffened the allied lines below Seoul, and by the end of January he led gallant fights back northward to the Han River, opposite the capital. After more weeks of hard fighting, UN forces recaptured Seoul, and in early April, American forces crossed the 38th parallel again. Later that month the last major Chinese offensive was turned back, and by the late spring of 1951 the fighting stabilized along lines similar to those that today mark the Korean demilitarized zone, with UN forces in occupation north of the parallel on the eastern side, and Sino–North Korean forces occupying swatches of land south of the parallel on the western side. That was about where the war ended after tortuous peace negotiations and another two years of bloody fighting (most of it positional, trench warfare reminiscent of World War I).

THE SUSPENSION OF THE WAR

On June 23, 1951, the Soviet UN representative, Adam Malik, proposed that discussions get started between the belligerents to arrange for a cease-fire. Truman agreed, suggesting that representatives find a suitable place to meet, which turned out to be the ancient Korean capital at Kaesong, bisected by the 38th parallel. Truce talks began on July 10, led initially by Vice Adm. C. Turner Joy for the UN side, and Lt. Gen. Nam Il of North Korea. The talks dragged on interminably, with several suspensions and a removal of the truce site to the village of Panmunjom (where it remains today). Proper and fair demarcation of each side's military lines caused endless haggling, but the key issue that drew out the negotiations was the disposition of huge numbers of prisoners of war on all sides. The critical issue was freedom of choice in regard to repatriation, introduced by the United States in January 1952; about one third of North Korean POWs and a much larger percentage of Chinese POWs did not want to return to Communist control. Meanwhile South Korea refused to sign any armistice that would keep Korea divided, and in mid-June 1953, Syngman Rhee abruptly released some 25,000 POWs—leading the United States to develop plans ("Operation Everready") to remove Rhee in a coup d'état, should he try to disrupt the armistice agreement again. As usual, though, Rhee got his way: the Eisenhower administration bribed him with promises of a postwar defense treaty and enormous amounts of "aid"—and even then he refused to sign the armistice.

The UN negotiating team. Paek Son-yop is in the front row. *U.S. National Archives*

The North Koreans had abused many American and allied POWs, harshly depriving them of food and especially sleep, and subjecting many to political thought reform that was decried as "brainwashing" in the United States. Meanwhile, in spite of endless American statements of their allegiance to individual rights, human dignity, and the Geneva convention, a virtual war ensued in the South's camps, as pro-North, pro-South, pro-China, and pro-Taiwan POW groups fought with one another, and for the allegiance of other POWs. Against American presuppositions, the Communists were more discriminating in the violence they dealt out to POWs, whereas the South routinely murdered captives before they could become POWs and tortured and mentally tormented the ones they let live. Right-wing youth groups—the familiar ones from the turmoil of the 1940s—tried to organize anti-Communist prisoners but generally dealt in haphazard mayhem. Both sides sought to "convert" POWs politically, but the Communists had a positive message

North Korean head negotiator Nam Il at Panmunjom. *U.S. National Archives*

and genuinely seemed to believe in what they said, whereas youth group leaders simply demanded automatic obedience (one of the best sources for all this remains *General Dean's Story*). Even after years in the camps, the ROK put liberated POWs through six more months of "reeducation" before dismissing them to their families. Sixty individuals remained detained because they had not yet shed their Communist "brainwashing."[33]

The POW issue was finally settled on June 8, 1953, when the Communist side agreed to place POWs who refused repatriation under the control of the Neutral Nations' Supervisory Commission for three months; at the end of this period those who still refused repatriation would be set free. Two final and costly Communist offensives in June and July sought to gain more ground but failed, and the U.S. Air Force hit huge irrigation dams that provided water for 75 percent of the North's food production. On June 20, 1953, *The New York Times* announced the execution of the accused Soviet spies Julius and Ethel Rosenberg at Sing Sing prison; in the fine print of daily war coverage the U.S. Air Force stated that its planes bombed dams at Kusong and Toksan in North Korea, and in even finer print the North Korean radio acknowledged "great damage" to these large reservoirs. Two days later the *Times* reported that the State Department had banned several hundred American books from overseas libraries of the U.S. Information Service— including Dashiell Hammett's *The Maltese Falcon.*

The fighting could have come to an end much earlier, but both Moscow and Washington had interests in keeping it going since Korea no longer threatened to erupt into general war. Some historians think that Stalin's death in March 1953 and the Eisenhower administration's escalation of the air war in May and June finally brought the hot war to a conclusion, while others argue that it easily could have ended in 1951. But as the war dragged on, the United States also brandished the biggest weapons in its arsenal. On May 26, 1953, *The New York Times* featured a story on the first atomic shell shot from a cannon, which exploded at French Flat, Nevada, with ten-kiloton force (half the Hiroshima yield). A few days later came the "mightiest atom blast" ever exploded at the Nevada test site; some speculated that it might have been a hydrogen bomb. Formerly secret materials illustrate that in May and June 1953 the Eisenhower administration sought to show that it would stop at nothing to bring the war to a close. In mid-May Ike told the National Security Council that using nukes in Korea would be cheaper than conventional weaponry, and a few days later the Joint Chiefs recommended launching nuclear attacks against China. The Nevada tests were integral to this atomic blackmail, a way of getting a message to the enemy that it had better sign the armistice. Nonetheless, there is little evidence that Ike's nuclear threats made any difference in the Communist decision to end the war, which had come some months before (since 1953, however, it remains true that *The Maltese Falcon* has subverted many innocents).

On July 27, 1953, three of the four primary parties to the war signed the armistice agreement (the ROK still refusing). It called for a 2.5-mile-wide buffer zone undulating across the middle of Korea, from which troops and weapons were supposed to be withdrawn. Today this heavily fortified "demilitarized zone" still holds the peace in Korea, as does the 1953 cease-fire agreement. No peace treaty has ever been signed, and so the peninsula remains in a technical state of war.

Various encyclopedias state that the countries involved in the three-year conflict suffered a total of more than 4 million casualties, of which at least 2 million were civilians—a higher percentage than in World War II or Vietnam. A total of 36,940 Americans lost their lives in the Korean theater; of these, 33,665 were killed in action, while 3,275 died there of nonhostile causes. Some 92,134 Americans were wounded in action, and decades later, 8,176 were still reported as missing. South Korea sustained 1,312,836 casualties, including 415,004 dead. Casualties among other UN allies totaled 16,532, including 3,094 dead. Estimated North Korean casualties numbered 2 million, including about 1 million civilians and about 520,000 soldiers. An estimated 900,000 Chinese soldiers lost their lives in combat.[34]

Washington, D.C., reporters wrote, met the war's end with "a collective shrug of the shoulders." In New York, TV camera crews showed up at Times Square to find desultory citizens who had to be coaxed into shouting approval of the peace; fewer people were on the streets because subway fares had just gone up to fifteen cents. The next day an Iowa court ruled that there had been no state of war in Korea, since Congress never declared one to exist.

The point to remember is that this was a civil war[35] and, as a British diplomat once said, "every country has a right to have its War of the Roses." The true tragedy was not the war itself, for a civil conflict purely among Koreans might have resolved the extraordinary tensions generated by colonialism, national division, and foreign intervention. The tragedy was that the war solved nothing: only the status quo ante was restored, only a cease-fire held the peace.

CHAPTER TWO

THE PARTY
OF MEMORY

Ghosts of those shot, pierced and even battered,
ghosts of those bombed by planes overhead,
ghosts hit by wagons, tanks, trucks, or trains...
ghosts still resentful, ghosts far from home,
all those who linger, each with its own tale...
—HWANG SOK-YONG, *The Guest*

On April 25, 2007, *The New York Times* carried a photo of North Korean soldiers goose-stepping through Pyongyang, on the seventy-fifth anniversary of the founding of their army. The *Times* noted that the regime itself was founded only in 1948, but carried no more information. Another article announced the arrival of the Japanese prime minister, Abe Shinzo, in Washington to visit George W. Bush. Neither there, nor in any article that I saw in the press after Abe came to power, were these two events connected. Abe is the grandson of the class-A war criminal and postwar prime minister Kishi Nobosuke, who was head of munitions in Manchuria in the 1930s.

Another recent prime minister, Aso Taro, also had direct links to Japan's empire. He was heir to a rich mining fortune, from a family company that used thousands of Korean forced laborers during the war, and which had a particular reputation for brutality and terrible working conditions. Allied POWs, mainly Australian and British, were also forced to work there. As the grandson of Prime Minister Yoshida Shigeru, Aso's lineage traces back to leaders of the Meiji Restoration, and he is related by marriage to Kishi and Sato Eisaku (another prime minister), to Abe Shinzo, and indeed to the emperor's family.[1] If the DPRK features hereditary communism, postwar Japan is hereditary democracy—often 70 to 80 percent of their parliamentarians have inherited seats from their fathers or come from politically prominent families. When a person like Abe or Aso comes to power in Japan, Pyongyang remembers what others don't know or forgot: their genealogy.

It would be difficult to exaggerate the ingrown solipsism of North Korea's leaders, but it is often matched on the right wing of the Liberal Democratic Party. In 2008 the chief of staff of the Air Self-Defense Force, Tamogami Toshio, a man known to be close to Mr. Abe, published an essay that might well have been entitled "Everything I Ever Wanted to Declare About Japan's Wars Since 1895 but Was Afraid to Say." Like many members of the Japanese elite, Gen. Tamogami is an entirely unreconstructed believer in the virtues of Japan's colonial mission and the justice of its wars against China and the United States. In 1937 Japan was lured into the Sino-Japanese War by a Comintern-manipulated Chiang Kai-shek, he claimed; a Kremlin conspiracy carried out by its spies in Washington (such as Harry Dexter White) initiated U.S. entry into World War II (and thus "Japan was drawn into it"); Roosevelt was duped because he "was not aware of the terrible nature of communism." In passing, Tamogami lauded "Col. Kim Suk Won," who led a thousand Japanese troops and "trampled the Army from China, the former suzerain state that had been bullying Korea for hundreds of years. He was decorated by the emperor for his meritorious war services."[2] Gen. Tamogami not only poured salt into Korean wounds by lauding their Benedict Arnold, but had spoken so clearly that dismissal (on October 31, 2008) was the prime minister's only option. But his essay still won the top prize ($30,000) in a contest sponsored by a wealthy hotel and condominium owner.

As for Mr. Abe, he selected March 1, 2007, to announce that "no evidence" existed to show that any women were "forcibly" recruited into the multitudinous ranks of Pacific War "comfort women" (*ianfu* in Japanese; sex slaves to everyone else). That is to say, "forcible in the narrow sense of the word," he elaborated, and then proceeded to try to clarify that opaque distinction for many succeeding days and weeks—and ultimately just "apologized" for himself on March 26, 2007 (while never retracting his original formulation). "I apologize here and now," he said, without really indicating what he was apologizing for, and then said, "I express my sympathy toward the comfort women and apologize *for the situation they found themselves in.*" Here Mr. Abe pays fealty to his departed comrades in arms: former

"Comfort women" in Burma, 1944. *U.S. National Archives (courtesy of Sarah Soh)*

sex slaves often said that soldiers would clean up, button up, and then offer awkward apologies to them on the way out the door.

Japanese historians had written about the sexual slavery system for decades, but were told time and again by the authorities that no archival documents existed on it. In 1992 the historian Yoshiaki Yoshimi walked into a military library and found many such documents just sitting on the shelf. His 1995 book, *Comfort Women: Sexual Slavery in the Japanese Military During World War II,* is now a standard source, but his findings were also a direct impetus to Foreign Minister Kono Yohei's 1993 apology, stating that many were recruited "against their will" through coaxing and "coercion." (Abe essentially repudiated this statement.) Dr. Yoshiaki and other historians determined that somewhere between 50,000 and 200,000 women were in the system by the time it was fully established, the vast majority of them Korean. Of course, many were lured or tricked into service with promises of ordinary jobs, before being compelled into slavery.[4]

It is difficult to think of a more sordid transgression by a modern army than this one, trampling the lives and decency of such a multitude of racially despised women. Korea's venerable tradition of female chastity is still reflected in common names given to babies, in the chadorlike head-to-toe garments worn by elite women when they ventured out of their home in the old days, and the female inner sanctum of the home: the character for peace and tranquillity depicts a woman under a roof. But in the past century millions of foreign soldiers have had their way with Korean women. Sarah Soh has shown that the actual number of sex slaves was perhaps 50,000 (still a terrible figure), that the first documented comfort station was established in Manchukuo in 1932–33, and as early as 1938 about 30,000 to 40,000 women, "primarily Korean," were already in this system in China. Her book also illustrates in detail that many procurers—more than half—of candidates for Japanese military brothels were in fact Koreans.[5] Korean men also joined the Japanese military in great numbers—but as soldiers, a minority as volunteers and a majority as draftees. About 187,000 Korean soldiers and an additional 22,000 sailors served during the war—and also availed themselves of comfort stations. The South Korean army then set up a similar comfort system during the Korean War, sometimes using women kidnapped from the North.[6] Many sex slaves were utterly ruined individuals, dared not return to their families, and thus had no alternative but to continue working in the fetid brothels alongside U.S. military bases in Japan, Okinawa, Korea, and the Philippines.

Mr. Abe's "forcible in the narrow sense of the word" turned out to mean that military officers did not kick down the doors of homes and drag teenage women off by the hair—but it was "forcible in the broad sense of the word," Abe later acknowledged, in that civilian brokers, colonial stooges, lying pimps, or businessmen claiming to have good factory jobs inveigled young women into this degradation most foul (initiation usually meant rape, especially if the victim was a virgin). If for once Mr. Abe could put himself in the shoes of a young woman fooled into a "job" taking on forty or fifty soldiers a day, held as a prisoner for months and years, given only a bare subsistence living, he would drop to his knees and beg forgiveness. Scholarship on this subject, almost always done by women, illustrates the awful life chances, family catastrophes, and casual degradations that lead women into prostitution in East Asia (or anywhere else).[7] Of course, only a minority of *ianfu* were prostitutes in the first place. And many *were* forced into it "in the narrow sense of the word": a dominant clan in a Korean village would tell a Japanese official and a Korean policeman where to find a pretty young girl among the residents of the subordinate clan households, and she was either inveigled with promises of education or a job, or just thrown bodily into the back of a truck.

Prime Minister Abe's fumbling and craven performance took place on a national holiday in Korea, marking the countrywide uprising against Japanese colonial rule that began on March 1, 1919. March 1 is also the day in 1932 that Japan chose to inaugurate Manchukuo (after seizing northeastern China). Imagine that this debate were in Germany, Tessa Morris-Suzuki wrote, and the leader in question were named Krupp.[8]

Americans shouldn't comfort themselves and feel unconnected to all this, or point out how awful the Japanese are compared to the Germans (who have sincerely tried to come to terms with their history, and so on). We are the ones who organized a unilateral occupation of Japan, provided it with a remarkably soft peace, refused war reparations to its near neighbors, and put people such as Kishi back into power (as Herbert Bix illustrated in his prizewinning book, *Hirohito and the Making of Modern Japan*). Americans also sometimes appear oblivious to wounds of empire that are still raw in Korea, and that haunt present-day relations with Japan.

ORIGINS AND BEGINNINGS

Friedrich Nietzsche famously questioned the origin of human events—the search for origins pushes ever backward in time, and is subject to endless revision—but he does not say that *beginnings*

never occur. The beginning for his *On the Genealogy of Morals* is the
Bible and two millennia of (mis)interpretations of its teaching. The
beginning for the Korean War was in 1931–32, after Japanese forces
invaded the northeast provinces of China and established the puppet state of Manchukuo. They quickly faced a huge if motley army
of guerrilla, secret society, and bandit resistance in which Koreans
were by far the majority, constituting upward of 90 percent of enti-
ties such as the Chinese Communist Party (partly because the
eventual top leaders and thus the main historical lineage of this
party resided in southeast China in the early 1930s). They quickly
found a tiny minority of Koreans who would collaborate with them
in killing these resisters. By the mid-1930s the man who took the
nom de guerre Kim Il Sung was a well-known and formidable
leader of guerrillas. At that time the head of the Central Control
Committee of Police Affairs for Manchukuo and concurrent
provost marshall of the Kwantung Army (the name of Japan's
armed forces in Manchuria) was Gen. Tojo Hideki, in command
when Japan attacked Pearl Harbor, and subsequently sentenced to
death for his war crimes by the U.S. occupation under Gen. Douglas MacArthur. Tojo played a crucial role in unifying ordinary police with the feared military police (*kempeitai*). Among the Koreans
tracking down and killing Korean and Chinese guerrillas was
Tomagami's hero Kim Sok-won, who commanded the 38th parallel
in the summer of 1949 (from the Southern side, of course).[9] This
Manchurian crucible produced the two most important leaders of
postwar Korea, Kim Il Sung and Park Chung Hee, and several key
leaders of postwar Japan (for example, Kishi Nobosuke not only
was responsible for munitions in Manchukuo, but later worked together with Shiina Etsusaburo and several others in the mid-1950s
to form the mainstay of the Liberal Democratic Party, long the core
of Japan's peculiar one-party democracy).[10]

To the North Koreans it is less the Japanese than the Korean
quislings that matter: blood enemies. They essentially saw the war
in 1950 as a way to settle the hash of the top command of the South

Korean army, nearly all of whom had served the Japanese. During the Korean War this was barely known to Americans, and when known was deemed to be of dubious import because by then Japan was our ally. This is not a matter of what we think, however, but what *they* think. The Japanese occupation of Korea from 1910 to 1945 is akin to the Nazi occupation of France, in the way it dug in deeply and has gnawed at the Korean national consciousness ever since. Manchuria is also "greater Korea" to patriots who remember the wide sway that the Koguryo kingdom (37 B.C.–A.D. 668) had in the region—and Koguryo begins Pyongyang's lineage of critical Korean antecedents for its own republic.

Kim Il Sung began fighting the Japanese in Manchuria in the spring of 1932, and his heirs trace everything back to this distant beginning. After every other characteristic attached to this regime—Communist, nationalist, rogue state, evil enemy—it was first of all, and above all else, an anti-Japanese entity. A state narrative runs from the early days of anti-Japanese insurgency down to the present, and it is drummed into the brains of everyone in the country by an elderly elite that believes anyone younger than they cannot possibly know what it meant to fight Japan in the 1930s or the United States in the 1950s (allied with Japan and utilizing bases all over Japan)—and, more or less, ever since. When you combine deeply ingrained Confucian patriarchy and filial piety with people who have been sentient adults more or less since the Korean War began in 1950, you have some sense of why North Korea has changed so little at top levels in recent decades, and why it is highly unlikely to change radically before this elite—and its relentlessly nationalist ideology—leaves the scene. The average age of the top twenty leaders in North Korea in 2009 was seventy-five. Of the top forty leaders in 2000, only one was under sixty: Kim Jong Il. This gerontocracy draws a straight line from 1932 onward, brooking no deviation from this most important of all North Korean legitimations. Diane Sawyer may not be the best example, but when she took an ABC crew to North Korea in late 2006, she interviewed

Gen. Yi Chan-bok, who commands the DMZ on the northern side. How long have you been there, she asked sweetly. "Forty years," he replied, to her amazement. He has been getting up every morning to riffle through the enemy's order of battle since the year before the Tet offensive effectively ended the American effort in Vietnam.

For decades the South Korean intelligence agencies put out the line that Kim Il Sung was an impostor, a Soviet stooge who stole the name of a famous Korean patriot. The real reason for this smoke screen was the pathetic truth that so many of its own leaders served the Japanese (but think of the contradiction: there *was* someone named Kim Il Sung heroically fighting the Japanese, even if it was somebody else—and what were you doing, sir?). This canard quickly took on the glow of truth; thus, when the leading scholar of Korean communism, Dae-sook Suh, was finally allowed to explain the real story to a large audience of young people in Seoul in 1989, upon hearing that Kim Il Sung was in fact a hero of the resistance they all burst into applause. Meanwhile the North Koreans took Kim's admirable record and piled on enough exaggeration and myth to insult the intelligence of a ten-year-old. But somewhere along the yawning chasm between the desperate lies of former South Korean governments and the ceaseless hyperbole of the North Koreans, there is a truth.

Two Koreas began to emerge in the early 1930s, one born of an unremittingly violent struggle in which neither side gave quarter; truths experienced in Manchukuo burned the souls of the North Korean leadership. The other truth is the palpable beginning of an urban middle class, as people marched not to the bugle of anti-Japanese resistance but into the friendly confines of the Hwashin department store, movie theaters, and ubiquitous bars and tearooms. The complexities of this moment in Korea, when 75 percent of the population were still peasants and a burgeoning working class bustled alongside a tiny middle class in the streets of Seoul, were brilliantly captured in Kang Kyong-ae's 1934 novel, *From Wonso Pond.*[11] A writer and quintessential "new woman" (*shin yosong*), at one point

Kang wanted to join the guerrillas in Manchuria, and she later worked with hundreds of other young women in a new textile factory in Inchon (the port of Seoul). With an acute critical sensibility Kang charted the arrival of urban modernity, the travails of "modern boys" and "modern girls," while saving her fury for the fraught lives of Korean women and her satire for the alienated suffering of the "blasted intellectuals, all words and no action." Even when they spoke out and went to prison, she wrote, they "converted" under Japanese suasion and got off scot free. No earlier generation of Korean women could possibly have had her experiences—her Brechtian experiences.

THE MEASURES TAKEN

> Your report shows us what is needed to change the world:
> Anger and tenacity, knowledge and indignation
> Swift action, utmost deliberation
> Cold endurance, unending perseverance
> Comprehension of the individual and comprehension of
>   the whole:
> Taught only by reality can
> Reality be changed.
>
> BERTOLT BRECHT

Brecht began his 1931 play with this: "The revolution marches forward even in that country. The ranks of fighters are well organized even there. We agree with the measures taken." He wrote about Communist agitators dispatched from Moscow to Manchuria to fight the oppressors. But the agitators also killed a comrade ("we shot him and cast him into a lime-pit"). Why? "He endangered the movement." Thus the play begins; it ends with the lines above.[12] Like Antigone, the fallen comrade was cast into a pit. Like Sophocles, Brecht thrusts the reader into a widening gyre of power and justice: Were "the measures taken" right or wrong? But he doesn't render a definitive judgment, unlike Sophocles. Instead he left the dilemmas for the cast and the audience to sort out, every evening *The Measures Taken* was staged.

Brecht could not have known how fitting his play would seem a few months later, when Korean agitators took up arms against the new puppet state of Manchukuo. They found themselves ensnared by pitiless overlords, a complex mix of Korean immigrants, and a local Chinese population filled with ethnic hatred, yielding a daily bread of life-and-death risks, dubious if not foolhardy odds, bad moral choices and worse moral choices. Brecht's play appears to be the opposite of *Antigone:* instead of justifying individual resistance against the state, all measures must be taken to assure the revolution's victory, even if it means sacrificing the individual. That isn't quite what he meant—he wanted the audience to grapple with the terrible dilemmas of revolutionary action versus the daily violence of the status quo in extremis: Hitler's rising power, the demise of any liberal option, and the alternative of Communist revolution.

This political milieu of bleak choices between the extremes of right and left inhabited most of Europe and East Asia during the Great Depression, and it is in this milieu that the North Korean leadership came of age and established itself. Korean resisters faced militarists capable of anything, and quickly concluded that violent struggle was their only viable option. Nearly eighty years later that state still stands, likewise against all odds, still arrayed against Japanese militarism (and against American power). But these distant origins in a barely known struggle in an obscure corner of the Pacific War ("even in that country") hold a key to why American leaders have consistently underestimated their opponents who hold power in Pyongyang.

Over time the Japanese built a textbook case of how to fight an insurgency by any means necessary, and the Koreans founded the nucleus of a "guerrilla state" that would come to power amid the ashes of Japan's defeat at the hands of American power. Japanese counterinsurgency was premised on using climate, terrain, and unflinchingly brutal methods to separate guerrilla bodies from their peasant constituents, and harsh interrogation and thought control to poison and destroy their minds. Winter drastically shifted the advantage to suppression forces: it made guerrillas stationary and the counterinsurgents mobile, as former Japanese army officers put it; the guerrillas holed up in winter shelters that well-fortified and protected troops sought out and burned. Rebuilding them was next to impossible "because everything is frozen." Frigid weather denied guerrillas the protection of thick foliage and undetected movement, military encirclement and blockade isolated base areas and prevented resupply of food and weaponry. Large armies established the blockades between the mountains and the low-lying fields and villages; small search-and-destroy units then entered the mountains to ferret out guerrillas, often by tracking their footprints in the snow.[13]

Japanese imperial forces were willing to go to any lengths to break the relationship between guerrillas and the sea of people in which they swam: slaughtering suspected peasant collaborators (millions of Chinese died in "kill-all, burn-all, loot-all" campaigns, as they were called), relocating large populations into concentrated or protected villages, and either executing or "converting" captured guerrillas. Japanese counterinsurgency experts told Americans that because of the close relations between guerrillas and peasants, "semi bandits [*sic*] must be abolished."[14] Who were "semi bandits"? Peasants who supported guerrillas by refusing to give information on guerrillas or pay taxes; in other words, almost anybody in a peasant village. The Japanese established "white cells" of supportive collaborators to counter guerrilla "red cells." Once guerrillas were captured, they were either routinely shot or put through intensive "thought reform" methods to turn them around (the Japanese term is *tenko*); they would then become leaders or members of anti-Communist groups, or of so-called Concordia associations promoting Japanese-Korean unity. When Japan's bacteriological warfare criminals in Unit 731 in Harbin needed more "logs" (*maruta*) on which to do live experiments, they would call the local prison and say, "Send us more Communists."

Careful scholarship in recent years, made possible by the availability of new Korean, Chinese, Japanese, and Soviet documentation and by the hard labors and open minds of a younger generation of historians, has now made clear that Koreans formed the vast majority of resisters to the Japanese takeover of Manchuria, native home for the rulers of the Qing dynasty (1644–1911). By the early 1930s half a million Koreans lived in the prefecture of Kando (Jiandao in Chinese) alone, long a Korean immigrant community just across the border in China, and since 1949 an autonomous Korean region in the People's Republic of China (PRC). Most Koreans had moved to Kando in hopes of escaping Japanese oppression, although some previous emigrants had also gotten wealthy developing the fertile soils of Manchuria, yielding tales that farming families could double or triple their income by relocating there. By and large, though, these Koreans were very poor and thoroughly recalcitrant in their hatred of the colonizers, and remained so in 1945 when U.S. intelligence estimated that 95 percent of the nearly two million Koreans in Manchuria were anti-Japanese, and only 5 percent were sympathizers and collaborators. Japanese officials saw their Korean colony as a model for Manchuria, and encouraged Korean allies to think that if they helped colonize Manchukuo, Korea itself might get closer to independence.

A certain degree of collaboration, of course, was unavoidable given the carrot-and-stick combination of considerable economic development and ruthlessness that characterized Japan's rule, especially in the last decade of this colony when Japan's expansion across Asia caused a shortage of experts and professionals throughout the empire. Ambitious Koreans found new careers opening to them just at the most oppressive point in this colony's history, as Koreans were commanded not to speak Korean and to change their names, and millions of Koreans were used as mobile human fodder by the Japanese. Koreans came to constitute about half of the hated National Police, and young Korean officers joined the aggressive Japanese army in Manchuria. Pro-Japanese aristocrats were rewarded with special titles, and some of Korea's greatest early nationalists and intellectuals, such as Yi Kwang-su, came out in public support of Japan's empire. If collaboration was inevitable, its considerable scale was not. Nor was it ever fully and frankly debated in South Korea or punished, leaving the problem to fester until 2004, when the government finally launched an official investigation of collaboration—along with estimates that upward of 90 percent of the pre-1990 South Korea elite had ties to collaborationist families or individuals.

Japanese forces launched their first major antiguerrilla campaign in April 1932 in Kando, killing anyone said to be a "Communist" or aiding Communists; many victims were innocent peasants. North Korean sources say that 25,000 died, perhaps an exaggeration, but it surely was an unholy slaughter. This experience became the most famous North Korean opera, *Sea of Blood* (*Pibada*),[16] and it happened amid a drastic fall in peasant livelihoods, brought on by the depression and the collapse of the world economy. Take a look at your dollar bill: you'll see George Washington. Looking at the North Korean equivalent, one will notice on the right side the heroine of *Sea of Blood*. You will also see her etched into a massive tile mural across from the Pyongyang Hotel and in many other iconic places in North Korea.

THE MANCHURIAN CANDIDATE

Kim Il Sung, who organized his first guerrilla unit in that same spring of 1932, was the Manchurian candidate—master of the measures taken. But he did not make a name for himself until a battle at Dongning in September 1933, when Chinese leaders mounted an unusually large attack on this city, aided by two Korean guerrilla

Kim Il Sung with his wife and son, Kim Jong Il, circa 1947. *U.S. National Archives*

companies led by Kim. His units rescued a Chinese commander (Shih Chung-hung) in this battle, and from then on Kim was a confidant of top Chinese leaders—which saved Kim when he himself was arrested by Chinese comrades on suspicion of being a traitor. Commander Shih declared that "a great figure like Kim Il Sung" could not be "a Japanese running dog," and said he would take his guerrillas and leave the Communist Party if it convicted Kim.[17]

Kim took a leading role in trying to forge Sino-Korean cooperation in the Manchurian guerrilla struggle, helped along by his fluency in Chinese. After the establishment of Manchukuo around 80 percent of anti-Japanese guerrillas and upward of 90 percent of the members of the "Chinese Communist Party" were Korean. By February 1936 a formidable Sino-Korean army had emerged, with Kim commanding the 3rd Division and several Chinese regimental commanders under him. Koreans were still the largest ethnic force in the late 1930s, constituting 80 percent of two regiments, 50 percent of another, and so on. By this time Kim was "the leader

North Korean Defense Minister Choe
Yong-gon, circa 1948. *U.S. National
Archives*

of Korean communists in eastern Manchuria with a great reputation and a high position," in the estimation of Han Hong-koo.
"Kim Il Sung fought all during 1938 and 1939," Dae-sook Suh
wrote, "mostly in southern and southeastern Manchuria. There
were numerous [published] accounts of his activities, such as the
Liudaogou raid of April 26, 1938, and his raid into Korea once
again in May 1939."[18]

He was not alone, though, working with other Korean guerrilla
leaders with their own detachments, such as Choe Yong-gon (minister of defense when the Korean War began), Kim Chaek, and
Choe Hyon. Kim's reputation was also plumped up by the Japanese,
whose newspapers featured the conflict between him and the Korean quislings whom the Japanese employed to track him down and
kill him, such as Col. Kim Sok-won (then known as Kaneyama
Shakugen); he reported to Gen. Nozoe Shotoku, commander of the
"Special Kim Detachment" of the Imperial Army. Colonel Kim's

greatest success came in February 1940, when he killed Yang Jingyu, a famous Chinese guerrilla and close comrade of Kim Il Sung. In April, Nozoe's forces captured Kim Hye-sun, thought to be Kim's first wife; the Japanese tried in vain to use her to lure Kim out of hiding, and then murdered her.[19] Maeda Takashi headed another Japanese Special Police unit, with many Koreans in it, that tracked Kim's guerrillas for months in early 1940. Maeda's forces finally caught up with Kim when his guerrillas attacked them on March 13, 1940. After both sides suffered casualties, Kim's group released POWs so they could move faster; Maeda pursued him for nearly two weeks, stumbling into a trap on March 25. Kim threw 250 guerrillas at 150 soldiers in Maeda's unit, defeating them and killing Maeda, fifty-eight Japanese, and seventeen others attached to the force, and taking thirteen prisoners and large quantities of weapons and ammunition.

In September 1939, the month when Hitler invaded Poland and started World War II, the Japanese mobilized a "massive punitive expedition" consisting of six battalions of the Kwantung Army and 20,000 men of the Manchurian Army and police force in a six-month guerrilla-suppression campaign, the main target being those led by Kim Il Sung and Choe Hyon. In September 1940 an even larger force embarked on a counterinsurgency campaign against Chinese and Korean guerrillas:

> The punitive operation was conducted for one year and eight months until the end of March 1941, and the bandits, excluding those led by Kim Il Sung, were completely annihilated. The bandit leaders were shot to death or forced to submit.[20]

In other words, massive counterinsurgency punctuated the last two years of this conflict, which lasted until the eve of the German onslaught against the Soviet Union. Kim Il Sung's unit had grown to 340 fighters by July 1940, when it again became the target of General

Nozoe's expeditionary force, but soon many of his comrades were killed and Kim was forced into "small-unit" operations thereafter.[21] Thousands of guerrillas were wiped out, and could be added to the estimates of about 200,000 guerrillas, Communists, secret society members, and bandits slaughtered by the Japanese going back to the Manchurian Incident in 1931.

The disunity of the Korean diaspora—ordinary farmers seeking their livelihood, merchants trying to start a business, lesser and greater collaborators with the Japanese, a resistance made up of Communists, nationalists, bandits, and criminals—left Kim Il Sung with a conviction: unity above all else, and by whatever means necessary (taking Brecht literally). From then onward the North Korean leadership promoted a totalized politics: no dissent, no political alternatives, our way or the highway. Almost as soon as they came into power they put key guerrilla leaders in charge of almost everything (Choe Yong-gon, for example, was installed as head of the main Christian democratic party in the North). However lamentable outsiders may find this, it has been a core element of North Korean politics since the 1930s. The dilemma of political means and ends, for them, is defined by being at war with either Japan or the United States ever since. "Nothing is more important than learning to think crudely," Brecht once said. "Crude thinking is the thinking of great men." So was the milieu of crisis in which he wrote, and Koreans fought: crude, illiberal, murderous.

Kim Il Sung, Kim Chaek, Choe Hyon, Choe Yong-gon, and about two hundred other key Korean leaders were the fortunate survivors of pitiless campaigns that dyed the hills of Manchukuo with Korean blood. But in 1945 these guerrillas came back to Pyongyang, colonized the regime, and in typical Korean fashion began intermarrying, producing children, and putting them through elite schools. Their descendants are the power holders in North Korea today. Regardless of Pyongyang's preposterous and ceaseless hagiography, in short, Kim Il Sung has an impeccable pedigree in the resistance. So did his family: his father was jailed for

what does this mean

anti-Japanese activities in 1924; he died soon after his release two years later. Kim's middle brother, Chol-ju, reportedly died at the age of twenty in Manchukuo after his arrest in 1935 by the Japanese. Kim's uncle Kang Chin-sok, elder brother to his mother, was arrested in 1924 and served thirteen years in a Japanese prison. The North foregrounds hundreds of similar family stories. Chu To-il, subsequently a vice-marshal of the KPA, lost one of his brothers in a Japanese "pacification" campaign, two others died as guerrillas on the battlefield, and his mother starved to death at a blockaded guerrilla base. Yi O-song's father also starved to death in a guerrilla base, even though he was in charge of food supplies. Yi's brother-in-law was executed, and his two sisters, part of his guerrilla group, both died of starvation. Extremely malnourished himself, Yi never reached full adult growth. In 1971 Yi, by then a lieutenant general in the KPA, became headmaster at the Mangyongdae Revolutionary School, successor to the School for the Offspring of Revolutionary Martyrs first established in 1947 for the hundreds of orphans collected by then. The devastation of the Korean War sent many more thousands of children to this parentless haven, and into the leadership. This is the central educational institution for the North Korean power elite, and the symbolic crucible for molding the astonishing "family state" created out of the ashes of two devastating wars.

The paramount interest of this elite was to have the big army and the full panoply of military equipment that they so sorely lacked in the 1930s. At the founding of the KPA on February 8, 1948 (many years later they changed the founding date to April 25, 1932), the essential features of this garrison state were on full display. Only Kim Il Sung's portrait was put out, instead of the usual tandem portraits with Stalin. Kim's speech laid emphasis on the necessity for a self-reliant nation to have its own army. "At all times and in all places our Korean people must take their fate into their own hands and must make all plans and preparations for building a completely self-reliant, independent nation in which they alone are the masters, and a government unified by their own hands." The KPA, he said, grew out of the Manchurian guerrilla struggle, with a tradition of "a hundred battles and a hundred victories." He made no reference to Soviet help in building the KPA.[22] A year later, on the first anniversary of the KPA, Kim was for the first time referred to as *suryong*, an ancient Koguryo term meaning "supreme" or "great leader" that had been reserved for Stalin until then. This was a complete heresy in the Communist world of that time, but it became his title thereafter, down to his death in 1994.

THE SOVIETS AND KIM IL SUNG

After the USSR collapsed in 1991 a picture emerged of Kim Il Sung in a Soviet uniform with some kind of medal on his lapel. Like Ho Chi Minh, Kim had a "dark period," whereabouts unknown (in the latter's case, 1941–45), and when some hard evidence finally turned up of a clear connection to Moscow, it was munched over time and again.[23] In my reading, this information was never balanced with hard facts that we learned long ago—in the work of the Soviet dissident Roy Medvedev, for example—that Stalin ordered every last Korean agent in the Comintern shot in the late 1930s and began his many mass deportations of subject populations by moving some 200,000 Koreans from the Soviet Far East to Kazakhstan and Uzbekistan (tens of thousands of whom died on this forced exodus),[24] in both cases on the racist grounds that they might be Japanese spies, subject to Japanese influence, or generally unreliable—plus one couldn't tell them apart from Japanese. Kim's relationship with the Soviets turns out to have been quite modest and uneasy.[25]

Andrei Lankov has proved, based on Soviet internal materials, that Moscow had no "clear-cut plan or a predetermined course of action" when it occupied the North in August 1945, and proceeded for many months to improvise and get by with daily ad hoc decisions taken on the ground, with little direction from Moscow. Kim Il Sung was not handpicked by the Russians, but for a number of months was subordinate in Russian minds to the nationalist leader Cho Man-sik; Kim was going to be the defense minister under an interim regime headed by Cho. By February 1946 Kim was at the top of the power structure, "almost by accident," in Lankov's words.[26] Even if, however, Stalin had handpicked Kim Il Sung and installed him in Pyongyang as his faithful servant, that would not have been too surprising, since he did that throughout Eastern Europe. Still, it would be entirely biased not to point out that the United States engaged the services of an exile politician who had spent the previous thirty-five years in America, named Syngman Rhee, and that the main wartime spy outfit, the Office of Strategic Services, had deposited him in Seoul in an intelligence operation designed (1) to get him there before any other exile leaders, and (2) to make an end run around State Department objections to favoring any particular politicians—especially Rhee, who had angered Foggy Bottom by pretending to be "Minister Plenipotentiary" of a "Korean Provisional Government" that never governed any Koreans.[27]

CHAPTER THREE

THE PARTY
OF FORGETTING

Man...braces himself against the great and ever greater pressure of what is past; it pushes him down and bends him sideways, it encumbers his steps as a dark, invisible burden.

—NIETZSCHE

It is a matter for wonder: a moment, now here and then gone, nonetheless "returns as a ghost"—and then "the man says 'I remember' and envies the animal." Cattle grazing and cavorting in a field live in the present, they cannot dissimulate, they cannot but be honest. The child, playing between the hedges, is likewise oblivious to past and present. But his play, too, will be disturbed and he will come to understand the words "it was." *It was*—"words that cause a man conflict, suffering, satiety, and fulfillment"—thus "to remind him what his existence fundamentally is—an imperfect tense that can never become a perfect one."[1]

Gustav Meyrink wrote that "knowledge and memory are one and the same thing."[2] A soldier has knowledge of a battle at Hill 79, and memory of it. But Meyrink is not quite right. Knowledge is of course about memory, but memories also have histories. They come and go, often without our sensing *where* they come from—or where they go; they are unstable, they change, they evolve, they mutate in ways independent of thought. Temporal and physical dislocation, displacement, oscillation, movement forward and back, confidence, panic, experiences acquired and lost—the human memory recapitulates the lived experience of the refugee. Michel Foucault's reasoning closely followed Nietzsche's on the inaccessibility of the origin and the discontinuous development of human consciousness—one that acquires experience, forgets, dissembles, remembers, represses, blots out one memory with another—in an unsteady progress toward a settled mind of integrity, remembrance, and wisdom. Memory comes down to us through "sedimented layers" of previous apprehension and interpretation, as people experience history, lodge it in memory, and then rewrite it to suit their needs—particularly where individual complicity in crimes is at stake. This plastic power preserves psychic peace at the cost of repression, but it is also a positive trait—"a testament to the creativity and ingenuity of the species," as Tina Rosenberg put it. Yet people strive against all odds to preserve "the sovereignty of the subject," a life narrative with a beginning, middle, and end.[3]

The opposite of remembrance, or of keeping promises, is forgetfulness. It allows us "to close the doors and windows of consciousness for a time," Nietzsche wrote; as an active faculty, forgetting is "like a doorkeeper, a preserver of psychic order, repose, and etiquette." Human beings need forgetting, just as its opposite, memory, is an act of will; it requires one "to think causally," to compute, to reflect, and to anticipate—this is "the long story of how *responsibility* originated." To be responsible is to be serious about husbanding memory. Forgetfulness is a matter of will, too, "an active and in the strictest sense positive faculty of repression." We humans are weak; we need to forget. However, people cannot but remember that which is "burned in"; only that which "never ceases to *hurt* stays in the memory"—pain is the most powerful aid to mnemonics. Virginia Woolf had the same insight: trauma confers memory, "an underground river of recollection." Here, in essence, is the reason why Koreans remember, and Americans forget.

The Korean War, more than any other war in modern times, is surrounded by residues and slippages of memory. The Great War's place is indelible "in modern memory," its annihilating violence a permanent reminder of war's carnage. World War II was the good war, an outright victory to be celebrated. Vietnam tore the United States apart. With Korea there is less a presence than an absence; thus the default reflexive American name: "the forgotten war." Its veterans feel neglected and misunderstood—they are also forgotten. South Koreans experience a knot of terrible loss, tragedy, bitterness, fate, invisible burdens, an inner negation pushing them down and bending them inward, which they call *han*. North Koreans remember a scourge that claimed, on average, at least one member from every family. But here is the party of memory—laser-focused, burned-in remembrance of things past.

For years I rejected the "forgotten war" rubric; the *unknown war* seemed much better. But for Americans Korea is both: a forgotten war and a never-known war. The war began to disappear from consciousness as soon as the fighting stabilized: the first time it was named "forgotten," to my knowledge, came in May 1951 as the title of an article in *U.S. News & World Report.* (Likewise, as early as 1973 Martha Gellhorn wrote that "consensual amnesia was the American reaction, an almost instant reaction, to the Vietnam War"; television reinforced the forgetting by maintaining "a respectful silence" after U.S. troops departed in 1973, even though this suddenly "forgotten war" was hardly over.[5]) Veterans also decided that this sobriquet fit Korea—based on their hard-won experience in the field, and their uncomprehending reception when they came home. "Now that the war is over," says the Chorus in *Antigone,* "forget war." But if the war is never over, how can it be forgotten?

For Americans Korea is just one among several wars best forgotten, since we are batting only one for four in big wars since 1945, just another transient episode among a myriad of interventions in Third World countries that do not bear close examination if one cares about amour propre, but have unsettling ways of coming back to haunt us—in Iran, for example, or Guatemala. Yet a surfeit of information and experience leaves even the most inquiring person with "a huge quantity of indigestible stones of knowledge," so we would rather let our knowledge rest quietly within, "like a snake that has swallowed rabbits whole and now lies in the sun and avoids all unnecessary movement." It is a strange and disturbing thing, this human-all-too-human failing—because "one would think that history would encourage men to be *honest.*"[6]

A CIVIL WAR

The American "perfect tense" leads with a complete automaticity toward the dogma that the Korean War was started in 1950 by Stalin and Kim Il Sung, it ended in 1953 (whether as a victory, stalemate, or defeat depends on your partisan politics), and its sobriquet ever since has been "the forgotten war." But let us assume that all we need know is the alpha: Kim Il Sung, aided by Stalin, pushed the button on June 25 and that's how this war started. We successfully contained him and restored South Korea—the omega. A nagging problem still remains: unlike Hitler invading Poland, Tojo attacking Pearl Harbor, or Saddam Hussein invading Kuwait, Koreans invaded Korea. What do we make of that? In the midst of the terrible crisis in December 1950 that ineluctably followed upon the American decision to "liberate" the North, another view surfaced: that of Richard Stokes, the British minister of works, who intuited a paradox. The 38th parallel decision in 1945, taken unilaterally by Americans, was "the invitation to such a conflict as has in fact arisen":

> In the American Civil War the Americans would never have tolerated for a single moment the setting up of an imaginery [*sic*] line between the forces of North and South, and there can be no doubt as to what would have been their re-action if the British had intervened in force on behalf of the South. This parallel is a close one because in America the conflict was not merely between two groups of Americans, but was between two conflicting economic systems as is the case in Korea.[7]

Ever since 1950 this civil war analogy has been like a Rumpelstiltskin for the official American view that Kim committed international aggression: say it and the logic collapses, the interpretation loses its power. But Stokes carried his argument one step further:

not just a civil war, but a war between two conflicting social and economic systems.

Stokes happened to have been right: the longevity of this conflict finds its reason in the essential nature of the war, the thing we need to know first: it was a civil war, a war fought primarily by Koreans from conflicting social systems, for Korean goals. It did not last three years, but had a beginning in 1932, and has never ended. In the early 1970s, when the Vietnam War was clearly lost, even an anti-Communist scholar such as Adam Ulam (who in the 1990s called Korea "Stalin's war") could reflect that the North's attack across the 38th parallel was no different than Mao's legions crossing the Yangtze River into south China,[8] and we can add Hanoi's regular armies roaring out of the central highlands in 1975: the civil wars in China and Vietnam ended with infantry invasions—and Korea would have, too, if we think of June 1950 as an end to decades of intra-Korean conflict, a dénouement instead of a beginning.

For Americans a discrete encapsulation limits this war to the time frame of June 1950 to July 1953. This construction relegates all that went before to mere prehistory, June 25 is original sin, all that comes after is postbellum. It also presumes to demarcate the period of active American involvement; before June 1950, it is Syngman Rhee against Kim Il Sung backed or controlled by Stalin and/or Mao; after July 1953, it is Rhee against the same people, his fledgling republic ever under threat. This construction focuses the bright glare of our attention on the question of who started the war, on the presupposition that the correct answer to this question furnishes answers to all the other questions. What is highlighted here obscures all that went before and all that came after, placing it in the shadows of irrelevance. In this manner a wrongly conceived and never-known civil conflict disappears before our very eyes, as an American construction that only an American would believe; but American amour propre remains firmly intact. The American focus on "who started it" is a political and often an ideological position, a point of honor that abstracts from and makes easy and comprehensible the politically shaped verdicts that began with Washington's official story on June 25, 1950.

The Korean War was (and is) a civil war; only this conception can account for the 100,000 lives lost in the South *before* June 1950 and the continuity of the conflict down to the present, in spite of assumptions that Moscow's puppets in Pyongyang would surely collapse after the USSR itself met oblivion in 1991. It is therefore instructive to see what Thucydides, the first philosopher of war, had to say about fratricidal conflict. Perhaps the most famous line from his book, "war is a stern teacher," comes from the civil war in Corcyra:

> War is a stern teacher. So revolutions broke out in city after city.... What used to be described as a thoughtless act of aggression was now regarded as the courage one would expect to find in a party member; to think of the future and wait was merely another way of saying one was a coward; any idea of moderation was just an attempt to disguise one's unmanly character; ability to understand a question from all sides meant that one was totally unfitted for action. Fanatical enthusiasm was the mark of a real man, and to plot against an enemy behind his back was perfectly legitimate self-defense. Anyone who held violent opinions could always be trusted, and anyone who objected to them became a suspect.[9]

This passage fits the Korean civil war with no necessity to dot "i"s or cross "t"s, and it explains the continuing blight on the Korean mind drawn by that war, just like a doctor drawing blood: to understand the Korean War "from all sides" is still to go to jail in the North, and to risk oblivion in the now (and finally) democratic South. It also fits the American civil war, by far the most devastating of all American wars to Americans, but one that happened long enough ago that most Americans have no idea what it means to have warfare sweeping back and forth across the national territory, or to have brother pitted against brother

Oh What a Literary War

This was Paul Fussell's title for the Great War.[10] It would never occur to anyone to say that about Korea; if this war exists in American literature, it is usually wallpaper for people who may or may not have fought there, but came of age in the 1950s. From this war came nothing like Norman Mailer's *The Naked and the Dead,* Joseph Heller's *Catch-22,* or Michael Herr's *Dispatches.* Neither a victory like World War II nor a defeat like Vietnam, it struck a glancing blow at young people who looked up to their parents who fought in the big war, had yet to encounter Vietnam, and seem ultimately to have been bewildered by Korea, not to have *seen* the war in its fullness, and quickly to have passed it by (if they didn't fight in it). The war was and remains, after all, a stark counterpoint to the halcyon 1950s—the easy "I like Ike" years of nearly full employment, Hollywood in Technicolor and James Dean in full adolescent sulk, TV in its *Ozzie and Harriet* phase of light family entertainment, Detroit turning out brilliantly painted and chromed lead sleds, cars with rocketlike tail fins and busty Marilyn Monroe front bumpers—it was all there by 1955 (the year Newt Gingrich once nominated as the apex of the American dream). This nostalgia elides segregation, a stultifying conformity, and of course the Korean War. But most young people loved these years. To experience Elvis and Little Richard and Fats Domino when nothing like them had ever appeared on the horizon (of white folks), with every fond hope for the future—it's just another reason why the war got buried.

James Salter's beautiful memoir, *Burning the Days,* briefly recounts his six months in Korea—a substitute for World War II, since he got his pilot's wings just as that war ended. This memoir might be the script for *The Bridges at Toko-Ri.* Probably the best-known Hollywood film of the war, the action takes place mostly in Japan, the narrative line is World War II—and Toko-ri is the Japanese pronunciation of a Korean village. It appeared when Hollywood "felt itself besieged" by McCarthyism, and neatly avoided all the controversies of this war.[11] Likewise, the country and the people leave not a bare trace on Salter's mind. He remembers cold winter mornings, anonymous Korean women serving him "bunja [orange] juice" at breakfast (or not—in which case they say "hava-no bunja"), headings for his bombing runs into the North, the girls at Miyoshi's in Japan. "There remains with me not the name of a single battle of the time or even general other than Van Fleet." What he discovered in Korea he also kept hidden, because it was so hard to articulate—"a deep attachment—deeper than anything I had known—to all that had happened," and to the self he became, "based on the risking of everything." It was the "great voyage" of his life, the burning days of youth, but it just happened to have happened in Korea. There are not many American memoirs of this war, but nearly all of them also follow a Toko-ri narrative: Korea is a never-known nightmare to be escaped in one piece; Japan is civilized, beautiful, with a petite culture only to be admired—not to mention the floor shows, the Ginza, the golf courses.[12]

Philip Roth's *Indignation* appears at first to reinhabit the territory of his collegiate days at Bucknell, a return to the terrain of his first novel, *Goodbye, Columbus:* the Midwest. Marcus Messner, a butcher's son from Newark, goes off to Winesburg College near Cleveland, studies the usual literary suspects, fumbles with girls in the backseats of cars, and ends up on the dean's list—his shit list: Korea beckons. Roth's novelistic treatment of the war he lived through does not go beyond the tropes and stereotypes of the time: "swarms" of Chinese, snow, "wave after wave" of Chinese, more snow, "a thousand screaming Chinese soldiers come swarming down on you"—and it's still snowing. What was the war about? It remains a mystery. So the Chinese swarm and the snows fall, but

Roth's climactic "coldest winter" comes in the Winesburg blizzard of '51, ostensibly a panty raid gone wild that gets him kicked out of college unfairly—and Korea awaits him. The war is reduced to the Chinese hordes and "some barbed wire on a spiny ridge in central Korea," but there his young life is snuffed out and his ghost reflects on what his father, a simple butcher, had tried to teach him: "the terrible, the incomprehensible way one's most banal, incidental, even comical choices achieve the most disproportionate result."

Roth interrupts his narrative, however, with a discourse on memory as "the all-embracing medium in which I am sustained as 'myself' " and the receptacle for life: "Who could have imagined that one would have forever to remember each moment of life down to its tiniest component?" It slowly dawns on the reader that Roth is writing posthumously—he is dead, and his afterlife is experienced in memories—"an imperishable fingerprint of an afterlife unlike anyone else's." It is an afterlife, but it is his own, uniquely, in a permanent condition of "memory upon memory, nothing but memory." He is right: memory is synonymous with oneself. His memory is immortal; the war is not—it recedes into oblivion.

No other American journalist so fully inhabited his time and ranged so widely, from the seriousness of *The Best and the Brightest* and courageous reporting from Vietnam to barnstorming with the Chicago Bulls or the New England Patriots, than David Halberstam. What other journalist so deeply explored the history through which he lived? Phillip Roth and Don DeLillo do this in fiction, but who else in nonfiction? Whether it was in Saigon or the ballpark, David was the one. I met David twice, first when I invited him to the University of Chicago and the next when we spent an afternoon talking about the Korean War. He left a message saying he was doing a book on the war and wanted to talk. I was flabbergasted that I could call back his published Manhattan number, and he picked up! He was charming, gracious, vital, engaging—and we didn't see eye to eye about the war. Then came the coldest April in 2007, when he died en route to interview the legendary quarterback Y. A. Tittle. A shocking, capricious, tragic auto accident stilled his resonant journalist's voice for the first time since his high school days.

Although the Korean War ended only a few years before Vietnam, it is as if a generation intervened between these two wars. Type "Korean War" on the Amazon website, and a few books come up that are still in print—usually by veterans or military historians. On Amazon.com a person named Edmund Burke listed "The Ten Best Books on the Korean War." All but one are by Americans or Westerners, and that one is a novel by Ha Jin (Koreans presumably do not write about their own war). Most of the books are decades old, and no books by scholars make the list.[13] Browse a library, and you will find rack after rack on the Vietnam War, and just one or two for the Korean War. Halberstam actually counted them, in a public library in Key West: eighty-eight books on the Vietnam War, four on Korea.

It took years of research to find out that Marilyn Monroe was discovered during the Korean War and dubbed "Miss Flamethrower," or that Margaret Bourke-White took hundreds of photos for *Life* not just of the war and the soldiers, but of the unknown guerrilla war in the South. It was only when Picasso died that I learned, in the fine print of his obituary, about his mural *Massacre in Korea,* in the style of *Guernica.* *M*A*S*H* remains an all-time popular TV series, because it may be set in Korea, but it's really about the Vietnam War—it has that sensibility. So it is to Halberstam's great credit that he did his last book on this war (of course, we all know it wouldn't have been close to his last book).

David Halberstam would have been the first to say that if someone thinks that Ted Williams's .406 batting average in 1941 is not awe-inspiring, well, you might not necessarily want to talk baseball with that person. Unfortunately, *The Coldest Winter* is full of passages that strike a historian in the same way. For example, that Dean Acheson made "a colossal gaffe" at the Press Club in January 1950 by leaving South Korea out of his defense perimeter, or that Kim Il

Sung was a dependent plaything of the Russians and Chinese, or that the invasion of the North in the fall of 1950 was MacArthur's idea, or that the June 1950 invasion started this conflict. Exactly two Korean names from the South show up in his book—Syngman Rhee, the president, and Paek Son-yop, the all-purpose former general trotted out for every prominent visiting journalist since the war ended, who fought alongside imperial Japan and was for decades a close associate of Japanese war criminals such as Sasakawa Ryoichi and assorted unrepentant Nazis.[14] Halberstam mentions the U.S. Military Government from 1945 to 1948, which deeply shaped postwar Korean history—in one sentence. There is absolutely nothing on the atrocious massacres of this war, or the American incendiary bombing campaign. Instead Korea is "a shrimp among whales" (a stereotype from 1900), an insignificant country with a bunch of leaders who, it seems, are hard to take seriously—and so on. *The Coldest Winter* is one of the best in a peculiar but common American genre: accounts of the war that evince almost no knowledge of Korea or its history, barely get past two or three Korean names, focus on the American experience in a war where Koreans and Chinese were much more numerous, and fail to question the accumulated baggage of 1950s stereotypes about the good guys and bad guys.

Nonetheless this genre exercises a strong influence in the United States, perhaps a subliminal one in that extensive knowledge of the war is not required, perhaps a hegemonic one in that well-known analysts easily perform its logic in a few sentences. Not many writers were better or more perspicacious guides to the George W. Bush administration and the wars in Iraq and Afghanistan than Hendrik Hertzberg of *The New Yorker*. He recently wrote that two of our five big wars since 1945 were good ones—Korea and the Gulf War (1991)—because they were "legitimate in their origins" and "scrupulous in their execution." Both were fought "in response to armed aggression across international borders," and in both American leaders "resisted powerful political pressures to expand its objective to include the destruction and conquest of the regime responsible for the original aggression."[15] The reader can judge how well these generalizations hold up as this book unfolds.

Acheson's Press Club speech was the opposite of an ill-considered gaffe: instead it unlocks key aspects of U.S. policy toward Korea before the war. Why did he not include Korea in his perimeter? The best answer is that Acheson "wanted to keep secret the American commitment to Korea's defense." Acheson implied that should an attack come there, the United States would take the problem to the UN Security Council—which is what Dean Rusk had secretly recommended to him nearly a year before the war, in July 1949, and exactly what Acheson did when the war erupted. In the many drafts leading up to this speech, South Korea was consistently seen as a direct American responsibility, along with Japan. But Acheson did not want to say this publicly, lest Syngman Rhee be emboldened to start a war; that is also why he blocked tanks and an air force for the ROK. Interestingly, when the North Koreans commented on this speech they had South Korea *included* in the defense perimeter. Why? Because for weeks there was no official transcript of the speech, and the North Koreans probably read *The New York Times*—which in the Sunday "Week in Review" section after the speech also had Korea included in the defense line. In the end it all worked beautifully for Acheson, who was seeking ambiguity and trying to keep both the Communists and volatile allies such as Syngman Rhee and Chiang Kai-shek guessing about what the United States would do if South Korea or Taiwan were attacked. The British War Office said in a December 1949 estimate that the Northern forces would have little difficulty in winning a war—and "on the question of aggression," there can be "no doubt whatever that their ultimate object is to overrun the South." The Americans had thought that the South could defend itself, the War Office said, but recently "they have been coming round to our way of thinking." This was an accurate reflection of Acheson's suppositions. As for Stalin, thanks to Kim Philby and other spies he was reading Acheson's secrets with his breakfast, and had no reason to pay attention to speeches for public consumption.[17]

The Coldest Winter is best at examining the major American protagonists, through deftly written portraits: Acheson, Truman, Kennan, MacArthur—and especially "Pinky" MacArthur, his mother. It was the "Age of Acheson," Halberstam correctly said; he dominated the basic decisions about the war and could do so because he had "a constituency of one"—Harry Truman. Halberstam's subtle portrait of George Kennan is one of the best in the literature, and explains why he was the only top American leader who understood that invading North Korea was a disastrous idea. He catches MacArthur well, but a bit too perfectly, overestimating his influence. MacArthur made no decision that was central to the war, except his fateful one to split his army corps as they marched into the North. The Inchon landing, which Halberstam presents as "a brilliant, daring gamble" and a total surprise to the North Koreans, was neither: a Pentagon war plan issued in mid-June 1950 prefigured it, and a host of captured documents show Pyongyang knew it was coming by the end of August, if not earlier—but could do little about it.

Halberstam brings into focus the views of many American veterans, whom he clearly enjoyed interviewing about this "puzzling, gray, very distant conflict, a war that went on and on, seemingly without hope or resolution, about which most Americans...preferred to know as little as possible." It was a war, he thought, "orphaned by history." True in the 1950s perhaps, but a full shelf of books by historians in the United States and around the world reclaimed it decades ago. Had Halberstam read this work seriously, he could not have written *The Coldest Winter*. Had someone written a book like this about the Vietnam War, he would have been the first to criticize it. Rather, his book illustrates the war's impact on a particular generation, those too young for World War II, in school while Korea raged, and professionally engaged by the time Vietnam became an issue. In the same way that no archival document could ever convince me of Richard Nixon's essential goodness, no historian was going to tell David Halberstam that Dean Acheson and Harry Truman were not the good guys, and MacArthur not the author of the war's essential failure. Halberstam ends Part I with this from Acheson: "We sat around like paralyzed rabbits while MacArthur carried out this nightmare." Here we witness nothing more than the brilliance of Acheson's ventriloquy and dissembling.

Melvin Horwitz was a bright young doctor assigned to a MASH unit near the front in 1951–52, and his loving letters to his wife reflect his complicated experience. His original image of the Far East, formed by Hollywood movies, was about places "where terrorists lurked in dark shadowed alleys." Korea existed somewhere between an occupied Japan that he could enjoy and appreciate, and American stereotypes of Chinese laundrymen ("Boysan, boysan, makee with rubber," he wrote about some sandals; the *san* honorific is, of course, Japanese). Like most other Americans in the last two years of the war, his contacts with Koreans were minimal—houseboys employed full-time for $2.25 a month, maids, wounded ROK soldiers muted by the language barrier. He rode through the countryside like a tourist, enjoying the beauty of the mountains and rice paddies, and the glint of red pepper drying on golden thatched roofs. The one city that escaped the war, Pusan, was for him a nightmare of refugees, gangs of ragged children and kids pimping ("Me pimpo…nice girl. Blow job."). Like most of the soldiers he knew, he fought in a war "that no one really believes in," especially the "pain and death" along a front that rarely moved more than a few miles. Syngman Rhee, the George Washington of Korea to American politicians, was "a tyrant and as fascistic as Chiang." Korea was "yet one more war that shouldn't have happened."[18] Salter, Roth, Halberstam, and Horwitz are markers for a generation that will pass away (like the rest of us), and after that no American will again bury this distant war in the nostalgia of young men and their formative experiences.

Gregory Henderson was one of the very few among the millions of Americans to have served in Korea both before and during the war (six million in the war years alone[19]) to have been moved by the country, to learn the language and culture, to have made of it a second home—first as a diplomat, then as a scholar. His *Politics of the Vortex* remains one of the best books on twentieth-century Korea, and it is particularly acute on those years he himself experienced. Everyone knew everyone else in Seoul, a city so centralized that it was the core of his "vortex"; Henderson's job was to get to know the elites even better, on behalf of his country. His eye fell on anomalies that others missed; for example, the Japanese military service of the high command of the ROK Army, the quiet pride they took in having fought for the emperor and remained loyal. (Park Chung Hee served a different emperor, P'u Yi, the titular leader of Manchukuo, from whom Park received a gold watch.) Henderson likened the ROK to the "Southern way of life" in the United States, an apt analogy given the prevalence of landed estates served by multitudes of peasant tenants; if this was hardly Athens, the North was much like its opposite: "steelier, more Spartan, more hardbitten, more ideological and less yielding and opportunistic."[20]

THROUGH CHINESE EYES

In contrast to the ephemeral traces Korea made on American minds, Ha Jin's novel *War Trash* rings true on every page, a closely observed and much-pondered experience. An interested, fair, discerning observer—so shocked by what he saw—he embraces the odd mass of humanity clustered in Korea during the war. His protagonist's unit crossed the Yalu to find empty land, "with at least four-fifths of the houses leveled to the ground." The farther south they went, even fewer houses remained. The image of a blind woman "in a ruffly white dress" picking through a garbage dump, a toddler strapped to her back, remains with him forever as a sign of human resilience. Even amid the blasted landscape, Korean women sang songs, sometimes for hours in the evening, and remained so fond of cosmetics that most had a pouch of stuff to make up their faces (few Chinese women over forty bother with wearing skirts, let alone makeup). He came upon a prison camp holding hundreds of women guerrillas; women sang there, too; "their voices transported me into reveries." He noticed that Chinese and North Korean soldiers paid for what they took from civilians, whereas South Korean troops just took. How is it that a Chinese foot soldier sees these things, but Americans apparently didn't? Then after he was captured, he wondered why American doctors and nurses were so kind to him.[21]

Ha Jin re-creates fictionally the notorious episode when North Korean POWs captured Brig. Gen. Francis T. Dodd on May 8, 1952, during riots on Koje Island. North Koreans in the camps looked more like highly organized militias than POWs, Ha Jin thought; women were their communication channel to guerrillas on the island and to their superiors in the North. A Korean People's Army colonel named Lee had fought for many years against the Japanese in Manchukuo, and spoke fluent Chinese; he and others explained that Kim Il Sung had ordered them to open "a second front" inside the camps. The POWs spit out bitterness at General Dodd: Why did American soldiers make North Korean soldiers strip naked after their capture? Why did their jets erase villages? After Dodd was released, American forces used flamethrowers to retake the camp, leaving seventy-seven dead among the POWs.[22]

In 1987 I was able to interview Pak Chang-uk in Pyongyang, a double-amputee who rose from his chair to a standing position by throwing his trunk forward and leveraging his wooden legs under his weight; he provided a blow-by-blow description of the Dodd capture and the subduing of North Korean POWs in Camp 76, in a presentation so striking that he seemed ready to fight it all out again. After the war he sired three daughters and a son, the eldest daughter an architect and the son a railway engineer.

CHAPTER FOUR

CULTURE
OF REPRESSION

The titular leader of the North Korean puppet regime and ostensible commander of the North Korean armies is Kim Il Sung, a 38-year-old giant from South Korea, where he is wanted as a fugitive from justice. His real name is supposed to be Kim Sung Chu, but he has renamed himself after a legendary Korean revolutionary hero...and many Koreans apparently still believe that it is their "original" hero and not an imposter who rules in North Korea.

—*New York Times* EDITORIAL, JULY 27, 1950

The Korean War is an unknown war because it transpired during the height of the McCarthy era (Julius and Ethel Rosenberg were indicted when the war began and executed just before it ended), making open inquiry and citizen dissent improbable. This home front was a repressed but also fascinating place, with Hollywood films that replayed the script of World War II in Korea, weekly magazines with articles and photos that documented a new and very different kind of war (anticipating Vietnam), and shocking stories that threatened and frightened all Americans (not unlike the period since 9/11): a menacing Communist bloc unified from Berlin to Canton, crushing and incomprehensible defeats on the battlefield, fiendish "brainwashing," and the astounding defection to communism of twenty-one Americans at the end of the war (all of whom ended up in China, and nearly all of whom eventually returned to the United States).

The known and observed Korean War occurred in the first six months, when some 270 journalists from nineteen countries followed the troops and the shifting battle lines, and sent mostly uncensored dispatches to their editors.[1] They instantly understood this to be a very different war from the global conflagration that ended five years earlier—and that most of them had also covered. It was obviously a smaller and more restricted war ("the limited war" was its name before Vietnam came along), but it was also something novel: a civil war, a people's war. The best of them was Reginald Thompson, an experienced British journalist who had reported on every important war of the twentieth century to that point and who covered Korea before censorship began. Honest, inquiring, investigative, confident in the truth seen by his own eyes, willing to say what he thought—he was what one wants in a war correspondent. Thompson's *Cry Korea* is the only Western book of the Korean War that can be compared to the classics of the Chinese civil war such as Graham Peck's *Two Kinds of Time* or Jack Belden's *China Shakes the World*. But another eyewitness account is almost as interesting: Gen. William F. Dean wandered around the hills near Taejon for more than a month after losing that battle, and then spent three years in a North Korean prison camp. His candid and thoughtful observations offer very little grist for the Cold War mill of Communist evil and free-world virtue. Instead both of them opened a window to eyewitness truth.

Early war coverage was fascinating and instructive, revealing its essential nature, its *civil* nature; war raged up and down the peninsula for six months, and everything was seen. Then for the last two years it was positional warfare along the DMZ, and Westerners had little contact with Koreans except as enemy, soldier, servant, or prostitute. Thompson was appalled by the ubiquitous, casual racism of Americans, from general to soldier, and their breathtaking ignorance of Korea. Americans used the term "gook" to refer to all Koreans, North and South, but especially North Koreans; "chink" distinguished the Chinese. Decades after the fact, many were still using the term in oral histories.[2] This racist slur developed first in the Philippines, then traveled to the Pacific War, Korea, and Vietnam. Ben Anderson called it a depository for the "nameless sludge" of the enemy, and it might be the namelessness of Koreans, in American eyes, that stood out then and still does today. Donald Knox's voluminous oral histories, for example, rarely if ever name any Koreans. But American soldiers do comment on the paradox that "their gooks" fought like hell whereas "our gooks" were cowardly, bugged out, never could be relied on. (General Dean sampled the fierce resentment that being called "gook" stirred in all Koreans, North and South.[3]) It did not dawn on most Americans that anticolonial fighters might have something to fight about.

In the summer of 1950 basic knowledge about the KPA and its leaders was treated as a revelation—for example, that the majority of its soldiers had fought in the Chinese civil war. Three months into the war, *The New York Times* found big news in a biography of Defense Minister Choe Yong-gon released by MacArthur's headquarters: it discovered that he had fought with the Chinese Communists, placing him in Yanan in 1931 (no mean feat, three years before the Long March). Also unearthed was the information that he was in overall command of the KPA, which appeared to suggest that international communism was allowing the locals to run some things. Two days later the *Times* turned up the news that the division commander Mu Chong had also fought in China, and that most of the KPA's equipment had been sold to it by the Russians in 1948. Ergo,

> With its peculiar combination of fanaticism, politics and just plain rudimentary fighting qualities of Orientals ... [the KPA] is a strange one. Some observers believe that, in the absence of good pre-war intelligence, we have just begun to learn about it.[4]

Early on, the *Times* had found a queer tone in North Korean statements to the United Nations: they "had a certain ring of passion" about them, as if they really believed what they were saying about American imperialism. The *Times*'s own rendering of the "imposter" Kim Il Sung read as follows:

> The titular leader of the North Korean puppet regime and ostensible commander of the North Korean armies is Kim Il Sung, a 38-year-old giant from South Korea, where he is wanted as a fugitive from justice. His real name is supposed to be Kim Sung Chu, but he has renamed himself after a legendary Korean revolutionary hero ... and many Koreans apparently still believe that it is their "original" hero and not an imposter who rules in North Korea.[5]

KPA soldiers captured during the Inchon operation. *U.S. National Archives*

Somehow the *Times*'s "all the news that's fit to print" seemed scripted by Syngman Rhee. The ordinary reader would believe that KPA soldiers were trouncing Americans and dying by the thousands, all for a poseur with a hyperactive pituitary, a John Dillinger on the lam from august organs of justice in Seoul.

Thompson's initial encounter with American racism was the appalling spectacle of MacArthur's greatest triumph, at Inchon. Why, after their defeat, he asked, were POWs paraded stark naked by the Americans? The dehumanization of "the gooks" was palpable whether in defeat (Taejon) or in victory (Inchon). But this slur "could not rob the slain or the living of their human kinship, nor the naked procession of prisoners, with their hands folded upon their heads—as though they might conceal weapons even in their bodies—of an uncouth and tragic dignity." Every other correspondent saw this naked parade of shame (but whose shame?); few of them commented on it. And then it turned out the nude men were young, inexperienced decoys; about two thousand North Koreans defended against seventy thousand UN forces in 270 ships. The actual Korean People's Army "had disappeared like wraiths into the hills." MacArthur's trap "had closed, and it was empty."[6]

Worst of all, in another reporter's eyes, were the Korean National Police. They ran rackets, procured destitute girls for brothels, blackmailed people by threatening to call them Communists, and executed thousands of political prisoners. In November 1950 an Australian journalist, Alan Dower, witnessed a retinue of hooded women, many with babies, roped together and dragged along by ROK police. He followed them until they were kneeling before "a deep freshly dug pit," ringed by machine guns. Dower pointed his rifle at the commander and said, "If those machine guns fire I'll shoot you between the eyes." And so he saved the women, at least for the moment. American soldiers also witnessed the summary execution of North Korean POWs, almost as a routine. Sometimes GIs turned a captive over to the Korean police, to be shot. Sometimes they just did it themselves. But sometimes they did the right thing. Pfc. Jack Wright witnessed a group of around a hundred civilians, including old men, pregnant women, and children as young as eight, digging their own graves as ROK policemen stood guard, ready to murder all of them. Wright told them to stop; the Korean in charge said he had his orders and planned "to execute these people." Wright pointed to a machine gun and told him not to move, as other GIs escorted the civilians to safety. "This kind of thing happened all over the front," he later said (meaning massacres rather than brave interventions).[7]

Similar atrocities occurred across Korea as the South recovered its own territory and marched through the North, but that was also the point where courageous and honest journalism came to an abrupt end. World outrage at the South's atrocities did change U.S.

The Reporter's faked article on Soviet puppetry. *Courtesy of the Howard Gotlieb Archival Research Center*

policy: in January 1951 "correspondents were placed under the complete jurisdiction of the army." Criticism of allies and allied troops was prohibited—"any derogatory comments" met the censor's black brush. American reporters were the most cowed and therefore, Philip Knightly thought, the most useless; worst of all, some U.S. journalists and editors even concocted false reports. Soon foreign reporters were so sick of UN Command "lies, half-truths and serious distortions" that they found Wilfred Burchett and Alan Winnington, both writing from the enemy side, more informative.[8]

What got past the censors was often killed on the McCarthy-terrorized home front; even Edward R. Murrow's reports were sometimes dead on arrival at CBS headquarters in New York. The fiercely independent and eagle-eyed I. F. Stone perused the global print media and wrote a famously contrary book, *The Hidden History of the Korean War*; twenty-eight publishing houses turned it down before Monthly Review Press brought it out in 1952.[9] For many years one of the few good sources on MacArthur's "my little fascist," General Willoughby, was a big exposé in *The Reporter*, a magazine that could be found on every liberal's coffee table in the 1950s. Yet it also ran articles faked by the CIA (one of them a cover story purporting to come from a Soviet defector who helped build up the North Korean army), and its crusading editor, Max Ascoli, had Allen Dulles (then a top aide in the CIA) check the page proofs of two long articles on the China Lobby; elements in the CIA probably informed parts of the articles, which did, indeed, contain much new information.[10]

It took more than a decade before Hollywood began to unlock this history in films (and in truth it never did). The singular classic film of the Korean War is *The Manchurian Candidate*, appearing in 1962 only to disappear for decades after it seemed to anticipate Kennedy's assassination. An odd mix of terror and high camp, its genius was to wrap the Orientalism and Communist-hating of the fifties in the black humor of the sixties, amid the self-congratulatory pillorying of the McCarthy character (presented as a henpecked fool and knave); the film allows one to be chic in one's prejudices. The battle itself is fleeting, haphazardly staged on a backlot. Yen Lo, the evil Oriental, superbly portrayed by Khigh Dhiegh, became a stunning media signifier for demonic Orientals thereafter. Dhiegh had a long career in similar Hollywood roles ("Wo Fat," "Four Finger Wu," "King Chou Lai," aka Chou En-lai; in his first film, *Time Limit*, he played Colonel Kim, a nasty interrogator of American POWs in Korea), but was otherwise known as Kenneth Dickerson—born in Spring Lake, New Jersey, of Syrian and Egyptian ancestry. *Candidate* is the one Korean War film of lasting significance, but it mostly reinforces stereotypes about Asian Communists and what the war was about.

INSTINCT FOR REPRESSION

As the year 1950 got going, Senator Joseph McCarthy remarked to a reporter, "I've got a sock full of shit and I know how to use it." Soon he rose to denounce 205, or 57, or, as it happened, a handful of vulnerable liberals in the State Department and elsewhere as "Communists and queers who have sold four hundred million Asiatic people into atheistic slavery."[11] McCarthy exemplified a destructive ideological era when labels stood in place of arguments and evidence made next to no difference. If the same phenomenon can be sampled today on our TV shouting matches, Tailgunner Joe and his allies dramatically wrenched the American political spectrum rightward, interrogating, castigating, and nearly burying the progressive forces of the 1930s. Their bludgeon was an undeniable global crisis detonated by the Soviet atomic bomb and the Chinese revolution, which seemed to spread red ink across half of the globe and jolted Americans, basking in their grand victory in 1945 but still remarkably unworldly, into thinking a handful of internal foreigners—traitors—had caused it all. On the very day McCarthy first rose in the Senate to denounce communism in government, Senator Homer Capehart of Indiana exclaimed, "How much more are we going to have to take? Fuchs and Acheson and Hiss and hydrogen bombs *threatening outside* and New Dealism eating away at the vitals of the nation! In the name of Heaven, is this the best America can do?"[12]

For Americans who had to be told what a Communist looked like,[13] McCarthy supplied plausible models: mainly Eastern establishment blue bloods, but also Foggy Bottom scribblers, tweedy professors, closet-bound homosexuals, and China experts who had been abroad too long—anyone who might be identified as an internal foreigner, alien to the American heartland. (*The Freeman* once said that Red propaganda appealed only to "Asian coolies and Harvard professors.") Almost anybody with a good education might qualify; thus the bane of the liberal in the fifties was the threat of mistaken identity.

Domestic politics in America is like rugby, slouching toward the goal line, hamstrung by constituents, lobbies, and the pulling-and-hauling of a thousand bargains, lacking autonomy. Foreign policy is like ballet, the long pass from quarterback, or the boxer with a knockout punch. McCarthy was a nihilist who believed in nothing; a breaker of Senate rules, he also broke free of the webs of domestic politics, taking a foreign-policy issue that hardly anyone understood and running with it. Drawing upon an aggrieved mass base, he escaped the slogging politics of Congress to launch ideological attacks on the Truman-Acheson executive, thus constraining the extraordinary autonomy foreign-policy elites had exercised since 1941, and placing distinct outer limits on the spectrum of "responsible" foreign-policy discourse which persist to this day.

McCarthy came from a farm constituency of Catholics and German-Americans, giving colorful voice to their hatred of the British and Anglophile easterners, for whom Acheson, with his phony British accent, waxed mustache, top hat and tails, was the flypaper. A bizarre sexual politics attended this farcical drama; McCarthy managed to make anyone with a Boston blue-blood accent, or with intellectual pretensions or worldly knowledge, seem like a sissy if not a homosexual (Everett Dirksen, a centrist, referred to the "Lavender Lads" in the State Department, and indeed the period saw widespread purges of homosexuals in government).

McCarthy was supplied documentation on alleged subversives, most of it classified, by J. Edgar Hoover, Willoughby and Whitney of MacArthur's staff, and even Walter Bedell Smith of the CIA. Willoughby had begun McCarthy-style investigations of his own in 1947, especially of scholars working for the extremely leftist Institute for Pacific Relations; his first case was Andrew Grajdanzev, the author in 1944 of what remains today one of the best English-language accounts of Japanese rule in Korea. Willoughby had him tailed, read his mail, and determined that he might be "a long-range Soviet agent"—the evidence being that Owen Lattimore, a professor at the Johns Hopkins University, had written a recommendation for him, and that he wanted to purge Japanese leaders with unsavory pre-1945 records whom MacArthur and Willoughby supported. Willoughby fingered crafty subversives such as Anna Louise Strong and Agnes Smedley who somehow, despite their blanketed obscurity, brought Mao to power by remote control. In a letter of May 1950 to the head of the House Un-American Activities Committee, Willoughby said that "American Communist brains planned the communization of China," fellow-traveling people who had "an inexplicable fanaticism for an alien cause, the Communist 'Jehad' of pan-Slavism for the subjugation of the Western world." Willoughby paid particular attention to names and birthplaces that might indicate Jewish origin.[14]

Owen Lattimore's experience says much about McCarthyism, the China Lobby, and its relationship to Korea. It is forgotten that McCarthy began his attacks well before the Korean War, that Lattimore's views on Korea were one of McCarthy's central subjects, and that by June 1950 McCarthyism seemed to be losing its momentum—its capacity to establish "China" as an issue in American politics. McCarthy first attacked Lattimore indirectly on March 13, 1950, alleged a week later that he had found a "chief Russian spy," and finally named Lattimore when information leaked from his committee. Beyond Lattimore stood Philip Jessup, "a dangerously efficient Lattimore front" (he was a professor of international law at Columbia then in the State Department), but ultimately his object was Acheson, whom McCarthy termed "the voice for the mind of Lattimore."[15] Acheson was his final target: Why? In part because by the spring of 1950 he was the last high official (besides Truman himself) standing between Chiang Kai-shek and the American backing he desperately needed to survive an impending Communist invasion.

In early April McCarthy claimed to have a document incriminating Lattimore as a Soviet agent prompting Lattimore to release it to the press—it was a memorandum he wrote for the State Department in August 1949, arguing that "the U.S. should disembarass itself as quickly as possible of its entanglements in South Korea." Lattimore saw Korea as "little China," and Rhee as another Chiang: If we could not win with Chiang, he said, how could we win with "a scattering of 'little Chiang Kai-sheks' in China or elsewhere in Asia"? Of greater moment, Lattimore's memo also implicitly criticized the developing bureaucratic momentum in the summer and fall of 1949 for not just containing communism, but rolling it back:

> It certainly cannot yet be said … that armed warfare against communism in the Far East … has become either unavoidable or positively desirable. Nor can it be said with any assurance that … the Far East would be the optimum field of operation. There are still alternatives before us—a relatively long peace, or a rapid approach toward war. If there is to be war, it can only be won by defeating Russia—not northern Korea, or Viet Nam, or even China.[16]

In mid-May 1950 McCarthy again attacked the "Acheson Lattimore axis" (or, the "pied pipers of the Politburo") on Korea policy, saying Lattimore's plans for Korea would deliver millions to "Communist slavery." Taking direct aim at the Nationalists' principal antagonist, Acheson, he blared, "fire the headmaster who betrays us in Asia."[17]

Lattimore's fuller views on Korea were given in the fall of 1949 when the State Department called in experts to consult with them on a new Asian policy. Generally speaking, liberal scholars such as Lattimore, Cora DuBois, and John K. Fairbank tried to point out that the revolution sweeping much of East Asia was indigenous, the culmination of a century of Western and imperial impact. Conservative scholars such as William Colegrove, David Nelson Rowe, and Bernard Brodie sought instead to argue that Soviet machinations were behind Asian communism. Liberals were dominant within scholarly circles, however, and in these meetings a consensus emerged, looking forward to the establishment of diplomatic relations with the PRC.

The United States should stand with progressive and liberal forces in Asia where they existed, Lattimore said, but should not place itself in the path of changes that were already faits accomplis, such as the Chinese revolution, which would be self-defeating and stupid. Meanwhile: "Korea appears to be of such minor importance that it tends to get overlooked, but Korea may turn out to be a country that has more effect upon the situation than its apparent weight would indicate." After this prophetic mouthful, he argued that the ROK politically was "an increasing embarrassment," an "extremely unsavory police state" where the

> chief power is concentrated in the hands of people who were collaborators of Japan.... Southern Korea, under the present regime, could not resume close economic relations with Japan without a complete reinfiltration of the old Japanese control and associations...the kind of regime that exists in southern Korea is a terrible discouragement to would-be democrats throughout Asia....Korea stands as a terrible warning of what can happen.

Once the war began, however, Lattimore expressed his support for the American intervention.[18]

In spite of the obviously political and mendacious nature of McCarthy's witch hunt against Lattimore, within a few weeks major organs of opinion were already giving the classic formulation that enabled them to escape McCarthy's gunsights: supporting Lattimore's right to his opinions, but condemning them as irresponsible or extreme. In mid-April *The New York Times* singled out his "unsound" position on Korea; it found Lattimore's view "quite shocking," saying that the State Department had "rejected flatly

Mr. Lattimore's advice to cut and run in Korea."[19] The historian Mary McAuliffe is right to say, "One of the major ironies of the period was the unexpected role which liberals played, first in constructing a new liberalism which rejected the American left, and then in accepting some of the basic assumptions and tactics of the Red Scare itself."[20]

In the atmosphere of McCarthyism, the British author Godfrey Hodgson wrote, "Liberals were almost always more concerned about distinguishing themselves from the Left than about distinguishing themselves from conservatives." Thus they joined "the citadel of... a conservative liberalism." If the fear of being investigated had shown the intellectuals "the stick" in the early 1950s, "the hope of being consulted had shown them the carrot" thereafter. Being an influential client meant accepting the confines of one's patronage.[21] But in 1950, it was the stick that counted, and a mighty one it was.

Let's say you supported North Korea or China in the war in Korea. What might an American citizen have faced if he or she demonstrated militantly in favor of that position? The United Nations determined that the invasion was a "breach of the peace," wrote Morris Amchan (deputy chief counsel for war crimes at the Nuremberg trials); it was therefore "aggressive and criminal." Any person who thereafter would "substantially participate" on the North Korean side "must be charged with knowledge of the fact that he is participating in the waging of an aggressive war and illegal aggression." All "high persons" doing this should be "held responsible before an international tribunal."[22] If you were a Korean or a Communist, mere pro–North Korean sentiments or mild protest brought a harsh penalty. The FBI investigated and deported several Koreans, permanent residents in the United States who were known as anti-Rhee leftists or who took the Northern side; the records are still classified on this, but it is alleged that some who were deported were subsequently executed in South Korea, and that others went to the North.[23]

The McCarran Internal Security Act, named for its sponsor, Patrick McCarran (D-Nevada)—the ignorant and corrupt inquisitor of China scholars, and the model for the senator in the film *The Godfather, Part II*—was passed on September 23, 1950, establishing among other things concentration camps for those construed as a threat to American security. Iconic liberals such as senators Paul Douglas (D-Illinois) and Hubert Humphrey (D-Minnesota) voted for it; a bipartisan coalition passed the bill. *U.S. News & World Report* published "rules for Communists" under the act: the government would not set up camps for Communists "right away." But, once they existed, who would go into them? "Many Communists and fellow travelers. Others would be rounded up, too. Anybody could be held if considered dangerous to U.S. security." The Ku Klux Klan would not count, however, because it lacked "connections with the Communists."[24] Readers who hasten to point out that no one was ever placed in the camps might recall that no one could have known that in September 1950.

Strangely enough, during the crisis occasioned by China's intervention in Korea—what Truman deemed a "national emergency"—McCarthy and his allies were curiously quiet. Perhaps it was because of MacArthur's palpable failure, or the enormous increases for defense spending happening under crypto-pink Democratic rather than patriotic Republican auspices. Or, it may simply have been that McCarthy was occupied with other matters. The Washington insider Drew Pearson had once again surfaced innuendos about McCarthy's manhood, stirring an important but subterranean sexual politics that animated the capital. On December 13, Pearson's fifty-third birthday, McCarthy cornered him in the cloakroom of the Sulgrave Club, kneed him twice in the groin in good Tailgunner Joe fashion, and slapped him to the floor. Whereupon Richard Nixon intervened: "Let a Quaker stop this fight."[25]

The United States during this period is not to be compared with authoritarian states such as prewar Japan or Germany, or the Soviet Union. It remained open, over the long term, to a reversal of some

President Truman signs declaration of National Emergency, December 1950. *U.S. National Archives*

of the worst excesses of the 1950s (although by no means all of them); the press was not muzzled and dissenters were not confined, unless they were the leaders of the Communist Party (and the Supreme Court later overturned their convictions under the Smith Act). But this is not really the point. Judged by the ideals America established for itself and its fight for freedom on a world scale, the early 1950s were a dark period indeed, a maximization of the potential for absolutist conformity that Tocqueville warned about. If critics were not shot or tortured, they nonetheless suffered loss of careers, ostracism, intense psychological pressures, and admonitions to change their thoughts or be excluded from the spectrum of political acceptability. Tailgunner Joe was a good marksman: he left a generation of liberals looking over their shoulder to the right, fearing yet another case of mistaken identity.

McCarthyism also served to draw attention away from the corruption and intrigue of high officials with the Nationalists and the China Lobby, including the filching of top-level secrets on behalf of a foreign government and U.S. agencies of justice working closely with sordid foreign secret police: in 1953, for example, the Justice Department worked with Willoughby, Ho Shih-lai, and Chiang Ching-guo on the cases of Lattimore and John Paton Davies—Chiang, of course, being the son of Chiang Kai-shek, with long experience in the KMT secret police. Perhaps most shocking, several of these investigations were faked.[26] Through McCarthyism a narrow set of interests combined to achieve (not single-handedly, of course) the result of maintaining American-Taiwan ties for two decades, wrecking the careers of nearly all government officials who had spoken the truth about China, and enriching the pockets of numerous hangers-on. Congress and the Justice Department should have been investigating this, and perhaps still should; but McCarthy's ferocious and wild attacks diverted attention all to the other direction.

ORIENT, OCCIDENT, AND REPRESSION: HOW THE BEST MINDS CREATE STEREOTYPES

The primary academic McCarthyite was Karl Wittfogel, who had a strange trajectory out of the same milieu as Bertolt Brecht: he was the leading ideologue of the German Communist Party in the early 1930s, and the leading proponent of Karl Marx's theory of "the Asiatic Mode of Production." Stalin purged him for reasons that are not entirely clear, and Wittfogel came to the United States and established himself as a scholar with his magnum opus, *Oriental*

Despotism.[27] Marx's theory appraised Asia by reference to what it lacked when set against the standard-issue European model of development: feudalism, the rise of the bourgeoisie, capitalism. A brutal satrap presided over a semiarid environment, running armies of bureaucrats and soldiers, regulating the paths of great rivers, and employing vast amounts of slave labor in gigantic public works projects (such as China's Great Wall). The despot above and the cringing mass below prevented the emergence of anything resembling a modern middle class.

Leon Trotsky, his biographer Isaac Deutscher, the Soviet dissident Nikolai Bukharin, and Wittfogel all likened Stalin to Eastern potentates, especially Genghis Khan, and thought his regime was a species of Oriental despotism, the worst features of the "Asiatic mode of production" coming to the fore. It is stunning to see Trotsky open his biography of Stalin with a first sentence remarking that the old revolutionist Leonid Krassin "was the first, if I am not mistaken, to call Stalin an 'Asiatic' "; Trotsky depicts "Asiatic" leaders as cunning and brutal, presiding over static societies with a huge peasant base.[28] "Cunning" and "shrewd" were standard adjectives in stereotypes of Asians, particularly when they were denied civil rights and penned up in Chinatowns by whites-only housing restrictions, leading to uniform typecasting from a distance—peering over a high board fence, so to speak. "Brutal" was another, at least since Genghis Khan, with Pol Pot and Mao reinforcing the image in our time. The broadest distinction, between static or indolent East and dynamic, progressive West, goes all the way back to Herodotus and Aristotle.

Marx never really investigated East Asia, but learned enough to know that if China fit his theory, Japan with its feudalism (and "petite culture") clearly did not. Wittfogel, however, applied his notions of Oriental despotism to every dynastic empire with a river running through it—China, tsarist Russia, Persia, Mesopotamia, Egypt, the Incas, even the Hopi Indians of Arizona. By this time he had done a full-fledged, high-wire *tenko* (Japanese for a political

[handwritten margin note: but US "supported" Pol Pot bc Vietnam]

flip-flop), reemerging as an organic reactionary and trying to re-produce himself in, of all places, Seattle—the most thoroughly middle-class city in America. Wittfogel wrote for many extreme-right-wing publications and played a critical role in the purges of China scholars and Foreign Service officers during the McCarthy period. Hardly any scholars would testify against Owen Lattimore, Senator Joseph McCarthy's prime professorial target, but the University of Washington furnished three: Wittfogel, Nikolas Poppe (a Soviet expert on Mongolia who had defected to the Nazis in 1943), and George Taylor, a British scholar-journalist.[29]

After teaching in the Philadelphia area in the mid-1970s—where I was pleased to meet Olga Lang, Wittfogel's first wife ("Why did you divorce?" I asked. "Irreconcilable political differences," she answered)—I wound up at the University of Washington, which has one of the oldest East Asian programs in the United States. Around that time Perry Anderson published *Lineages of the Absolutist State*. At the end of this magisterial book rests an eighty-seven-page "Note" on the theory of the Asiatic mode of production,[30] where Anderson shows that Marx's views on Asia differed little from those of Hegel, Montesquieu, Adam Smith, and a host of other worthies; they were all peering through the wrong end of a telescope, or in a mirror, weighing a smattering of knowledge about Asia against their understanding of how the West developed. Nor did Marx ever take the "Asiatic mode" very seriously; he was always interested in one thing, really, and that was capitalism (even when it came to communism). Anderson called Wittfogel a "vulgar charivari" and recommended giving this theory an unceremonious burial, concluding that "in the night of our ignorance . . . all alien shapes take on the same hue." I eagerly recommended his book to my colleagues: a good friend said, "He doesn't know any Chinese." Another responded, "Isn't he a Marxist?"—meaning Anderson, not Wittfogel.

The theory never really got a proper burial, though, it just reappears in less-conspicuous forms. It isn't politically correct to say "Oriental" or "Asiatic" anymore (even if some haven't gotten the message). Stalin is long dead, but Stalinism is apparently not, and it's still okay to say almost anything about Stalinism. Furthermore, lo and behold, one set of "Orientals" has kept it alive: journalists use the term time and again to describe North Korea, without any hint of qualifying or questioning their position. The idea that the DPRK is a pure form of "Stalinism in the East"[31] goes back to the 1940s, and was constantly reinforced by Berkeley's Robert Scalapino, a Cold War scholar who came along in the late 1950s and benefited as much as anyone from the post-McCarthy accommodation between the right and the middle.

North Korean political practice is reprehensible, but we are not responsible for it. More disturbing is the incessant stereotyping and demonizing of this regime in the United States. When Kim Il Sung died in 1994, *Newsweek* ran a cover story entitled "The Headless Beast." Assertions that his son is simply crazy abound, but when they enter the thinking of fine analysts such as Steven Coll in *The New Yorker*,[32] a magazine with a venerable tradition of fact-checking, you might ask which psychiatrist diagnosed Kim? Another expert recently wrote, as if everyone knows this, that North Korea is "a hybrid of Stalinism and oriental despotism."[33]

Kim Jong Il, of course, specializes in do-it-yourself stereotyping, masquerading as the Maximum Leader of a Communist opéra bouffe in elevator shoes and 1970s double-knit pants suit, fattening himself while the masses starve, which makes it hard to argue that "Oriental despotism" is not the name of his politics. But there is no evidence in the North Korean experience of the mass violence against whole classes of people or the wholesale "purge" that so clearly characterized Stalinism, and that was particularly noteworthy in the scale of deaths in the land reform campaigns in China and North Vietnam and the purges of the Cultural Revolution. Nonetheless, North Korea remains everyone's example of worst-case socialism and (until 1991) Soviet stoogery, leading American observers whether at the time or since to deem it impossible for the DPRK to have had any capacity for independent action in 1950.

In fact Kim and his late father, and the ideologues around them, continue the ancient monarchical practice in East and West of "the king's two bodies," a body politic and a "body natural." The latter is an ordinary, frail human being who happens to be king, who will go to his death like anyone else: Kim Jong Il, in short, with the dyspeptic, cynical, irritated face of a man who, from birth, had no chance of living up to his father—yet he has to be king. The other is a superhuman presence, an absolutely perfect body representing the god-king, maintained through the centuries as an archetype of the exquisite leader. (And with this you get North Korean inanities such as Kim Jong Il scoring eagles on his first golf round.) In death the body natural disappears, but the soul of the god-king passes on to the next king. In Pyongyang this translated into Kim Il Sung's "seed" bringing forth his first son, Jong Il, continuing the perfect "bloodlines" that his scribes never tire of applauding. The family line thus becomes immortal, explaining why Kim Il Sung was not just president-for-life, but remained president of the DPRK in his afterlife. The high-level defector Hwang Jang-yop told Bradley Martin that the two Kims "turned Stalinism and Marxism-Leninism on their heads by reverting to Confucian notions."[34]

North Korea is thus a modern form of monarchy, realized in a highly nationalistic, postcolonial state. "The social unity expressed in the 'body of the despot,' " Jameson pointed out, is political, but also analogous to various religious practices. That the favored modern practice of such regimes should be nationalism (the leader's body, the body politic, the national body) is also entirely predictable. But the Western left (let alone liberals) utterly fails to understand "the immense Utopian appeal of nationalism"; its morbid qualities are easily grasped, but its healthy qualities for the collective, and for the tight unity that postcolonial leaders crave, are denied.[35] When you add to postcolonial nationalism Korea's centuries of royal succession and neo-Confucian philosophy, it might be possible to understand North Korea as an unusual but predictable combination of monarchy, nationalism, and Korean political culture.

FALLS THE SHADOW

We who live in Western liberal society have our subconscious automatically (if imperfectly) produced from birth and we take for granted the relatively stable societies that we join as adults, so that we do what is expected without necessarily thinking about it. Civil society is thus internalized and reproduced, as an outcome of centuries of Western political practice. The creation of such habits, however, the spontaneous production of good citizens and good workers, loyal subjects who are also afforded the opportunity of disloyalty, appears as an opaque mystery where it does not exist— how can social exchange be so open, so fluid, so simultaneously orderly and threatening even to the powers, and yet so stable? "The ways by which people advance toward dignity and enlightenment in government," George F. Kennan wrote, "are things that constitute the deepest and most intimate processes of national life. There is nothing less understandable to foreigners, nothing in which foreign influence can do less good."[36] It is our blindness, our hidden complex of unexamined assumptions, that constitutes the core of Kim-hating—what makes him simultaneously so laughable, so impudent, and so outrageous; we revile him, while he thumbs his nose at us and our values and gets away with it. We have proved over seven decades that we do not understand North Korea and that we cannot do anything about it, however much we would like to. We can do something about our prejudices.

Korea is the place where the Cold War arrived first, where it never ended and never left, and where we can still see it on cable television. In Cold War bipolarity we are in the right, our motives are pure, we do good and never harm. They are a hateful mob, criminal when not just Communist, invisible (or even aliens and Martians in 1950s movies), grotesque, insane, capable of anything. We are human and dignified and open; they are inhuman, a mysterious, secluded Other with no rights worthy of our respect. We would happily go home if the enemy would only do the right thing and evaporate, disappear, efface themselves. But the enemy is obstinate, persistent, ever-present in its malevolence (in the summer of 2009, day in and day out, CNN presented news about the North under the title "North Korea Threat"). After seven decades of confrontation, the dominant American images of North Korea still bear the birthmarks of Orientalist bigotry.

CHAPTER FIVE

38 DEGREES OF SEPARATION: A FORGOTTEN OCCUPATION

At 11:00 A.M. on August 9, 1945, the B-29 nicknamed "Bock's Car" appeared over Nagasaki, with a bombardier named Kermit Beahan sitting in the Plexiglas nose of the plane. It was his twenty-seventh birthday. He released a plutonium-239 bomb called "the Fat Man," weighing nine thousand pounds. Dangling under a parachute, it took forty seconds to fall one and a half miles to its point of detonation, five hundred meters above the red domes of the Catholic church at Urakami, long admired as the most splendid Christian cathedral in East Asia. A thirty-six-year-old Catholic priest named Ishikawa was ministering to patients in Urakami Hospital on that hot, sultry morning. The day of the Ascension of the Virgin Mary approached, and his flock wanted to confess their sins in advance of the grand festival planned for August 1. Around eleven o'clock, as he returned to his room, "a sudden white flash filled the corridor with light," followed by "a great roar" that flung him through the air, where he struck his head on a concrete post. Somehow he stumbled back to the chapel, where nurses found him lying on the floor. They roused him and, in spite of his head wounds, he administered last rites to the walking dead who soon appeared at the doorstep of the hospital. A Korean, Father Ishikawa later returned to his homeland where he became a Catholic bishop and lived into the late 1970s.[1] (At least ten thousand Koreans, mostly conscripted laborers, perished at Hiroshima and Nagasaki.)

The next day John J. McCloy, then with the War Department, asked Dean Rusk and Charles Bonesteel to retreat to an adjoining room to find a place to divide Korea for the purposes of accepting the surrender of Japanese armed forces. They chose the 38th parallel because, as Rusk later said, it included the highly centralized capital at Seoul in the American zone. The United States consulted no other powers in coming to this decision, least of all any Koreans. But McCloy, of course, was already a charter "wise man," and he carried the day. This decision was embodied in General MacArthur's General Order Number One issued on August 15, 1945, a highly political demarcation that directed Japanese soldiers to surrender to Chiang Kai-shek in China and northern Vietnam (but not to Mao or Ho) and ended up being the first critical act in the Cold War division of East Asia. Soviet armed forces had entered northern Korea on August 8 and swept southward, but they accepted the 38th parallel decision silently, without comment or written agreement. The XXIV Corps on Okinawa, led by Gen. John Reed Hodge, drew occupation duty in Korea but could not disembark until September 8—in spite of so much prodding from Washington to get there quickly that Hodge later referred to it as "that scramble move." Soon this corps, composed of the 6th, 7th, and 40th infantry divisions, which had suffered grievous losses in the bloody "last battle" on Okinawa, was in full occupation of Korea south of 38 degrees—just as the State Department had long planned.

Most Americans seem unaware that the United States occupied Korea just after the war with Japan ended, and set up a full military government that lasted for three years and deeply shaped postwar Korean history. The laws of warfare and postwarfare distinguished between "pacific" (that is, peaceable) occupations of victimized populations, where interference in their internal affairs was prohibited, and "hostile" occupations in enemy terrain. The State Department instantly determined that Korea was a victim of Japanese aggression, but the occupation command time and again not only treated the South as enemy territory but at several points actually declared it to be such (especially in the southeastern provinces), and interfered in its politics to the degree that no other postwar regime was so clearly beholden to American midwifery.

The social and political forces that spawned the Korean civil war went back into the period of Japan's colonial rule in Korea and

Manchuria, particularly to land inequities, to the anti-Japanese resistance of some Koreans and the collaboration with Japan of others, and to the staggering dislocation of ordinary Koreans, particularly in the decade 1935–45, when millions were moved around to service Japan's vast industrialization and war mobilization efforts. By the end of the war fully one fifth of the population ended up abroad (usually in Japan or Manchuria) or laboring in a province other than their own (usually in northern Korea). The "comfort women" and the 200,000-plus Korean soldiers were the obvious victims, but millions of ordinary Koreans were exploited in mines, factories, forced labor details, and the like; tellingly, 10 percent of the entire population (2.5 million) was in Japan in 1945, compared with only 35,000 Taiwanese. Since the migrants were unlikely to be under twelve or over sixty, this was a very large chunk of a people that theretofore had clung tightly to the towns and villages of their birth. They all wanted to return to their hometowns when Japanese rule collapsed, and the vast majority were from southern Korea, home to major "surplus" populations.

After Pearl Harbor, American policy toward Korea shifted dramatically. The United States had never questioned Japanese control of Korea after 1905, when Theodore Roosevelt was awarded the Nobel Peace Prize for arranging the Portsmouth Treaty ending the Russo-Japanese War, and blessed what he took to be Japanese "modernizing" efforts in Korea. By mid-1942, however, State Department planners began to worry that a Korea in the wrong hands might threaten the security of the postwar Pacific, and made plans for a full or partial military occupation of Korea upon Japan's defeat. Franklin Roosevelt had a shrewder policy, a four-power "trusteeship" for Korea (the United States, the USSR, Britain, and Nationalist China) that would get Japanese interests out and American interests in, while recognizing the Soviet Union's legitimate concerns in a country that touched its border. Roosevelt had entirely unrealistic visions of how long a trusteeship might last (forty or fifty years, perhaps), but he pushed the idea several times in wartime discussions with Churchill and Stalin, and as the policy evolved it might have worked to keep Korea in one piece. The atomic bombings brought the Pacific War to an abrupt close, however, and with Truman now in the Oval Office, State Department bureaucrats pushed through an occupation policy.

Within a week of landing in Seoul, the head of XXIV Corps military intelligence, Col. Cecil Nist, had found "several hundred conservatives" who might make good leaders of postwar Korea. Most of them had collaborated with Japanese imperialism, he wrote, but he expected that taint soon to wash away. This pool of people held most of the leaders who would subsequently shape South Korean politics. The collaborationist nature of the anointed hundred led Hodge to seek a patriotic figurehead; the Office of Strategic Services found its man in Syngman Rhee, an exile politician who had haunted and irritated Foggy Bottom for decades. He was hustled aboard a military plane over State Department objections, flown to Tokyo, where he met secretly with MacArthur, and then deposited in Seoul by MacArthur's personal plane, *The Bataan*, in mid-October 1945. Rhee understood Americans and their reflexive, unthinking, and uninformed anticommunism, and made that his stock-in-trade until 1960, when the Korean people finally threw him out in a popular rebellion. Because he had been gone so long from Korea and had few relatives, he was also a master at manipulating the family and regional ties of those below him. An obstinate man known for pushing things to the brink, he quickly convinced Americans that after him came chaos, beyond his leadership was the abyss.

A short two years into the occupation, the fledgling CIA issued a report stating that South Korean political life was "dominated by a rivalry between Rightists and the remnants of the Left Wing People's Committees," described as a "grass-roots independence movement which found expression in the establishment of the People's Committees throughout Korea in August 1945." As for the ruling political groups,

Syngman Rhee (right), at the office of the Association of the Friends of Korea, Denver, in 1920. *Courtesy of An Hyong-Ju**

The leadership of the Right [*sic*] ... is provided by that numerically small class which virtually monopolizes the native wealth and education of the country. Since it fears that an equalitarian distribution of the vested Japanese assets [that is, colonial capital] would serve as a precedent for the confiscation of concentrated Korean-owned wealth, it has been brought into basic opposition with the Left. Since this class could not have acquired and maintained its favored position under Japanese rule without a certain minimum of "collaboration," it has experienced difficulty in finding acceptable candidates for political office and has been forced to support

*From An Hyong-Ju, *Pak Yong-man kwa Hanin sonyon pyonghakkyo.* (Pak Yong-man and the Young Koreans' Military School,* 2007.)

Syngman Rhee speaking at the welcoming ceremony for allied forces, October 20, 1945, with Gen. John Reed Hodge seated to his right. *U.S. National Archives*

imported expatriate politicians such as Rhee Syngman and Kim Koo. These, while they have no pro-Japanese taint, are essentially demagogues bent on autocratic rule.

The result was that "extreme Rightists control the overt political structure in the U.S. zone," mainly through the agency of the Japanese-built National Police, which had been "ruthlessly brutal in suppressing disorder." The structure of the southern governmental bureaucracy was "substantially the old Japanese machinery," with the Home Affairs Ministry exercising "a high degree of control over virtually all phases of the life of the people."[2] The late 1940s were indeed the crucible of Korean politics thereafter, with a tremendous and indelible responsibility left at the American doorstep.

Both powers, of course, set about supporting domestic forces that suited their respective interests and worldviews. But American

Kim Il Sung speaking at Pyongyang celebration of independence from Japan, October 14, 1945. The Soviet generals who were behind him on the platform have been whited out by North Korean censors. *North Korea; U.S. National Archives*

occupation leaders took several decisive actions late in 1945—reestablishing the colonial national police, setting up a fledgling army, bringing Syngman Rhee back from exile in the United States, and moving toward a separate southern government—that came more hastily than Soviet decisions to create a functioning government in the North. Furthermore, the United States had to impose its plans against a "Korean People's Republic," independent of the Northern version, that had been proclaimed in Seoul on September 6, and which spawned hundreds of "people's committees" in the countryside. In December 1945 at a foreign ministers' conference, the United States and the Soviets agreed on a five-year bilateral trusteeship for Korea, but actions taken by both commands in Korea made that agreement impossible to implement. By early 1946 Korea was effectively divided and the two regimes and two leaders (Rhee and Kim Il Sung) who founded the respective Korean states in 1948 were effectively in place.

The commander of the occupation, General Hodge, was a sin-

A Korean National Police unit at muster, circa 1946. *U.S. National Archives*

cere, honest, and unpretentious person with a sterling reputation as a warrior ("the Patton of the Pacific"). But as a military man he worried most about the political, social, and economic disorder that was everywhere around him. Within three months of his arrival he "declared war" on the Communist party (the one in the southern zone; he mistook a mélange of leftists, anticolonial resisters, populists, and advocates of land reform for "Communists"); in the spring of 1946 he issued his first warning to Washington of an impending North Korean invasion; and against direct instructions from Washington, at the end of November 1945 he began forming a native Korean army.

The English Language School for officers founded in December was father to the Korean Constabulary Training Center established in May 1946, which in turn was father to the Korean Military Academy, renamed just after Rhee was inaugurated in 1948 and modeled on West Point. This academy graduated the plotters of the ROK's first military coup in 1961 (led by the eighth class) and the subsequent military coup in 1980 (class of '55). Chong Il-gwon, for example, a captain in the Japanese Kwantung Army and (after the war) ROKA chief of staff and later prime minister, came out of the English Language School. In the fall of 1946 the second class of officers graduated from the academy: in it were Park Chung Hee, who led the 1961 coup, and the head of the Korean Central Intelligence Agency (KCIA) who murdered him in 1979, Kim Chae-gyu; both had been officers in the Japanese military in Manchukuo. The U.S.-sponsored Combat Intelligence School was renamed the Namsan (South Mountain) Intelligence School in June 1949, and later became the dreaded torture chamber of the KCIA.

Resistance to these outcomes was much greater in southern Korea than in the North. A major rebellion shook the American occupation to its roots in October and November 1946, and was the culmination of numerous conflicts over previous months with locally powerful people's committees. In October 1948 another big rebellion occurred in and around the southwestern port of Yosu, and after that guerrilla resistance developed quickly, most of it indigenous to the south. It had its greatest impact in southwestern Korea and on Cheju Island, and kept the U.S.-advised Korean Army and Korean National Police very busy in 1948 and 1949. Meanwhile, by early 1947 Kim Il Sung had begun to dispatch Koreans to fight on the Communist side in the Chinese civil war, and in the next two years tens of thousands of them gained important battle experience. These soldiers later became the main shock forces in the Korean People's Army, and structured several divisions that fought in the Korean War.

American policy toward Korea was driven by local events in 1945 and 1946, especially the strong left wing in the South that pushed the occupation toward a premature Cold War containment policy. Much of the occupation's de facto policymaking and its support for the Korean right wing was opposed by the State Depart-

ment; in this period southern Korea was a microcosm of policy conflicts and anti-Communist policies that would later mark U.S. policy throughout the Third World, but when containment became
the dominant policy in Washington in early 1947 it had the effect of
ratifying occupation actions. Internal documents show that South
Korea was very nearly included along with Greece and Turkey as a
key containment country; although never admitted publicly, in effect it became a classic case of containment in 1948–50, with a military advisory group, a Marshall Plan economic aid contingent,
support from the United Nations, and one of the largest embassy
operations in the world.

The new Korea policy derived from the Truman Doctrine and
the "reverse course" in Japan, which created a new logic of a regional political economy in which Japanese industry would again
become the workshop of East and Southeast Asia, requiring access
to its old colonies and dependencies for markets and resources, but
not eventuating in renewed Japanese militarism (since the United
States provided for Japan's defense—then and ever since). When
Secretary of State George Marshall wrote a note to Dean Acheson
on January 29, 1947, saying, "Please have plan drafted of policy to
organize a definite government of So. Korea and *connect up* [*sic*] its
economy with that of Japan," he captured with pith and foresight
the future direction of U.S. policy toward Korea from 1947 down to
the normalization of South Korean relations with Japan in 1965.
Acheson later became the prime internal advocate of keeping
southern Korea in the zone of American and Japanese influence,
and single-handedly scripted the American intervention in the Korean War.

The Republic of Korea, led by Syngman Rhee, was founded
on August 15, 1948, with MacArthur standing proudly on the
platform. Rhee was chosen by a legislature that emerged from a
UN-observed election in May 1948, a result that John Foster
Dulles had shepherded through the General Assembly. These elec-

tions corresponded to the very limited franchise established under the Japanese, with voting restricted to landowners and taxpayers in the larger towns, elders voting for everyone else at the village level, and gendarmes and youth groups around all the polling places. Likewise, the United Nations "was a relatively small body in 1947 and effectively dominated by the United States."[4] The Soviets could veto Security Council resolutions, but the United States controlled the General Assembly. Nonetheless, the UN commissioners declared the election to be a free and fair one in those parts of Korea to which they had access (that is, not the North), and thereby the UN imprimatur gave to the Republic of Korea a crucial legitimacy.

THE SOUTHWEST OF KOREA DURING THE MILITARY GOVERNMENT

A window into a different future for the American occupation of Korea was opened in the first year after Japan's defeat—a future that might not have concluded with a divided Korea and an internecine war two years later. The southwest was a microcosm of what happened throughout Korea after the liberation from Japanese imperialism, a fascinating time of crisis politics in action, a fundamental turning point unlike any other in modern Korean history. In South Cholla, later to become the most rebellious province, Americans worked with local leaders and, at least for a while, did not try to change the political complexion of local organs that reflected the will of the people. As the historian Kim Yong-sop has shown in his many works, South Cholla was the site of the Tonghak peasant war in the early 1890s because it occupied the confluence of great Korean wealth—the lush rice paddies of Honam, as the region is known—and Japanese exporters who sent that Korean rice flowing out of southwestern ports to Japan and the world economy. In other words, here was a concentrated intersection of modernity and empire: Korean desires for autonomy and self-strengthening that took the form of a proto-nationalist rebellion, and imperial interests (Japanese, American, Russian, British) competing with one another in the world economy and determined to take advantage of Korean wealth (and weakness). Long after the Tonghak rebellion was put down, Japanese travel guides in the 1920s still warned against going into the interior of South Cholla, and of course the provincial capital, Kwangju, was the site of a major student uprising against the Japanese in 1929 and an insurrection against the militarists in 1980.

When I toured South Cholla in the 1970s, riding on local buses through the countryside, local people frequently stared at me with uncomplicated, straightforward hatred, something I had rarely experienced elsewhere in Korea. The roads were still mostly hard-packed dirt, sun-darkened peasants bent over ox-driven plows in the rice paddies or shouldered immense burdens like pack animals, thatch-roofed homes were sunk in conspicuous privation, old Japanese-style city halls and railroad stations were unchanged from the colonial era. At unexpected moments along the way, policemen would materialize from nowhere and waylay the bus to check the identification cards of every passenger, amid generalized sullenness and hostility that I had seen before only in America's urban ghettos.

Things might have been different. It is a paradox of the American Military Government (AMG) that its most successful program in the first year of occupation was in South Cholla. After the Japanese defeat, local organs of Yo Un-hyong's founding organization had established themselves, and quickly came to be known as "people's committees." The late president Kim Dae Jung joined one in Mokpo at the time, something that the militarists in Seoul always held against him (and was part of his indictment for sedition by Chun Doo Hwan in 1980). These committees were patriotic and anticolonial groupings with a complicated political complexion, but Americans in Seoul quickly placed them all under the rubric of

Yo Un-hyong, founder of the Korean People's Republic (South).

"Communists." (Indeed, as we have seen, Hodge "declared war" on communism in the southern zone on the very early date of December 12, 1945.) But in the southwest, American civil affairs teams worked with local committees for more than a year (and for nearly three years on Cheju Island), something that I first learned about by reading E. Grant Meade's *American Military Government in Korea.*

American military forces did not arrive in the provincial capital of Kwangju until October 8, 1945 (a month after they got to Seoul), and civil affairs teams did not show up until October 22. They soon recognized that people's committees controlled almost the entire province. In charge in Kwangju was Kim Sok, who had spent eleven years as a political prisoner of the Japanese. But in Posong and Yonggwang, landlords ran the committee, and police who had served the Japanese remained in control of small towns. In the coal

town of Hwasun, miners ran the local committee. Several committee elections had been held since August 15 in Naju, Changhung,
and other places, excluding only officials who had served the Japanese in the previous decade. Americans in Kwangju, like those in
Seoul, wanted to revive the defunct Japanese framework of government and even retained the former provincial governor, Yaki
Nobuo, until December (he provided them with secret lists of co-
operative Koreans). Kim Sok was arrested on October 28 on
trumped-up charges of running an "assassination plot." His trial,
according to an American who witnessed it, was a complete trav-
esty. Soon he was back in his familiar surroundings of the previous
decade: prison.

Other Americans, however, recognized that the people's committees represented "a designation applied to some faction in every
town," with its influence and character varying from place to place:
"In one county, it represents the 'roughnecks'; in another, it is perhaps the only political party and represents no radical expressions;
in others, it may even possibly have the [former] county magistrate
as its party leader." Lt. Col. Frank E. Bartlett ran the 45th Military
Government team, one of the only such teams to have been trained
specifically for Korea (the vast majority had been trained for occupation duty in Japan), and urged his men to know the tenor of local
political opinion. This resulted in attempts to "reorganize" the
committees in several counties, but basically Bartlett's group allowed most committees in the province to operate until the fall of
1946. A key reason: the Americans could find no evidence that the
committees were controlled "from a strong central headquarters."[5]

It all ended in bloodshed a year later. I still remember the day
that I read in the National Archives a report entitled "Cholla-South
Communist Uprising of November 1946," thirty-nine pages long.[6]
Uprisings had begun in Taegu almost a month earlier, and had followed a classic pattern of peasant war: rebellions in one county
would move to the next and then the next, like billiard balls striking
each other. This major uprising was the result of intense Korean

frustrations with the first year of American occupation and the suppression of the people's committees in the southeastern provinces, and the increasing tendency for the same thing to happen in the southwest. It was entirely indigenous to the southernmost part of the peninsula, having nothing to do with North Korea or with communism. This report detailed more than fifty incidents in November 1945 of the following kind:

- Mob composed of people's committees types attacked police box; police fired into mob, killing six.
- 1,000 attacked police station ... cops fired 100 rounds into mob killing (unknown).
- Police fired on mob of 3,000, killing 5.
- Police fired into mob of 60 ... tactical [American] troops called out; captured 6 bamboo spears and 2 sabers.
- 600–800 marched on police; police killed 4.[7]

The report went on like this, listing a myriad of small peasant wars. When the reader finally reaches the end of the report, he realizes that he stares into an abyss containing the bodies of countless Cholla peasants. In recent years a single incident of this type would have gained national and international attention, but these distant events remain an unknown moment of history along the dusty roads and "parched hills" of Cholla that Kim Chi Ha commemorated in his poem "The Road to Seoul": except to those who witnessed them, or those who died.

What happened to the families of the dead—how do they commemorate a battle that no one ever heard of? How can Americans occupy a country and, a year later, find themselves firing on people about whom they know next to nothing, but conveniently label as faceless "Communists" or inchoate "mobs"? Are some of these same Americans not living still today, with memories of a peasant war in South Cholla in the fall of 1946? Were they never able to connect the dots between the indigenous organs of self-government that Koreans fashioned in the aftermath of four decades of brutal colonial rule, and the peasants armed with the tools of their trade, being cut down like rice shoots by the same treacherous Koreans who had served the Japanese?

The Liberation in Samchok

Samchok is a port on the upper east coast of South Korea, about fifty miles from the 38th parallel.[8] The large Japanese cement firm Onoda opened a number of plants in Korea during the colonial period; all were in northern Korea except for the one in Samchok. As in most factories elsewhere, a self-governing committee drawn from the factory workers immediately took over the factory on August 15, so that everything could be run by Koreans with their own hands. They proceeded to manage the factory for months and years, under the leadership of Oh Pyong-ho, who had come to the plant when he graduated from engineering school in 1943 and had moved rapidly upward during the war, as six Japanese engineers were drafted away for work in the army—a general pattern in the last decade of colonial rule. He had apprenticed under Kusugawa Shintaro, the head of the Engineering Bureau at the plant, a second-generation colonizer who began work at the Sunghori factory in the north in 1928. But Oh was still only twenty-five in 1945, the eldest son of a landed family from Chinju.

U Chin-hong was one of the skilled workers in the plant, having been born in Samchok in 1920 and later graduated from Sunlin Commercial Higher Common School in Seoul (where I happened to teach English when I was in the Peace Corps). By 1943 he was a skilled worker in the Engineering Bureau. Unlike in the north, where Japanese technicians were often kept on at the factories for up to three years, none were kept at the Samchok factory—and so

Koreans moved into technical and managerial positions instantly at liberation.

Around September 15, a Captain Chapman of a USAMGIK civil affairs team arrived in town, visited the factory, and said that from then on, every important decision at the factory should be discussed with him first; he took over the Onoda housing facilities for his team's headquarters. A short while later Oh Pyong-ho went to Seoul to ask the AMG for financial support to keep the factory going. He got some funds from Yu Han-sang of the Commerce and Industry Bureau, and on October 1 the plant was operating fully again, staffed by Korean engineers and factory workers. The next month organizers from the left-liberal Chonpyong labor union set up a branch at Onoda. According to U Chin-hong, 70 percent of the workers were "leftist," probably meaning that they wanted a union.

In December 1945 the Military Government issued Ordinance #33, prohibiting self-governing committees at all factories; it also announced that all former Japanese-owned public and private properties now would be vested in the occupation—about three thousand properties, including all the large factories. Politically connected people in Seoul then got about appointing factory managers; the one appointed to run Onoda was a close friend of Yu Han-sang. An absentee manager, he lasted about a year, as did the next one appointed from Seoul—another friend of someone, and another absentee.

The Military Government decided finally to eliminate leftist elements in the factory in 1947. It had outlawed Chonpyong more than a year earlier, but the union was still flourishing, as was the self-governing committee. Thirty so-called leftists and Red elements were arrested, including all the leaders of the factory committee. The engineer Oh Pyong-ho, still on the self-governing committee, was one of them. Over a period of years, U Chin-hong remembered, the politics of the workers slowly reversed; by the 1950s, 70 percent were so-called rightists. They also had no union.

When the conventional war opened in June 1950, most people from the self-governing committee rejoined the factory workforce. Some of the managers and engineers fled to the Pusan perimeter, but not all. From the fall of 1950 until April 1952, South and North Korean forces wrested the factory away from each other several times, southerners finally getting it and keeping it after North Korean forces, who had operated the factory for three straight months, departed for good. At length, Syngman Rhee's friends sold the factory in 1957 to the fifth Seoul-appointed absentee owner, Kang Chik-son. This was four years after the United States allocated $632,000 in United Nations relief funds to the factory, although the factory had not been destroyed in the war—supplies were pilfered, and the main crane was demolished, but otherwise it was intact. By the 1960s, the man tarred as a leftist and "Red element," Oh Pyong-hŏ, who had learned his profession at the knee of Kusugawa Shintaro, was chief cement engineer for all of South Korea. The so-called leftist U Chin-hong owned his own cement-related business in Samchok.

There are many points one might draw out of this story, so redolent is it of Korean history in the middle of the twentieth century, but one thing is clear: it may have been a cement factory, but this story is about a consequent politics—political choices that seem small on the day they are made (say, the day Captain Chapman arrived) but that loom very large later on. What if Captain Chapman had said, "Great job, Mr. Oh; keep up the good work—and by the way I'm a union man myself"? In these transactions there is no such thing as neutrality, evenhandedness, a polite demurral of noninvolvement, the American as innocent bystander in his own occupation government. Whatever Captain Chapman and his political superiors in Seoul did or did not do, they made choices. And it is those choices, made throughout the peninsula by Americans, Russians, and Koreans on those warm September days so long ago, that ultimately led to the civil conflict that Americans know as "the forgotten war."

THE CHEJU INSURGENCY

On Cheju Island something happened in "peacetime" under the American occupation—namely a major peasant war—and after decades of repression Cheju people are finally coming forward to tell their stories and demand compensation, and no special pleading about the exigencies of wartime will suffice to assuage the American conscience. What the formerly classified American materials document is a merciless, wholesale assault on the people of this island. No one will ever know how many died in this onslaught, but the American data, long kept secret, ranged from 30,000 to 60,000 killed, with upward of 40,000 more people having fled to Japan (where many still live in Osaka). More recent research suggests a figure of 80,000 killed. There were at most 300,000 people living on Cheju Island in the late 1940s.[9]

The effective political leadership on Cheju until early 1948 was provided by strong left-wing people's committees that first emerged in August 1945, and later continued under the American occupation (1945–48). The occupation preferred to ignore Cheju rather than do much about the committees; it appointed a formal mainland leadership but let the people of the island run their own affairs. The result was an entrenched left wing, one with no important ties to the North and few to the South Korean Workers' Party (SKWP) on the mainland; the island was also well and peaceably governed in 1945–47, when contrasted with the mainland. In early 1948, as Syngman Rhee and his American supporters moved to institute his power in a separate Southern regime, however, the Cheju people responded with a strong guerrilla insurgency that soon tore the island apart.

Before Rhee came to power, silenced his officials, and blamed the whole rebellion on alien Communist agitators, Koreans in USAMGIK attributed the origins of the insurgency to the long tenure of the Cheju governing committees and subsequent police and right-wing youth-group terrorism. General Hodge told a group of visiting American congressmen in October 1947 that Cheju was "a truly communal area that is peacefully controlled by the People's Committee without much Comintern influence." Shortly thereafter a Military Government investigation estimated that "approximately two-thirds of the populace" on the island were "moderate leftist" in their opinions. The chairman of a big leftist organization, a former Cheju governor named Pak, was "not a Communist and [was] very pro-American." The people were deeply separatist and did not like mainlanders; their wish was to be left alone. This survey determined, however, that Cheju had been subjected to a campaign of official terrorism in recent months. According to Counter-Intelligence Corps (CIC) information, the current governor, Yu Hae-jin, was an "extreme rightist," a mainlander with connections to right-wing youth groups; he was "ruthless and dictatorial in his dealing with opposing political parties." He thought anyone who did not support Syngman Rhee was "automatically leftist"; for months in 1947 he had sought to prevent "any meeting by any party except those he definitely approves."

An official investigation by the USAMGIK judge Yang Won-il conducted in June 1948 found that "the People's Committee of Cheju Island, which was formed after the Liberation...has exercised its power as a *de facto* government." He also found that "the police have failed to win the hearts of the people by treating them cruelly." A Seoul prosecutor, Won Taek-yun, said the troubles began because of official incompetence, not "leftist agitation"; Lt. Col. Kim Ik-yol, commander of Constabulary (military) units on the island when the rebellion began, said that the blame for the uprising "should be laid entirely at the door of the police force."

Governor Yu had filled national police units on the island with mainlanders and refugees from northern Korea, who worked together with "ultra rightist party terrorists." Some 365 prisoners were in the Cheju city jail in late 1947; an American investigator witnessed thirty-five of them crowded into a ten-by-twelve-foot cell. "Direct control of food rationing" had also been placed in the hands of "politicians" responsive to Yu, who operated out of township offices. Unauthorized grain collections had been five times as high as official ones in 1947. When Americans interviewed Governor Yu in February 1948 he acknowledged that he had utilized "extreme rightist power" to reorient the Cheju people, "the large majority" of whom were leftist, in his judgment. He justified this by saying that "there was no middle line" in island politics; one supported either the left or the right. He said the police controlled all political meetings, and would not allow the "extreme leftists" to meet. Although the author of the survey called for Governor Yu's dismissal, Gen. William F. Dean decided in late March 1948 not to remove him.[10]

Perhaps the affair that most inflamed the island population was the unleashing of the right-wing terrorist group known as the Northwest Youth Corps (NWY) to control and reorient leftists. In late 1947 the CIC had "warned" the NWY about their "widespread campaign of terrorism" on Cheju. Under the American command, these same youths joined the police and Constabulary in the Cheju guerrilla suppression campaigns. As a special Korean press survey put it in June 1948,

> Since the coming of a youth organization, whose members are young men from Northwest Korea, the feeling between the [island] inhabitants and those from the mainland has been growing tense.... They may have been inspired by the Communists. Yet, how shall we understand how over 30,000 men have roused themselves to action in defiance of gun and sword. Without cause, there can be no action.

The NWY was said to have "exercised police power more than the police itself and their cruel behavior has invited the deep resentment of the inhabitants."[11]

In the formerly secret internal reports of the U.S. occupation this outfit was routinely described as a fascist youth group engaged in terrorism throughout southern Korea. Its members primarily came from refugee families from the north, and the "youths" ran from teenaged to middle-aged thugs. To try to counter them the United States officially sponsored its own group, which modeled itself on Chiang Kai-shek's "Blue Shirts" (black, brown, and green having already been spoken for). In putting down one strike or uprising after another in the late 1940s (and there were many), this and other youth groups worked hand in glove with the hated National Police.

The documented violence was so extreme, so gratuitous, as to suggest a peculiar pathology. As I was getting to know the furious and unremittingly vicious conflicts that have wracked divided Korea, I sat in the Hoover Institution library reading through a magazine issued by the Northwest Youth Corps in the late 1940s. On its cover were cartoons of Communists disemboweling pregnant women, running bayonets through little kids, burning down people's homes, smashing open the brains of opponents. As it happened, this was *their* political practice. In Hagui village, for example, right-wing youths captured a pregnant twenty-one-year-old woman named Mun, whose husband was allegedly an insurgent, dragged her from her home, and stabbed her thirteen times with spears, causing her to abort. She was left to die with her baby half-delivered. Other women were serially raped, often in front of villagers, and then blown up with a grenade in the vagina.[12] This pathology, perhaps, has something to do with the self-hatred of individuals who did Japanese bidding, now operating on behalf of another foreign power, and with extremes of misogyny in Korea's patriarchal society.

After a March 1, 1948, demonstration against the separate elections on the mainland, the police arrested 2,500 young people; islanders soon fished the dead body of one of them out of a river: he had been tortured to death. This, Colonel Kim thought, was the incident that provoked the original rebellion on April 3 that subsequently marked the start of the insurgency.[13] The April 3 uprising

Women and children refugees from the insurgency on Cheju
Island, 1948. *U.S. National Archives*

occurred mostly along the north coast of Cheju, with attacks on
eleven police stations and various other incidents—roads and
bridges destroyed, telephone wires cut. The demonstrators de-
nounced the separate elections and called for unification with the
North. Three rebels died, as did four police and twelve rightists.
When news of the rebellion spread to the mainland, signal fires
were lit in the hills near the port of Mokpo, and demonstrators
came out to shout hurrah for "the Korean People's Republic" (the
one organized in Seoul in 1945, not the North Korean one).

In May, as the election proceeded on the mainland, the rebellion
spread to the west coast of the island, with some thirty-five police
and rightists killed by May 15; the next day police began rounding
up civilians, taking 169 prisoners in two villages thought to have assisted the guerrillas. No election could be conducted on the island.
By the end of May the violence had left only the eastern coast un-

touched; Constabulary units swept the mountains from east to west.[14]

A month later an American colonel, Rothwell H. Brown, reported that Korean and American military units had interrogated fully four thousand inhabitants of Cheju, determining that a "People's Democratic Army" had been formed in April, composed of two regiments of guerrillas; its strength was estimated at four thousand officers and men, although fewer than one tenth had firearms. The remainder carried swords, spears, and farm implements; in other words, this was a hastily assembled peasant army. Interrogators also found evidence that the SKWP had infiltrated no more than six "trained agitators and organizers" from the mainland, and none had come from North Korea; with some five hundred to seven hundred allies on the island, they had established cells in most towns and villages. Between 60,000 and 70,000 islanders had joined the party, Brown asserted, although it seems much more likely that such figures refer to long-standing membership in people's committees and mass organizations. "They were for the main part, ignorant, uneducated farmers and fishermen whose livelihood had been profoundly disturbed by the war and the post-war difficulties."[15]

Yi Tok-ku was the commander of the rebels. Born in Shinchon village on the island in 1924 into a family of poor fishermen-peasants, he subsequently went to Osaka as a child laborer, as did his brother and his sister. He returned to Sinchon just after the liberation, and became a Workers' Party activist. He was arrested and tortured for three months in 1947, and thereafter began organizing guerrillas.[16] The guerrillas generally were known as the *inmin-gun*, or People's Army, but they were not centrally commanded and operated in mobile units eighty or a hundred strong that often had little connection with other rebels. This, of course, was one of the elements that made the movement hard to suppress. CIC elements found no evidence of North Korean personnel or equipment.[17]

The police refused to admit any responsibility for the eruption of the violence, blaming agitators from North Korea for the trouble. These organizers were able to stir up the population, the police thought, because "the learned and wealthy" had the habit of living on the mainland, leaving "only the ignorant" people on Cheju. It was necessary to appoint officials from the mainland, the police said, because local people were all interrelated and would not work "strongly and resolutely" in dealing with unrest. The KNP superintendent recommended that "patriotic young men's associations" be promoted, and the institution of "assembly villages" to concentrate the population and drain rural support away from the guerrillas.[18]

In his own report Colonel Brown said that the rebellion had already led to "the complete breakdown of all civil government functions"; the South Korean Constabulary had adopted "stalling tactics," whereas "vigorous action was required." People on the island were panicked by the violence, but they also would not yield to interrogators, even under torture: "blood ties which link most of the families on the Island . . . make it extremely difficult to obtain information." Direct American involvement in suppressing the rebellion included the daily training of counterinsurgent forces, interrogation of prisoners, and the use of American spotter planes to ferret out guerrillas. One newspaper reported that American troops intervened in the Cheju conflict in at least one instance in late April 1948, and a group of Korean journalists even charged in June that Japanese officers and soldiers had secretly been brought back to the island to help in suppressing the rebellion.

On May 22, 1948, Colonel Brown developed the following procedures, to "break up" the revolt: "police were assigned definite missions to protect all coastal villages [from guerrillas]; to arrest rioters carrying arms, and to stop killing and terrorizing innocent citizens." The Constabulary was told to break up all elements of the guerrilla army in the interior of the island. Brown also ordered widespread, continuing interrogation of all those arrested, and efforts to prevent supplies from reaching the guerrillas. Subsequently he anticipated the institution of a long-range program "to offer positive proof of the evils of Communism," and to "show that the American way offers positive hope" for the islanders. From May 28 to the end of July, more than three thousand islanders were arrested.[19]

Following Japanese counterinsurgency practice, the entire island interior was declared an enemy zone, villagers were forcibly relocated to the coast, and the mountains—primarily the volcanic Mount Halla, which dominates the island—were blockaded. More than half of all villages on the mountain slopes were burned and destroyed, and civilians thought to be aiding the insurgents were massacred. Civilians were by far the largest category of victims, some killed by the insurgents, but the vast majority by police and right-wing youth squads. Women, children, and the elderly who were left behind were tortured to gain information on the insurgents, and then killed. Col. Kim Yong-ju brought three thousand soldiers in the Constabulary's 11th Regiment back to the mainland in early August, and told reporters that "almost all villages" on the island were vacant, the residents having fled either to the protection of guerrillas in the interior or to the coast. He implied that far more had gone into the mountains. "The so-called mountain man is a farmer by day, rioter by night," the Cheju Constabulary commander said; "frustrated by not knowing the identity of these elusive men, the police in some cases carried out indiscriminate warfare against entire villages." When the Constabulary refused to adopt the same murderous tactics, the police called them Communists. A KMAG account in late 1948 cited "considerable village burning" by the suppression command; three new Constabulary battalions were being recruited, the report said, "mainly from Northwest Youth." Islanders were now giving information on the guerrillas—apparently because their homes would be burned if they did not.[20]

The 9th Regiment of the Constabulary later got control of several points in the highlands, and herded village people toward the coasts, enabling them to starve out guerrillas and push them out of their mountain redoubts. Naval ships had completely blockaded the island, making resupply of guerrillas from the mainland impossible.[21] By early 1949 more than 70 percent of the island's villages had been burned out. In April things got worse:

> Cheju Island was virtually overrun early in the month by rebels operating from the central mountain peak...rebel sympathizers numbering possibly 15,000, sparked by a trained core of 150 to 600 fighters, controlled most of the island. A third of the population had crowded into Chejoo town, and 65,000 were homeless and without food.[22]

By this time 20,000 homes on the island had been destroyed, and one third of the population (about 100,000) was concentrated in protected villages along the coast. Peasants were allowed to cultivate fields only near perimeter villages, owing to "chronic insecurity" in the interior and the fear that they would aid the insurgents.[23]

Soon, however, the guerrillas were basically defeated. An American Embassy official, Everett Drumwright, reported in May 1949 that "the all-out guerrilla extermination campaign...came to a virtual end in April with order restored and most rebels and sympathizers killed, captured, or converted." Ambassador John Muccio wired to Washington that "the job is about done." Shortly it was possible to hold a special election, thus finally to send a Cheju islander to the National Assembly; none other than Chang Taeksang, the longtime head of the Seoul Metropolitan Police, arrived to run for a seat.[24] By August 1949 it was apparent that the insurgency had effectively ended and the rebel leader Yi Tok-ku was finally killed. Peace came, but it was the peace of a political graveyard.

American public sources reported in 1949 that 15,000 to 20,000 islanders died, but the ROK's official figure was 27,719. The North Koreans said that more than 30,000 islanders had been "butchered" in the suppression. The governor of Cheju, however, privately told American intelligence that 60,000 had died, and as many as 40,000 people had fled to Japan; officially 39,285 homes had been demolished, but the governor thought "most of the houses on the hills" were gone: of 400 villages, only 170 remained. In other words, one in every five or six islanders had perished, and more than half the villages were destroyed."

The Northwest Youth now ran Cheju and continued "to behave in a very arbitrary and cruel manner" toward the islanders, according to Americans on the scene; "the fact that the Chief of Police was a member of this organization made matters even worse." Like Stanley Kubrick's *A Clockwork Orange*, where the "droogies" turned into police, the NWY not only worked closely with the National Police, but soon entered its ranks wholesale. By the end of 1949, three hundred members of the Northwest Youth had joined the island police, and two hundred were in business or local government: "the majority have become rich and are the favored merchants." The senior military commander and the vice-governor were also from north Korea. Of course, "the rich men of the island" were once again influential, too, "despite the fact that governmental control has changed three times." About three hundred "emaciated" guerrillas remained in the Cheju city jail, and another two hundred were thought to be still on the loose, but inactive. Peasants and fishermen had to have daily police passes to work the fields or the ocean.[26]

Just before the war began in June 1950, a U.S. Embassy survey found the island peaceful, with no more than a handful of guerrillas. During the warfare at the Pusan perimeter, Americans reported that police had collected radios from the entire island population, so they could not find out about the North Korean advance on the mainland; the only telephone network was controlled by the police, and would be the main means of communication should the North Koreans seek to invade the island. Americans surmised, however, that a "subversive potential" still existed on Cheju, because of "an estimated 50,000 relatives of persons killed as Communist sympathizers in the rebellion." Fully 27,000 of the islanders had been enrolled in the National Guidance Alliance, an organization set up by the state to convert leftists. In 1954 an observer of Cheju wrote, "Village guards man watchtowers atop stone walls; some villages have dug wide moats outside the walls and filled them with brambles, to keep bandits out."[27]

Dr. Seong Nae Kim has given eloquent voice to Cheju survivors, whose repressed memories of violence surface in dreams or in sudden apparitions—ghosts, spirits, the conjurings of a shaman, or fleeting glimpses of loved ones "in blood-stained white mourning clothes." The widow of an insurgent is hounded by the police into autism, catatonia, and suicide. Families cannot even utter the name of the dead or perform ancestor rituals, for fear of blacklisting; if one relative was labeled a Communist, the entire family's life chances were jeopardized under the Law of Complicity (*yonjwa pop*). Forgetting was the immediate cure for such suffering, but its comforts were temporary. Memory surfaces apart from one's intentions, the deceased return in dreams, the terror recurs in nightmares. The mind compensates for loss and adapts to the dictate of the state: if your brother was killed by a right-wing youth squad, say the Communists killed him. Time passes, and the bereaved turns this reversal into the recalled truth. But the mind knows it is a lie, and so psychic trauma returns in terrible dreams, or the apparition of an accusing, vengeful ghost.[28]

THE YOSU REBELLION

As the Cheju insurgency progressed, an event occurred that got much more attention, indeed international coverage: a rebellion at the southeastern port city of Yosu that soon spread to other counties, and that for a time seemed to threaten the foundations of the fledgling republic. The proximate cause of the uprising was the re-

Gen. Chong Il-gwon at the Mount Chiri guerrilla suppression command. *U.S. National
Archives*

fusal on October 19, 1948, of elements of the 14th and 6th regiments of the ROK Army to embark for a counterinsurgency mission on Cheju. Here, too, the commanders who actually subdued
the rebels were Americans, assisted by several young Korean
colonels: Chong Il-gwon, Chae Pyong-dok ("Fatty" Chae to Americans), and Kim Paek-il. Gen. William Roberts, the KMAG commander, ordered Americans to stay out of direct combat, but even
that injunction was ignored from time to time. American advisers
were with all ROK Army units, but the most important ones were
Col. Harley E. Fuller, named chief adviser for the suppression,

Gen. Chae Pyong-dok, known as "Fatty" to Americans. James Hausman is second from right. Circa 1949. *U.S. National Archives*

Capt. James Hausman from KMAG G-3, and Capt. John P. Reed from G-2 (Army intelligence).[29]

On October 20 the American G-2 intelligence chief recommended that KMAG "handle [the] situation" and command the army in restoring order "without intervention of U.S. troops." Roberts said that he planned "to contain and suppress the rebels at [the] earliest moment," and formed a party to fly to Kwangju on the afternoon of October 20 to command the operation. It consisted of Hausman, Reed, and a third American from KMAG; also an American in the Counter-Intelligence Corps, and Col. Chong Il-gwon. The next day Roberts met with the Constabulary commander Song Ho-song and urged him "to strike hard everywhere... and allow no obstacles to stop him." Roberts's "Letter of Instruction" to Song read,

> Your mission is to meet the rebel attack with an overwhelm-
> ingly superior force and to crush it.... Because of their polit-

ical and strategic importance, it is essential that Sunchon
and Yosu be recaptured at an early date. The liberation of
these cities from the rebel forces will be moral and political
victories of great propaganda value.

American C-47 transports ferried Korean troops, weapons, and
other matériel; KMAG spotter planes surveilled the area throughout the period of the rebellion; American intelligence organizations worked intimately with U.S. Army and KNP counterparts.[30]

As guerrillas built up their strength on the mainland after Yosu,
American advisers were all over the war zones in the South, constantly shadowing their Korean counterparts and urging them to
greater effort. The man who distinguished himself in this was James
Hausman, one of the key organizers of the suppression of the Yosu
rebellion, who spent the next three decades as perhaps the most important American operative in Korea, the liaison and nexus point
between the American and Korean militaries and their intelligence
outfits. Hausman termed himself the father of the Korean Army in
an interview, which was not far from the truth. He said that everyone knew this, including the Korean officers themselves, but could
not say it publicly. In off-camera remarks, meanwhile, Hausman
said that Koreans were "brutal bastards," "worse than the Japanese";
he sought to make their brutality more efficient by showing them,
for example, how to douse corpses of executed people with gasoline, thus to hide the method of execution or blame it on Communists.[31] Back in the United States, hardly anyone has ever heard of
Hausman.

If the Rhee regime had one unqualified success, viewed through
the American lens, it was the apparent defeat of the southern partisans by the spring of 1950. A year before, it had appeared that the
guerrilla movement would only grow with the passage of time; but
a major suppression campaign begun in the fall of 1949 resulted in
high body counts and a perception that the guerrillas could no
longer mount significant operations when they would be expected

Rebels trussed up during the Yosu rebellion, 1948. *U.S. National Archives*

to—as the spring foliage returned in early 1950. Both Acheson and Kennan saw the suppression of the internal threat as the litmus test of the Rhee regime's continence: if this worked, so would American-backed containment; if it did not, the regime would be viewed as another Kuomintang (Chiang Kai-shek's Nationalist Party). Col. Preston Goodfellow, formerly the deputy director of the wartime OSS, had told Rhee in late 1948, in the context of a letter where he referred to his "many opportunities to talk with [Dean

Acheson] about Korea," that the guerrillas had to be "cleaned out quickly... everyone is watching how Korea handles the Communist threat." A weak policy would lose support in Washington; handle the threat well, and "Korea will be held in high esteem."[32] American backing was thus crucial to the very willingness of the ROK Army to fight the guerrillas, whether on Cheju or the mainland.

Americans sang the praises of the Rhee regime's counterinsurgency campaign, even as internal accounts recorded nauseating atrocities. As early as February 1949, Drumwright reported that in South Cholla "there was some not very discriminating destruction of villages" by the ROKA; but a week later he demonstrated his own support for such measures (if discriminate): "the only answer to the Communist threat is for non-Communist youth, after weeding out, to be organized just as tightly and for just as ruthless action as their Leftist counterparts." He also suggested that American missionaries be utilized for information on the guerrillas.[33] The Americans and the Koreans were in constant conflict over proper counterinsurgent methods, but out of this tension came a mix of American methods and the techniques of suppression the Japanese had developed in Manchuria, for combating guerrillas in cold-weather, mountainous terrain, implemented by Korean officers who had served the Japanese (often in Manchuria). Winter drastically shifted the advantage to suppression forces, as we have seen; large units established blockades while small search-and-destroy units scoured the mountains for guerrillas.[34]

The American journalist Hugh Deane argued presciently in March 1948 that Korea would soon come to resemble the civil wars in Greece or north China: as in Greece, "North Korea will be accused of sending agitators and military equipment south of the 38th parallel and the Korean problem will be made to look as if it were simply southern defense against northern aggression." Yet the worst problem, he thought, would come in the southwestern Chollas, as far from North Korea as any region save Cheju—which developed the biggest insurgency of all.[35] As it happened, Deane's prediction was right on all counts: this was where the insurgency was strongest, and this became the American line—and not only that, but the judgment of history. To the extent that anyone knows about the guerrilla conflict, it is assumed to be externally induced, by North Koreans with Soviet backing and weapons, with the Americans standing idly by while the Rhee regime fought the infiltrators. Yet the evidence shows that the Soviets had no involvement with the southern partisans, the North Koreans were connected mainly to attempts at infiltration and guerrillas in northeastern Kangwon province, while the seemingly uninvolved Americans organized and equipped the southern counterinsurgent forces, gave them their best intelligence materials, planned their actions, and often commanded them directly.

Walter Sullivan, a *New York Times* correspondent, was almost alone among foreign journalists in seeking out the truth of the guerrilla war on the mainland and Cheju. Large parts of southern Korea, he wrote in early 1950, "are darkened today by a cloud of terror that is probably unparalleled in the world." Guerrillas made brutal assaults on police, and the police took the guerrillas to their home villages and tortured them for information. Then the police shot them, and tied them to trees as an object lesson. The persistence of the guerrillas, he wrote, "puzzles many Americans here," as does "the extreme brutality" of the conflict. But Sullivan went on to argue that "there is great divergence of wealth" in the country, with both middle and poor peasants living "a marginal existence." He interviewed ten peasant families; none owned all their own land, and most were tenants. The landlord took 30 percent of tenant produce, but additional exactions—government taxes, and various "contributions"—ranged from 48 to 70 percent of the annual crop.[36] The primary cause of the South Korean insurgency was the ancient curse of average Koreans—the social inequity of land relations and the huge gap between a tiny elite of the rich and the vast majority of the poor.

Guerrilla suppression fort, 1949. *Walter Sullivan*

In the end upward of 100,000 Koreans in the southern part were killed in political violence *before* the Korean War; once the war began at least another 100,000 were killed, as we will see. The Spanish civil war is well known to have been fratricidal, bloody, and to have generated enmities that lasted for half a century. Recent scholarship on political killings under Franco's terror during and after this war (still not a full accounting and one covering just thirty-seven of fifty provinces) suggests that about 101,000 people were killed; factoring in the other thirteen provinces would suggest a total figure somewhere between 130,000 and 200,000.[37] Spain may be the best comparison for a Korean civil war that began well before June 1950 and still goes on today.

The insurrections on Cheju Island and in the southwest were inflamed by a brutal Japanese occupation that led to a vast uprooting of the population, the simple justice of the local administration that took effective power on the island in 1945 and held it until 1948, and the elemental injustice of the mainlander dictatorship that Syngman Rhee imposed and that the American legal authorities did nothing about—except to aid and abet it. It was on this hauntingly beautiful island that the postwar world first witnessed American culpability for unrestrained violence against indigenous peoples fighting for self-determination and social justice.

BATTLES ALONG THE PARALLEL

The ROK quickly expanded its armed forces in response to internal rebellion and the North Korean threat. By late summer 1949 it had upward of 100,000 troops, a figure the North would not reach until spring 1950. The United States, however, pursued a civil-war deterrent in Korea, hoping to restrain both the enemy and the ally; it therefore refused to equip this army with heavy weaponry that could be used to support an invasion of the North, such as tanks and an air force, and tried to keep hotheaded Southern commanders from provoking conflict along the 38th parallel. They did not succeed in the latter case; much of the extensive fighting along the border that lasted from May to December 1949 was said by internal American accounts to have been started by Southern forces, and was a major reason for the posting of UN military observers in Korea in 1950—to watch *both* the North and the South.

Although the South launched many small raids across the parallel before the summer of 1949, with the North happy to reciprocate, the important border battles began at Kaesong on May 4,

Kim Sok-won, right, with Defense Minister Yi Pom-sok, 1949.

1949, in an engagement that the South started. It lasted about four days and took an official toll of four hundred North Korean and twenty-two South Korean soldiers, as well as upward of a hundred civilian deaths in Kaesong, according to American and South Korean figures.[38] The South committed six infantry companies and several battalions, and two of its companies defected to the North (incongruous in their American military uniforms, Pyongyang made quick propaganda use of them). Months later, based on the defectors' testimony, the North Koreans claimed that several thousand troops led by Kim Sok-won attacked across the parallel on the morning of May 4, near Mount Songak, inaugurating border fighting that lasted for six months.[39] Kim was the commander of the critically important 1st Division; he was also from northern Korea and, as we have seen, had tracked Kim Il Sung at Japan's behest in the Manchurian wilderness in the late 1930s. Syngman Rhee came to rely on Kim and a small core of Manchurian officers after coming to power in 1948, mainly those who had experience in Japanese counterinsurgency. A few weeks after the Kaesong battle, Kim Sok-won gave the United Nations Commission on Korea (UNCOK) a briefing in his status as commander of ROKA forces along the 38th parallel: North and South "may engage in major battles at any moment," he said; Korea has entered into "a state of warfare." "We should have a program to recover our lost land, North Korea, by breaking through the 38th border which has existed since 1945"; the moment of major battles, Kim told UNCOK, is rapidly approaching.[40]

The worst fighting of 1949 occurred in early August, when North Korean forces attacked ROKA units occupying a small mountain north of the 38th parallel. It went on for days, right through an important summit conference between Syngman Rhee and Chiang Kai-shek. In the early morning hours on August 4 the North opened up great barrages of artillery and mortar fire, and then at 5:30 A.M. some 4,000 to 6,000 North Korean border guard soldiers attacked, seeking, in the KMAG commander Roberts's words, "to recover high ground in North Korea occupied by [the] South Korean Army." The southern side was "completely routed," according to Ambassador Muccio; two companies of ROKA soldiers in the 18th Regiment were annihilated, leaving hundreds dead and the North in occupation of the mountain.[41] On August 16, Muccio related that Rhee, in a conversation with him,

> ...threw out the thought that...he might replace [Chief of Staff] Chae [Pyong-dok] with General Kim Suk Wan [Kim Sok-won]....Kim Suk Wan has long been a favorite of Pres-

ident Rhee. Last fall prior to Yosu Rhee mentioned to General Coulter and myself that Kim had offered to "take care of the North" if he could be supplied with 20,000 rifles for Korean veterans of the Japanese Army who were burning with patriotism. The Minister of Defense, the Korean general staff and American advisors are all against General Kim. They do not consider him a good soldier but a blusterer. They have called my attention to his propensity for needling northern forces in his sector of the front, for resorting to Japanese banzai attacks and for deploying all his forces in a most hazardous manner right on the front without adequate reserves. They particularly object to his ignoring headquarters and going direct to President Rhee.[42]

General Roberts did indeed order Southern commanders not to attack and threatened to remove KMAG if they did; British sources said that ROKA commanders' heads "are full of ideas of recovering the North by conquest. Only the American ambassador's stern warning that all American aid would be stopped ... prevented the Army from attempting to attack across the parallel at another point when the Communists attacked at Ongjin."[43]

When we now look at both sides of the parallel with the help of some new (if scattered and selective) Soviet materials, we learn that Kim Il Sung's basic conception of a Korean War was quite similar to Rhee's, and was influenced deeply by the August 1949 fighting: namely, attack the cul-de-sac of Ongjin, move eastward and grab Kaesong, and then see what happens. At a minimum this would establish a much more secure defense of Pyongyang, which was quite vulnerable from Ongjin and Kaesong. At maximum it might open Seoul to his forces—that is, if the southern army collapsed, he could move on to Seoul and occupy it in a few days. And here we see the significance of the collapse of the ROK 2nd and 7th divisions in late June 1950, which opened the historic invasion corridor and placed the Korean People's Army in Seoul within three days, and why some people with intimate knowledge of the Korean civil conflict have speculated that these divisions may have harbored a fifth column.[44]

The critical issue in the Soviet documents[45] is a military operation to seize the Ongjin Peninsula. According to these materials, Kim Il Sung first broached the idea of an operation against Ongjin to Terenti Shtykov, the Soviet ambassador to Pyongyang, on August 12, 1949, right on the heels of the August 4 battle. Like Southern leaders, Kim Il Sung wanted to bite off a chunk of exposed territory or grab a small city—all of Kaesong, for example, or Haeju just above the parallel on Ongjin, which Southern commanders wanted to occupy in 1949–50. We also see how similar the Russians were in seeking to restrain hotheaded Korean leaders, including the chief of state. When Kim spoke about an invasion of Ongjin, two key Russian Embassy officials "tried to switch the discussion to a general theme." The Soviet documents also demonstrate the hard-won, *learned* logic of this civil war by late 1949; namely, that both sides understood that their big power guarantors would not help them if they launched an unprovoked general attack—or even an assault on Ongjin or Chorwon. A telegram from Shtykov to Moscow in January 1950 has Kim Il Sung impatient that *the South* "is still not instigating an attack" (thus to justify his own), and the Russians in Pyongyang tell him once again that he cannot attack Ongjin without risking general civil war. (The last Southern assault across the parallel was in December 1949, led by Paek Son-yop's brother, In-yop.)

North Korea was not ready for war, however, since it had tens of thousands of soldiers still fighting in China. It did not respond even to major provocations, such as several South Korean ships that invaded its waters and shelled a small port in the summer of 1949. Large numbers of battle-tested troops filtered back into Korea in August–September 1949, however, and again in early 1950, as the Chinese fighting ended, about 50,000 in toto (Zhang Shu-guang puts the number of Koreans fighting with the Chinese Communists against the Japanese in northeast China at 90,000, and the number that returned to Korea at 28,000 before September 1949—and tens of thousands more returned in early 1950).[46] The crack 6th Division, which acquitted itself very well in the early Korean War fighting, was wholly made up of China veterans and led by Gen. Pang Ho-san, who had gotten his original military training at the famed Whampoa Institute in the 1920s. In the spring of 1950 Kim Il Sung posted that division just above the small city of Haeju near the 38th parallel on the west coast.

Thus the 1950 logic for both sides was to see who would be stupid enough to move first, with Kim itching to invade and hoping for a clear Southern provocation, and hotheads in the South hoping to provoke an "unprovoked" assault, thus to get American help—for that was the only way the South could hope to win. Kim already had begun playing Moscow off against Beijing, too; for example, he let Shtykov overhear him say, at an apparently drunken luncheon on January 19, 1950, that if the Russians would not help him unify the country, "Mao Zedong is his friend and will always help Korea." In general these materials underline the influence that the victory of the Chinese revolution had on North Korea, and that North Korea's China connection was a trump card Kim could play to create some breathing room for his regime between the two Communist giants—and perhaps to bail his chestnuts out of an impending fire.

Kim also made several secret visits to Moscow and Beijing in early 1950, seeking support for an attack on the South. Based on the scattered evidence now available from Soviet archives, it appears that a wary and reluctant Stalin, who had restrained Kim for months before, changed his mind in early 1950 and approved an assault on the South. He offered Kim military equipment and sent advisers to help with planning the assault, but sought to distance the Soviet Union from Kim's adventurism (which became evident when Kim, at the last minute in June, changed a major assault on the South designed to seize Ongjin and Kaesong, and perhaps

Seoul, into a general invasion). Little definitive information has appeared about Kim's talks with Mao, but other evidence from the time suggests that Mao was probably more supportive than Stalin of Kim's plans.[47]

In 1949–50 Syngman Rhee also tried mightily to get elements of the Truman administration (especially in the intelligence agencies and the Pentagon) to back an invasion of the North, but through the intervention and multiple visits to Seoul by his patron M. Preston Goodfellow, Rhee was told that Washington would not come to the aid of his regime unless it were attacked without provocation. Goodfellow returned from Seoul in December 1949 and had discussions with the Chinese nationalist ambassador; the momentum for attack had shifted, Goodfellow told him:

> ... it was the South Koreans anxious to go into N.K., because they were feeling sharp with their army of well-trained 100,000 strong [*sic*]. But U.S. Govt was most anxious to restrain any provocation by the S.K. and Goodfellow had gone there lately to do just that. I asked how great was the possibility or danger of war breaking out in Korea. G[oodfellow] said U.S. Govt. position is this: avoid any initiative on S. Korea's part in attacking N.K., but if N.K. should invade S.K. then S.K. should resist and march right into N.K. with III World War as the result but in such a case, the aggression came from N.K. and the Am[erican] people would understand it.[48]

By the end of May 1950 Rhee's government was in total disarray, having lost many seats in an election for the legislature, and with devastating internal squabbles between different factions in the forces of order. The Korean ambassador to the United States, Chang Myon, made American officials aware of this crisis—which was the main reason John Foster Dulles decided to visit Seoul one week before the conventional war began.

The conflicts examined in this chapter were punctuations in a civil war that began in 1945 with political struggles, deepened in the next two years as battles over the people's committees culminated in a major rebellion in the fall of 1946, and then escalated to the limited warfare of guerrilla and border conflict in 1948–50. The June invasion was itself a culmination, a dénouement, that took the internal struggles to a new and decisive level, which would have ended them without outside intervention. June 25 was truly pivotal, therefore, because what might have been an ending for Koreans was the beginning for Americans—and has remained so ever since, a lightning bolt on a Sunday morning because Acheson and Truman chose to make it so. Their initial response was a limited war to restore the 38th parallel that Americans had drawn five years earlier. Soon, however, there seemed to be no limit on how this war was prosecuted.

CHAPTER SIX

"THE MOST DISPROPORTIONATE RESULT": THE AIR WAR

A characteristic of air wars is that those who sow the wind do not reap the whirlwind and those who reap the whirlwind did not sow the wind.

—JÖRG FRIEDRICH

Americans now in retirement will remember, perhaps, that we never won the Korean War. We helped the South defend itself in a successful war to contain communism in the summer of 1950, and then we lost our attempt to invade and overthrow communism in the North in the terrible winter of 1950–51. As the war dragged on it became as unpopular as Vietnam was by 1968, and made Harry Truman as disliked as any American president in history, with a 23 percent approval rating in December 1951 (until George W. Bush beat him).[1] What hardly any Americans know or remember, however, is that we carpet-bombed the North for three years with next to no concern for civilian casualties. Even fewer will feel any connection to this. Yet when foreigners visit North Korea, this is the first thing they hear about the war. The air assaults ranged from the widespread and continual use of firebombing to threats to use nuclear and chemical weapons, finally to the destruction of huge North Korean dams in the last stages of the war. It was an application and elaboration of the air campaigns against Japan and Germany, except that North Korea was a small Third World country that lost control of the air to the United States within days of the war's start.

After much experimentation and scientific study by Germany, Britain, and the United States, by 1943 it became clear that "a city was easier to burn down than to blow up." Combinations of incendiaries and conventional explosives, followed up by delayed-detonation bombs to keep firefighters at bay, could destroy large sections of a city, whereas conventional bombs had a much more limited impact. Magnesium-alloy thermite sticks, manufactured by the million and bundled together, did the trick; when supplemented by mixtures of benzol, rubber, resins, gels, and phosphorus, they formed unprecedentedly destructive blockbuster flaming bombs that could wipe out cities in a matter of minutes (seventeen in the case of the attack on Wurzburg, March 16, 1945). The creation of urban "annihilation zones" destroyed masses of civilian lives, an outcome accepted by all sides in the war—and "by the people, parliaments, and armed forces." And with that, in Jörg Friedrich's words, "modernity gave itself up to a new, incalculable, and uncontrollable fate."

Pretensions of precision targeting were put out for public consumption, while secret estimates showed that fewer than half the large bombs hit their targets. But in favorable atmospheric conditions these bombs ignited firestorms that razed Darmstadt, Heilbronn, Pforzheim, Wurzburg, and, of course, Hamburg (40,000 deaths), Dresden (12,000), and Tokyo (88,000). Or in Winston Churchill's words, "We will make Germany a desert, yes, a desert" through the power of incendiary bombing—only "an absolutely devastating, exterminating attack by very heavy bombers" would finally bring Hitler to his knees. The goal was to destroy the morale of the enemy and the people, a horizon that receded even as the attacks intensified.[2] The postwar *U.S. Strategic Bombing Survey* demonstrated that enemy morale was mostly unaffected by the bombing, but also that the actual level of civilian deaths was less than predicted—that is, "far removed from the generally anticipated total of several millions." Morale was not broken, and even the harvest of blackened, scorched, blasted, or asphyxiated human beings was anticlimactic (not even several millions). Furthermore, both countries were democracies, so some rose up to criticize mass attacks against civilians (Bishop George Bell told the House of Lords that "to obliterate a whole town" because it may have some industrial targets violated "a fair balance between the means employed and the purpose achieved"[3]).

Herblock's depiction of bombing of civilians by Franco's Spain and by Japan, 1937. *Copyright by the Herb Block Foundation*

Top air force officers decided to repeat "the fire" in Korea, a wildly disproportionate scheme in that North Korea had no pretense or possibility of a similar city-busting capability. Whereas German fighter planes and antiaircraft batteries made these allied bombing runs harrowing, with high loss of life among British and American pilots and crew, American pilots had virtual free-fire zones until later in the war, when formidable Soviet MIGs were deployed. Curtis LeMay subsequently said that he had wanted to burn down North Korea's big cities at the inception of the war, but the Pentagon refused—"it's too horrible." So over a period of three years, he went on, "We burned down *every* [*sic*] town in North Korea and South Korea,

Part of the city of Wonsan, under siege for 273 days. *U.S. National Archives*

too.... Now, over a period of three years this is palatable, but to kill a few people to stop this from happening—a lot of people can't stomach it."[4] To take just one example of these "limited" raids, on July 11, 1952, an "all-out assault" on Pyongyang involved 1,254 air sorties by day and 54 B-29 assaults by night, the prelude to bombing thirty other cities and industrial objectives under "operation PRESSURE PUMP." Highly concentrated incendiary bombs were followed up with delayed demolition explosives.

By 1968 the Dow Chemical Company, a major manufacturer of napalm, could not enter most college campuses to recruit employees because of napalm's use in Vietnam, but oceans of it were dropped on Korea silently or without notice in America, with much more devastating effect, since the DPRK had many more populous cities and urban industrial installations than did Vietnam. Furthermore, the U.S. Air Force loved this infernal jelly, its "wonder weapon," as attested to by many articles in "trade" journals of the

Part of the city of Pyongyang, at the end of the war. *Courtesy of Chris Springer*

time.* One day Pfc. James Ransome, Jr.'s unit suffered a "friendly" hit of this wonder weapon: his men rolled in the snow in agony and begged him to shoot them, as their skin burned to a crisp and peeled back "like fried potato chips." Reporters saw case after case of civilians drenched in napalm—the whole body "covered with a hard, black crust sprinkled with yellow pus."[5]

Korea recapitulated the air force's mantra from World War II, that firebombing would erode enemy morale and end the war sooner, but the interior intent was to destroy Korean society down to the individual constituent: General Ridgway, who at times deplored the free-fire zones he saw, nonetheless wanted bigger and better napalm bombs (thousand-pound versions to be dropped from B-29s) in early 1951, thus to "wipe out all life in tactical locality and save the lives of our soldiers." "If we keep on tearing the

---

* J. Townsend, "They Don't Like Hell Bombs," *Armed Forces Chemical Journal* (January 1951); "Napalm Jelly Bombs Prove a Blazing Success in Korea," *All Hands* (April 1951); E. F. Bullene, "Wonder Weapon: Napalm," *Army Combat Forces Journal* (November 1952).

place apart," Secretary of Defense Robert Lovett said, "we can make it a most unpopular affair for the North Koreans. We ought to go right ahead." (Lovett had advised in 1944 that the Royal Air Force had no restrictions on attacks against enemy territory, so the American bombers should "wipe out the town as the RAF does.")[6]

Another irony of the air war against Germany and Japan is that the worst civilian losses came after Arthur Harris, RAF Bomber Command chief, and Carl Spaatz, commander of U.S. Army Air Forces, had run out of targets—months before the most destructive incendiary attacks in March 1945. Cities were razed "because the bombing offensive had long ago become an end in itself, with its own momentum, its own purpose, devoid of tactical or strategic value, indifferent to the needless suffering and destruction it caused."[7] Within months few big targets remained in Korea, either; in late 1951 the air force judged that there were no remaining targets worthy of using the "Tarzon," its largest conventional bomb at 12,000 pounds, which had been deployed in December 1950 to try to decapitate DPRK leaders in deep bunkers. Twenty-eight of them had been used in the war.[8]

The opening of North Korean dams was another carryover from World War II. In May 1943 when the water level was highest (as in Korea), "Operation Chastise" attacked two dams on the Ruhr; the Moehne dam had a height of 130 feet and was 112 feet thick at its base; the Eder River dam held 7 billion cubic feet of water. "A tidal wave of 160 million tons of water, with a vertex thirty feet high," inundated five towns. The Royal Air Force considered this to be its "most brilliant action ever carried out." Friedrich concluded that total war consumes human beings totally—"and their sense of humanity is the first thing to go."[9]

Air force plans for attacks on North Korea's large dams originally envisioned hitting twenty of them, thus to destroy 250,000 tons of rice that would soon be harvested. In the event, bombers hit three dams in mid-May 1953, just as the rice was newly planted: Toksan, Chasan, and Kuwonga; shortly thereafter two more were attacked, at

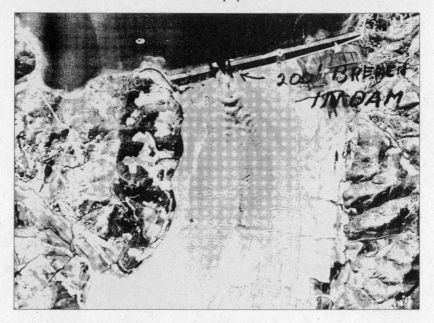

The Toksan Dam, breached by American bombers. *U.S. Air Force and U.S. National Archives*

Namsi and Taechon. These are usually called "irrigation dams" in the literature, but they were major dams akin to many large dams in the United States. The great Suiho Dam on the Yalu River was second in the world only to Hoover Dam, and was first bombed in May 1952 (although never demolished, for fear of provoking Beijing and Moscow). The Pujon River dam was designed to hold 670 million cubic meters of water, and had a pressure gradient of 999 meters; the dam's power station generated 200,000 kilowatts from the water.[10] According to the official U.S. Air Force history, when fifty-nine F-84 Thunderjets breached the high containing wall of Toksan on May 13, 1953, the onrushing flood destroyed six miles of railway, five bridges, two miles of highway, and five square miles of rice paddies. The first breach at Toksan "scooped clean" twenty-seven miles of river valley, and sent water rushing even into Pyongyang. After the war it took 200,000 man-days of labor to reconstruct the reservoir.

But as with so many aspects of the war, no one seemed to notice back home: only the very fine print of *New York Times* daily war reports mentioned the dam hits, with no commentary.[11]

THE ULTIMATE FIRE

The United States also considered using atomic weapons several times, and came closest to doing so in early April 1951—precisely the time that Truman removed MacArthur. It is now clear that Truman did not remove MacArthur simply because of his repeated insubordination, but also because he wanted a reliable commander on the scene should Washington decide to use nuclear weapons: that is, Truman traded MacArthur for his atomic policies. On March 10, 1951, MacArthur asked for a " 'D' Day atomic capability," to retain air superiority in the Korean theater, after intelligence sources suggested the Soviets appeared ready to move air divisions to the vicinity of Korea and put Soviet bombers into air bases in Manchuria (from which they could strike not just Korea but also American bases in Japan), and after the Chinese massed huge new forces near the Korean border. On March 14, Vandenberg wrote, "Finletter and Lovett alerted on atomic discussions. Believe everything is set." At the end of March, Stratemeyer reported that atomic bomb loading pits at Kadena Air Base on Okinawa were operational; the bombs were carried there unassembled, and put together at the base— lacking only the essential nuclear cores, or "capsules." On April 5 the JCS ordered immediate atomic retaliation against Manchurian bases if large numbers of new troops came into the fighting, or, it appears, if bombers were launched against American assets from there.

That same day Gordon Dean, chairman of the Atomic Energy Commission, began arrangements for transferring nine Mark IV nuclear capsules to the air force's 9th Bomb Group, the designated carrier of the weapons. General Bradley (JCS chairman) got Truman's approval for this transfer of the Mark IVs "from AEC to military custody" on April 6, and the president signed an order to use them against Chinese and North Korean targets. The 9th Bomb Group deployed to Guam. "In the confusion attendant upon General MacArthur's removal," however, the order was never sent. The reasons were two: Truman had used this extraordinary crisis to get the JCS to approve MacArthur's removal (something Truman announced on April 11), and the Chinese did not escalate the war. So the bombs were not used. But the nine Mark IVs remained in air force custody after their transfer on April 11. The 9th Bomb Group remained on Guam, however, and did not move on to the loading pits at Kadena AFB in Okinawa.[12]

The Joint Chiefs again considered the use of nuclear weapons in June 1951, this time in tactical battlefield circumstances, and there were many more such suggestions as the war continued to 1953. Robert Oppenheimer went to Korea as part of Project Vista, designed to gauge the feasibililty of tactical use of atomic weapons. In early 1951 a young man named Samuel Cohen, on a secret assignment for the Defense Department, observed the battles for the second recapture of Seoul, and thought there should be a way to destroy the enemy without destroying the city. He became the father of the neutron bomb.[13]

Most daunting, perhaps, was Operation Hudson Harbor. It appears to have been part of a larger project involving "overt exploitation in Korea by the Department of Defense and covert exploitation by the Central Intelligence Agency of the possible use of novel weapons." This project sought to establish the capability to use atomic weapons on the battlefield, and in pursuit of this goal lone B-29 bombers were lifted from Okinawa in September and October 1951 and sent over North Korea on simulated atomic bombing runs, dropping "dummy" A-bombs or heavy TNT bombs. The project called for "actual functioning of all activities which would be involved in an atomic strike, including weapons assembly and testing, leading, ground control of bomb aiming," and the like. The project indicated that the bombs were probably not useful, for purely technical reaons: "timely identification of large masses of enemy troops was extremely rare."[14] But one can imagine the steel nerves required of leaders in Pyongyang, observing a lone B-29 simulating the attack lines that had resulted in the devastation of Hiroshima and Nagasaki just six years earlier, each time unsure of whether the bomb was real or a dummy.

Violet Ashes

After his release from North Korean custody Gen. William F. Dean wrote that "the town of Huichon amazed me. The city I'd seen be-fore—two-storied buildings, a prominent main street—wasn't there any more." He encountered the "unoccupied shells" of town after town, and villages where rubble or "snowy open spaces" were all that remained.[15] The Hungarian writer Tibor Meray had been a corre-spondent in North Korea during the war, and left Budapest for Paris after his participation in the 1956 rebellion against Communist rule. When a Thames Television team interviewed him, he said that how-ever brutal Koreans on cither side might have been in this war, "I saw destruction and horrible things committed by the American forces":

> Everything which moved in North Korea was a military tar-get, peasants in the fields often were machine gunned by pi-lots who, this was my impression, amused themselves to shoot the targets which moved.

Meray had arrived in August 1951 and witnessed "a complete dev-astation between the Yalu River and the capital," Pyongyang. There were simply "no more cities in North Korea." The incessant, indis-criminate bombing forced his party always to drive by night:

> We traveled in moonlight, so my impression was that I am traveling on the moon, because there was only devasta-tion... every city was a collection of chimneys. I don't know

Rebuilding Pyongyang after the war, 1957. *Courtesy of the artist, Chris Marker, and Peter Blum Gallery, New York*

why houses collapsed and chimneys did not, but I went through a city of 200,000 inhabitants and I saw thousands of chimneys and that—that was all.[16]

A British reporter found communities where nothing was left but "a low, wide mound of violet ashes." At 10:00 P.M. on July 27 the air attacks finally ceased, as a B-26 dropped its radar-guided bomb load some twenty-four minutes before the armistice went into effect.

In the end the scale of urban destruction quite exceeded that in Germany and Japan, according to U.S. Air Force estimates. Friedrich estimated that the RAF dropped 657,000 tons of bombs on Germany from 1942 to 1945, and the total tonnage dropped by the UK and the United States at 1.2 million tons. The United States dropped 635,000 tons of bombs in Korea (not counting 32,557 tons of napalm), compared to 503,000 tons in the entire Pacific theater in World War II. Whereas sixty Japanese cities were destroyed to an average of 43 percent, estimates of the destruction of towns and cities in North Korea "ranged from forty to ninety percent"; at least 50 percent of eighteen out of the North's twenty-two major cities were obliterated. A partial table looks this:[17]

Pyongyang, 75%
Chongjin, 65%
Hamhung, 80%
Hungnam, 85%
Sariwon, 95%
Sinanju, 100%
Wonsan, 80%

As another official American history put it,

> So, we killed civilians, friendly civilians, and bombed their homes; fired whole villages with the occupants—women and children and ten times as many hidden Communist soldiers—under showers of napalm, and the pilots came back to their ships stinking of vomit twisted from their vitals by the shock of what they had to do.

Then the authors ask, was this any worse than "killing thousands of invisible civilians with the blockbusters and atomic bombs...?" Not really, they say, because the enemy's "savagery toward the people" was even worse than "the Nazis' campaign of terror in Poland and the Ukraine."[18] Apart from this astonishing distortion, note the logic: they are savages, so that gives us the right to shower napalm on innocents.

After the war the air force convinced many that its saturation bombing forced the Communists to conclude the war. The air force general Otto Weyland determined that "the panic and civil disorder" created in the North by round-the-clock bombing was "the most compelling factor" in reaching the armistice.[19] He was wrong, just as he had been in World War II, but that did not stop the air force from repeating the same mindless and purposeless destruction in Vietnam. Saturation bombing was not conclusive in either war—just unimaginably destructive.

The United Nation's Genocide Convention defined the term as acts committed "with intent to destroy, in whole or in part, a national, ethnical, racial or religious group." This would include "deliberately inflicting on the group conditions of life calculated to bring about its physical destruction in whole or in part." It was approved in 1948 and entered into force in 1951—just as the USAF was inflicting genocide, under this definition and under the aegis of the United Nations Command, on the citizens of North Korea. Others note that area bombing of enemy cities was not illegal in World War II, but became so only after the Red Cross Convention on the Protection of Civilians in Wartime, signed in Stockholm in August 1948.[20] Neither measure had the slightest impact on this air war, which operated with a mindless and implacable automaticity.

CHAPTER SEVEN

THE FLOODING
OF MEMORY

The country at this time took ye Alarm and were immedi-
ately in Arms, and had taken their different stations behind
Walls, on our Flanks, and thus we were harassed in our
Front, Flanks, and Rear...it not being possible for us to
meet a man otherwise than behind a Bush, Stone hedge or
Tree, who immediately gave his fire and went off.

—A BRITISH OFFICER AT LEXINGTON

Ambrose Bierce once wrote a short story called "An Occurrence at Owl Creek Bridge." Like the late Joseph Heller, the books by Paul Fussell on his experience in World War II, or Michael Herr's wonderful Vietnam memoir, *Dispatches*, the realities of the battlefield turned Ambrose Bierce into a specialist in black humor, if not cynicism, about the human condition. Bierce is best known for a handful of short stories—"Owl Creek Bridge," "Chickamauga," "The Mocking-Bird," "Three and One Are One," "An Affair of Outposts"—all of them drawn from his experience in the American civil war. That was the last war to rage back and forth across American soil. Six hundred thousand Americans lost their lives in it, more than the total number of American deaths in all the wars of the twentieth century, from World Wars I and II through Korea, Vietnam, and the Persian Gulf War. The civil war pitted brother against brother, son against father, mother against herself. Memories of that war lasted so long that we still have a bitter controversy about the flag of the Confederacy that flies over the Mississippi statehouse. I first went to the South when I was twelve years old, to spend some time with relatives in Memphis, and my shock at seeing Jim Crow in action was only slightly greater than my shock at finding out I was a Yankee—almost a century after the war ended.

Bierce specialized in surprise endings to his stories, ones that drove home a truth about the human nature of civil war: in "The Mocking-Bird," Private Grayrock of the Federal Army, posted as a sentinel, sees something moving in the woods of southwestern Virginia and fires his musket. Convinced that he actually hit something, he spends hours scouring the area. In the end John Grayrock finds the body, a single bullet hole marking the gray uniform. Inside the uniform is William Grayrock, his brother.

In the course of this sad story, Bierce refers without explanation to the "unconverted civilians" of southwestern Virginia in 1861, who torment John Grayrock's mind in their imagined multitude, materializing from all angles to kill him—peeping from behind trees, rushing out of the woods, hiding in a home. In "The Story of a Conscience" a man kills himself after realizing that he has killed an enemy spy who once spared his own life, earlier in the war. In "Chickamauga," a soldier dreams so vividly that we believe him to be reunited with his family and kinsmen, but the story ends with the man standing over his mother's dead body, her hands clutched full of grass, beside the burned-out remains of his childhood home.

In "An Occurrence at Owl Creek Bridge," Peyton Farquhar, a well-to-do Alabaman and "southern planter," that is to say, slave-holder, is about to be hanged from a railroad bridge. This is Bierce's most famous story, so many would know that it also involves an elegiac dream of reuniting with his beloved family after the rope snaps and plunges him into the raging river below, followed by a justly famous surprise ending—when the rope breaks the man's neck. Less well known, perhaps, is that the Yankee commandant had "issued an order, which is posted everywhere, declaring that any civilians caught interfering with the railroad, its bridges, tunnels or trains will be summarily hanged."[1]

In the summer of 2000, and for every summer of the previous half century, a soldier named Art Hunter awakened in the middle of the night with cold sweats, imagining the faces of two old people, a man and a woman, hovering above his bed. These two weathered faces had made his life "a living hell," and when they haunted him he would arise, get his hunting rifle, go sit on the porch, and smoke a cigarette. In 1991 the former soldier Hunter finally got the U.S. government to give him full disability pay for his severe post-traumatic stress disorder, but the nightmares still came to him in his home in the foothills of Virginia's Blue Ridge Mountains.[2]

On September 30, 1999, a woman named Chon Chun-ja appeared on the front page of *The New York Times*, dressed as if she were yet another middle-aged and middle-class Korean housewife going shopping. Instead she stood at the mouth of a tall tunnel in Nogun village and pointed to a hill where, she alleged, in July 1950 "American soldiers machine-gunned hundreds of helpless civilians under a railroad bridge." She and other survivors went on to say that they had been petitioning their government and the American government for years, seeking compensation for this massacre; they had been completely stonewalled in both Seoul and Washington. Meanwhile, the article also carried the testimony of American soldiers who did the firing, who said that their commander had ordered them to fire on civilians.[3] Art Hunter was one of those soldiers, shooting into a white-clad mass of women, children, and elderly people gathered under the railroad bridge.

The *Times* did not produce this story, but rather front-paged an Associated Press account of the massacre. In subsequent days and weeks it did no follow-up reporting, to my knowledge, except periodically to update its readership on what the Associated Press was saying about the reaction in the Pentagon, or Seoul, the announcement of an investigation into the survivor's claims, and the like. Two months after this story broke, Doug Struck, a reporter for *The Washington Post*, learned that civilians were huddled in the railroad tunnel for as much as three days, while American soldiers repeatedly returned: Chong Ku-hun, then seventeen years of age, told Struck, " 'They were checking every wounded person and shooting them if they moved.' Other soldiers climbed down toward a drainage pipe where dozens of villagers had taken shelter and began shooting into families, according to the accounts of other survivors." Yang Hae-suk, then a girl of thirteen, was also in the tunnel: "Suddenly there were planes and bombs. My uncle covered his child, and I heard him say, 'Oh, my God.' I looked and saw his intestines had come out. The bullet had passed through his back and killed his daughter." A few moments later the young teenager also got hit and lost her left eye. Mr. Struck said investigators "face the delicate task of measuring a dirty war by standards that officials here say were violated by all sides during the three-year conflict."[4] This account carried the story a very troubling step further: not only were the American GIs ordered to shoot at civilians, they returned again and again to make sure they were all dead. This suggests, of course, that they wanted to assure themselves that there would be *no* survivors to tell the tale of Nogun-ri.

This element of the Korean War has disappeared from the collective memory, as if Vietnam were the only intervention where "My Lais" occurred. But in 1950, the people in "white pajamas" and what they provoked in Americans was as accessible as the neighborhood barbershop reading table. For example, John Osborne of *Life* told readers of the August 21, 1950, issue that American officers had ordered GIs to fire on clusters of civilians; a soldier said, "It's gone too far when we are shooting children." It was a new kind of war, Osborne wrote, "blotting out of villages where the enemy *may* be hiding; the shelling of refugees who *may* include North Koreans." As I. F. Stone put it, the air raids and the sanitized reports issued to the press "reflected not the pity which human feeling called for, but a kind of gay moral imbecility, utterly devoid of imagination—as if the flyers were playing in a bowling alley, with villages for pins."[5]

The military historian Walter Karig, writing in *Collier's*, likened the fighting to "the days of Indian warfare" (a common analogy); he also thought Korea might be like the Spanish civil war—a testing ground for a new type of conflict, which might be found later in places such as Indochina and the Middle East. "Our Red foe scorns all rules of civilized warfare," Karig wrote, "hid[ing] behind women's skirts"; he then presented the following colloquy:

> The young pilot drained his cup of coffee and said, "Hell's fire, you can't shoot people when they stand there waving at you." "Shoot 'em," he was told firmly. "They're troops." "But,

hell, they've all got on those white pajama things and they're straggling down the road"..."See any women or children?" "Women? I wouldn't know." "The women wear pants, too, don't they?" "But no kids, no, sir." "They're troops. Shoot em."[6]

Eric Larrabee, writing in *Harper's*, began by quoting an English captain who subdued the Pequot Indians in 1836: "the tactics of the natives...far differ from Christian practice." He recalled the reflections of a British officer at Lexington during the American revolution:

> The country at this time took ye Alarm and were immediately in Arms, and had taken their different stations behind Walls, on our Flanks, and thus we were harassed in our Front, Flanks, and Rear...it not being possible for us to meet a man otherwise than behind a Bush, Stone hedge or Tree, who immediately gave his fire and went off.

A marine in Korea told him, "In Tarawa you could at least see the enemy. Here the gooks hide in the bushes." What was a limited war for Americans, Larrabee wrote, was a people's war for Koreans (much like the American war against the British), and he said it could not be fought with a "brutal and senseless display of technical superiority"—instead, without using the terms, he called for the development of rapidly deployable special forces to fight the people's wars of the future, where the object would be winning the people over to our side.[7]

Reginald Thompson wrote that war correspondents found the campaign for the South "strangely disturbing," different from World War II in its guerrilla and popular aspect. "There were few who dared to write the truth of things as they saw them." GIs "never spoke of the enemy as though they were people, but as one might speak of apes." Even among correspondents, "every man's dearest wish was to kill a Korean. 'Today . . . I'll get me a gook.' " GIs called Koreans gooks, he thought, because "otherwise these essentially kind and generous Americans would not have been able to kill them indiscriminately or smash up their homes and poor belongings."[8]

Americans still seem to have difficulty looking with open eyes on the record of the Korean War. Why did *The New York Times* and other papers find massacre stories fit to print in 1999, but not fit to print for the previous forty-nine years? In one sense it *is* a "forgotten war"; U.S. reporters of the first rank often know nothing about it. Forgotten, unknown, never-known: and thus Nogun-ri becomes interesting and salient, because it suggests to reporters of the younger generation not Korea but the Vietnam War and the My Lai massacre—and we thought things like that happened only in Vietnam (and really, only once). So, in this curious American lexicon, civilian massacres—about which one could read in *Life* in the summer of 1950—disappear into oblivion because of a false construction of the nature of the Korean War; they get lost for a sufficiently long time, such that when they resurface they appear to contradict much of the received wisdom on this war.

Art Hunter surely knew the truth of what happened in Nogun village so many years ago, but why did it haunt him? I think it is because a young man on the giving end of a rifle intuits a fundamental human truth about warfare, that the soldier is there to kill, but also to save and protect:

> The soldier, be he friend or foe, is charged with the protection of the weak and unarmed. It is the very essence and reason for his being. When he violates this sacred trust he not only profanes his entire culture but threatens the very fabric of international society.

The author of this moving statement went on to say that "the traditions of fighting men are long and honorable, based upon the no-

blest of human traits—sacrifice." He was General of the Army
Douglas MacArthur.[9]

Jesus

POLITICAL LINEAGE, ANCESTRAL LINEAGE

When we examine these events more closely they help us to un-
ravel certain truths about the Korean War. What happened in
Nogun-ri grew out of the legacy of the suppressed aspirations of
Koreans in 1945; local guerrillas in 1950 were remnants of the communal hopes of Koreans when they were liberated from Japan.
Nogun village is located a couple of miles down the road from the
county seat of Yongdong, in a remote and mountainous region
where the borders of three provinces meet, and where a strong, indigenous left wing emerged just after Japanese imperialism collapsed in Korea in August 1945. A county people's committee took
power from the Japanese, and then two months later watched as
American civil affairs teams retrieved the reins of government
from it, as part of the establishment of the U.S. Military Government. The Americans on the scene quickly reemployed Koreans
who had served in the colonial police, and of course suppressed
the people's committee. But the committee kept coming back to
power, according to internal American reports. The U.S. Counter-
Intelligence Corps found that Yongdong still had a strong people's
committee in the autumn of 1948, at the time of the Yosu rebellion,
and guerrilla war emerged in and around Yongdong, long before
the ostensible "Korean War" began.[10] An American doctor named
Clesson Richards ran a Salvation Army hospital in Yongdong from
1947 until leaving just before the war. "Guerrilla warfare was around
us all the time," he told a reporter. "We had many Commies as
patients. . . . The police would keep an eye on them, grill them and
when they had all possible information, take them out and stand
them before a firing squad. This wall was near the hospital. We
could hear the men being shot." This he said matter-of-factly, since

not soviet

hated

in Dr. Richards's opinion "the Commies were ruthless" (although they "had no anti-foreign feeling and did not bother us"). Americans such as KMAG officer James Hausman directed much of the counterinsurgency in 1948–49, and knew Yongdong county well as a hotbed of resentment and insurrection—it was long called a "red county"—while noting that all the guerrillas were indigenous and had no direction from North Korea. Rather, their grievances harkened back to the shattered hopes of liberation in 1945, and the extreme poverty of the tenant farmers in the area.[11] But when the conventional warfare opened in June 1950, this history meant that Yongdong was targeted as a dangerous place for Americans.

Nogun-ri is a very old village in Korean records, the earliest mention in gazetteers coming in the eleventh century. With the typical landholding patterns of the 1940s in which families would have owned land going back centuries (usually to the time of the warlord Hideyoshi's invasions in the 1590s, when gazetteers say Nogun village was laid waste), it is not surprising that most people in this ancient village did not want to move out of their homes, in spite of American and South Korean demands that they do so; this would mean leaving not just the land, but the ancestral tombs that dot the hills near Korean villages.

WHAT IS TRUTH? OUR SREBRENICA

In July 2008 the world media heralded the arrest of "the world's most wanted war criminal," the Bosnian Serb leader Radovan Karadzic. He had been in hiding for thirteen years, ever since he was charged with genocide by the United Nations war crimes tribunal in The Hague for his role in the massacre of some eight thousand Muslim men and boys in Srebrenica. These events were subsequently termed "Europe's worst slaughter of civilians since World War II."[12] Fifty-eight years earlier, in another murderous July, as the North Korean People's Army bore down upon the city of Taejon, south of Seoul, police authorities removed political prisoners from local jails, men and boys along with some women, massacred them, threw them into open pits, and dumped the earth back on them. Somewhere between four thousand and seven thousand died, and their stories remained buried for half a century. American officers stood idly by while this slaughter went on, photographing it for their records but doing nothing to stop it. A few months later the JCS classified the photos, not to be released until 1999. Then official American histories blamed the massacre on the Communists.

South Korea has illustrated that mutual understanding and rapprochement between enemies needs to be preceded by a process of truth and reconciliation; that is, a scrupulous, penetrating, forensic look at the past that investigates and acknowledges buried and suppressed aspects of history. And so, mostly unbeknownst to the American people or press, the Korean Truth and Reconciliation Commission has dredged up and verified the massacres of tens of thousands of its own citizens by the Syngman Rhee regime (including one that appears to have been larger than the Taejon massacre, at Changwon[13]), various villages blotted out by American napalm (in the *South*), and has reexamined massacres by North Korean and local Communists (these were the cases endlessly propagandized since the war ended).

The Koreans found their primary model in the truth and reconciliation process in South Africa, which defined that vexing term, "truth," in at least four ways: forensic truth (dig up and examine the bodies; forensic evidence is "embodied memory": violence is written, inscribed, even performed on the body, living or dead[14]); eyewitness truth (let the victims speak); scholarly truth (historians and archival documents); and perpetrators' truth—get them on the stand, let them speak too, and then let the others respond. It is a method for letting all the relevant parties have their say, for achieving a social or "dialogue" truth, a healing or restorative truth, a way to allocate justice and assess punishment, all in the interest of reconciliation rather than revenge or self-justification. South Africa

Woman guerrilla captured in 1949. *U.S. National Archives*

adopted its commission in 1995, predicated on public deliberations, truth established in these ways, official investigations using fair procedures, testimony from planners, perpetrators, and victims alike; and amnesty for those who disclosed the full facts and recognized their complicity.[15] The same kind of inquiry is needed into American massacres such as Nogun-ri, the unrelenting firebombing of the North, and one of the most astonishing cover-ups in postwar U.S. history, the black-and-white reversal of the truth of what happened in Taejon.

In early August 1950, Alan Winnington published an article in the London *Daily Worker* hyperbolically titled "U.S. Belsen in Korea," alleging that ROK police under the supervision of KMAG advisers had butchered seven thousand people in a village near Taejon, during the period July 2–6. Accompanying KPA troops as a war correspondent, Winnington found twenty eyewitnesses who said that on July 2, truckloads of police arrived and made local people build six pits, each two hundred yards long. Two days later political prisoners were trucked in and executed, both by bullets to the head and decapitation by sword, and then layered on top of one another in the pits "like sardines." The massacres continued for three days. The witnesses said that two jeeps with American officers observed the killings.[16] North Korean sources said four thousand had been killed (changing it some months later to seven thousand), mostly imprisoned guerrillas from Cheju Island and the Taebaek Mountains, and those detained after the Yosu rebellion in 1948. They located the site differently than Winnington, however.[17]

The American Embassy in London called the Winnington story an "atrocity fabrication" and denied its contents. The official American history of the early stages of the Korean War by Roy Appleman made no mention of any ROK atrocities, and instead claimed that the North Koreans carried out this massacre—perpetrating "one of the greatest mass killings" of the war in Taejon, with between five thousand and seven thousand people slaughtered and placed in mass graves.[18] Most Western histories do the same: Max Hastings, as we have seen, paid attention only to Communist atrocities (even though he does not catalog or verify them in any detail) because they gave to the UN cause in Korea "a moral legitimacy that has survived to this day."

The evidence shows that Winnington was more truthful in 1950, during the heat of war, than Appleman and Hastings were with the benefit of hindsight and classified documentation. U.S. Army intelligence on July 2 rated as "probably true" a report that the Korean National Police in Taejon were "arresting all Communists and executing them on the outskirts of the city." The CIA stated the next day that "unofficial reports indicated that Southern Korean police are executing Communist suspects in Suwon and Taejon, in an effort both to eliminate a potential 5th column and to take revenge for reported northern executions in Seoul." Neither report gave numbers, however.[19] British officials in Tokyo who talked to Supreme Command, Allied Powers (SCAP) officers said that "there may be an element of truth in [Winnington's] report," but SCAP thought it was a matter to be handled between London and Washington. Alvary Gascoigne, a British representative at MacArthur's headquarters, said that reliable journalists have "repeatedly" noted "the massacre of prisoners by South Korean troops," but one "J. Underwood" of the U.S. prisoners of war mission told British sources that he doubted seven thousand prisoners could even have been assembled in Taejon, as not more than two thousand were in the city's prisons.[20] Underwood would have done better to admit that this incident was not simply a merciless slaughter of political prisoners, but the murder of people rounded up during the American occupation for protesting against the conditions that Americans fostered or created. Americans conducted the various rounds of suppression in the period 1945–50 or supported those Koreans who did, and then stood idly by to watch this slaughter in July 1950, photographing it but doing nothing about it.

In his 1981 book a former U.S. Central Intelligence Agency operative gave witness to the systematic slaughter of political prisoners near Suwon, just south of Seoul, in the first week of July 1950:

> I stood by helplessly, witnessing the entire affair. Two big bull-dozers worked constantly. One made the ditch-type grave. Trucks loaded with the condemned arrived. Their hands were already tied behind them. They were hastily pushed into a big line along the edge of the newly opened grave. They were quickly shot in the head and pushed into the grave.[21]

A psychologist in New York by the name of Do-young Lee finally got photos of this particular tragedy declassified, and they are dramatic evidence of American complicity. The most striking fact, uncovered by the Associated Press, was that in September 1950 the U.S. government at the highest level (in this case the Joint Chiefs of Staff) chose to suppress the photos, never to be revealed until 1999. And then the Pentagon subsidized official histories that blamed every civilian atrocity at this time, including Taejon, on the North Koreans, and got Humphrey Bogart to narrate a 1950 film, *The Crime of Korea*, which had the most extensive public film footage of the Taejon massacre—layered corpses stretching across football-field-length trenches: "Taejon: men, women and children murdered cold-bloodedly, deliberately, butchered to spread terror" by "Communist monsters" and "primitive North Koreans." In time, Bogart went on, "we'll get a careful tabulation...certified by the UN Commission on Korea—each case will be thoroughly documented."[22]

Instead the UN did nothing and decades of stonewalling by two governments followed, right up to the Pentagon's claim for two years (1997–99) that it found "no information that substantiates the claim" of the Nogun village survivors. The offending 1st Cavalry Division wasn't even in the area, they said. Yet it took me exactly five minutes to find Clay Blair's statement in *The Forgotten War*, based on declassified unit records, that "the 1st Cav[alry] would relieve the shattered 24th Division at Yongdong" on July 22. But then the Pentagon had to prevaricate and refuse to compensate the survivors because there were so many similar incidents during the war, and who knows how many claimants for compensation.[23]

The day after the Taejon massacre story broke, I got a phone call from an American woman in Los Angeles whose father was one of the victims. In 1947 she was a Korean citizen of the American Military Government, one of six children of a factory owner in a town near Taejon. He had prospered during the Japanese period, and at liberation thought it desirable to share some of his wealth. He was arrested for giving money to "Communists" in the raucous summer of 1947 (when hundreds if not thousands of Koreans died at the hands of the occupation's National Police) and was still in jail in early July 1950. This woman (a registered nurse) and her four sisters and one brother have never been able to tell anyone outside the family how their father died. For half a century they had agonized over the loss of the patriarch of the family, but privately—even among themselves—no one ever talked about it. She was weeping over the phone for half an hour about her experience. Do-young Lee's father also perished in a massacre in August 1950, but he had the courage to come forward with his photos; subsequently he tracked down and confronted the Korean Army officer who killed his father.

The Korean Truth and Reconciliation Commission investigations of the Taejon massacre are not complete, but by now have determined that at least four thousand people died at the hands of the ROK authorities, and that later the North Koreans killed yet more (but not thousands), and may have buried them in the same pits. Lee Yoon-young was a prison guard who had the courage to step forward at the age of eighty-five and testify to what he saw decades earlier: "Ten prisoners were carried to a trench at a time and were made to kneel at the edge. Police officers stepped up behind them, pointed their rifles at the back of their heads, and fired."

MEASURES TAKEN: THE SOUTHWEST DURING THE WAR

Political massacres began as soon as Seoul looked like it might fall. Official Australian sources pointed to "the stupid order of the Rhee Government to execute about 100 communists in Seoul before it evacuated" the city in June 1950; United Press International (UPI) stated that ninety to a hundred had been executed in this episode, including "the beautiful 'Mata Hari' " of Korean communism, Kim Su-in.[25] Many more were murdered at the same time in the port city of Inchon. American internal sources reported that Southern authorities imprisoned most known leftists as towns fell to the KPA: "Our information is that these prisoners are considered as enemies of South Korea and disposed of accordingly, before the arrival of North Korean forces."[26] American occupation authorities in Tokyo (or SCAP) said that a "guerrilla riot" occured in Inchon on June 30, resulting in the arrest of three hundred people. The North Koreans later claimed to have found eyewitnesses to the slaughter of a thousand political prisoners and alleged Communists in Inchon, perpetrated in the period June 29 to July 1 (they alleged that this was done on the order of an American in KMAG). The State Department's Office of Intelligence Research (OIR) noted these North Korean charges, but dismissed the affair as "nothing more than an ROK police action against rebellious elements attempting a prison break and other dissidents aiding them."[27] Things got much worse as North Korean forces entered the stronghold of the left wing in the southwestern Chollas, a week into the war.

As this happened, Gen. Yi Ung-jun declared martial law in the region and authorized capital punishment for subversive and sabotage activities, and for "anyone considered a political criminal by the commander." Who was he? After pledging his fealty to the emperor in blood, he graduated from the Japanese Military Academy in 1943 and was a colonel when the war ended. He then helped the U.S. occupation develop military forces in the south in November 1945, was the first ROK Army chief of staff in 1948, and was remembered by the wife of an American official as having seen "a great deal of action with the Japanese troops in China"; with his jackboots and riding crop he "retained some of the arrogance of the Jap military." When the North invaded he was commander of the 2nd Division, responsible for the east side of the Uijongbu corridor. Ordered to attack with his whole division, he refused to attack even with a couple of battalions. Soon the whole division was routed.[28]

The massacres in Suwon and Taejon came in the midst of American troops reeling backward by the hour. At Taejon came the clearest and in some ways worst defeat of American troops, at the hands of KPA commanders who have prized that victory ever since. The 24th Infantry Division suffered a "ghastly" defeat at Taejon, "one of the greatest ordeals in Army history."[29] As the backpedaling American forces tumbled southward from Taejon, they soon arrived in Yongdong. North Korean sources said it had been "liberated" by local guerrillas before they arrived, something corroborated by Walter Sullivan. He reported that some three hundred local guerrillas in and around Yongdong harassed the retreating Americans, and that they would take over local peacekeeping duties once the North Koreans passed through. "The American G.I. is now beginning to eye with suspicion any Korean civilian in the cities or countryside," Sullivan wrote; " 'Watch the guys in white'— the customary peasant dress—is the cry often heard near the front." The diary of a dead Korean named Choe Song-hwan, either a North Korean soldier or a local guerrilla, noted on July 26 that American bombers had swooped over Yongdong and "turned it into a sea of fire."[30]

Meanwhile, to the west, in the same week of July the 6th Division of the KPA swept through the southwestern Cholla provinces, clearing them in forty-eight hours—essentially for three reasons: first, the 6th Division was a crack unit led by Pang Ho-san, who a year earlier had led this same division when it was the 166th Division of the Chinese People's Liberation Army, made up almost entirely of Koreans who fought in the Chinese civil war. They had transferred back to North Korea as the war in China wound down, and in May 1950 North Korean commanders positioned this division just north of Haeju, across the 38th parallel on the Ongjin Peninsula. It was these and other China-blooded troops that underpinned North Korea's war plan in 1950, a battle that would have happened earlier, perhaps, if those troops had been available in the summer of 1949. Second, the 6th Division cleared the Chollas so quickly because the forces of order of the Rhee government evacuated so quickly. Third, the North Koreans were met by thousands of local guerrillas who rose up as North Korean forces drew near, seizing villages and towns, the residue of the guerrilla conflict that was strong in the Chollas in 1948 and 1949. These troops then turned and began a daunting march eastward, occupying Chinju by August 1 and thereby directly menacing Pusan.

The rapid advance of the 6th Division southward and eastward threatened a full envelopment of the peninsula as early as July 26 (the time of the Nogun-ri incident), when General Walker ordered a military withdrawal from Taegu. On the same day the ROK government announced that any civilian "making enemy-like action" would be shot; all civilians now had to travel by special trains, and people in the battle area would be allowed to leave their homes for only two hours each day. "All those found violating these regulations will be considered enemies and will be executed immediately." In essence this meant that a free-fire zone now surrounded the front lines. Really, though, they were only following American orders in the Chollas: guerrilla infiltration led to General Dean's decision "to force every Korean out of the division's area of responsibility, on the theory that once they were removed, any Korean caught in the area would be an enemy agent." This order was issued to the Korean Army and to the National Police.[31]

The next day MacArthur flew over to Korea and demanded that further withdrawals cease, and shortly thereafter the 2nd Infantry Division landed at Pusan and was rushed up to the line at Chinju. The 6th Division had just "beat hell out of us" there, an American officer related; the next day the KPA occupied Masan and American forces retreated to the Naktong River, employing a "scorched earth" policy that led to the burning of many villages harboring guerrillas: "smoke clouds rose over the front from Hwanggan to Kumchon."[32] Soon, however, the war front stabilized at the Pusan perimeter.

Ever since this early and determining point South Korean politics has had a suppressed "third force," with strong roots in the southwest, but a presence all over the country. If we locate these forces on the "left," we reduce them to the polarized and caricatured constructions of the Cold War in which any kind of mayhem committed by the right is insufficient truly to distance them from American support, so long as they remain firmly anti-Communist. For decades these political and social forces resided of necessity in the long memories of participants in the local committees, labor and peasant unions, and rebellions of the late 1940s, harboring many personal and local truths that could not be voiced. For the next fifty years, the acceptable political spectrum in the South consisted of the ruling forces and parties of Rhee, Park, Chun, Roh, and Kim Young Sam, and an opposition deriving from the Korean Democratic Party founded in September 1945, led by figures such as Kim Song-su, Chang Taek-sang, and Chang Myon. The ROK did not have a real transition to the opposition until Kim Dae Jung's election in 1998, and it did not have a president who was not part of the political divide (and political system) going back to the U.S. occupation until February 2003. (Kim Dae Jung got his political start in the self-governing people's committees that sprouted near the southwestern port of Mokpo; the right always used that against him to claim that he was a Communist or pro-North, but in fact he made his peace with the existing system in the late 1940s, and was an establishment politician thereafter, however much he was hounded by the militarists.) The late president Roh Moo Hyun was the first of the ROK's leaders not to have a recognizable lineage back to the 1940s. His lineage was more recent, to the extraordinary turmoil of the 1980s, when he put his career and his life in danger to defend labor leaders and human rights activists; but through marriage he is also connected to a family blacklisted politically for events going back decades—Roh's father-in-law was a member of the South Korean Workers' Party, outlawed under the U.S. occupation; he was arrested for allegedly helping the North Koreans during the war, and died in prison.

MR. MASSACRE

Kim Chong-won got the name "Tiger" for his service to the Japanese Army; after 1945 he liked journalists to call him "the Tiger of Mount Paekdu." He volunteered for the Imperial Army in 1940, served in New Guinea and the Philippines, and rose to sergeant, "a rank which epitomized the brutality of the Japanese Army at its worst," in Ambassador Muccio's words. He was with the Korean National Police at the Eastgate Station in 1946, then for eight months in 1947 he was Chang Taek-sang's personal bodyguard (Chang was head of the Seoul Metropolitan Police). He then entered the army, where he rose quickly through the ranks in the counterinsurgency campaigns; Americans remembered him for his brutality in the suppression (Muccio called it "ruthless and effective"), and for his refusal to take American orders. An American in 1948 termed him "a rather huge, brute of a man"—after witnessing Kim and his men "mercilessly" beat captured Yosu rebellion prisoners, including women and children, "with cot rounds, bamboo sticks, fists." He worked closely with Kim Paek-il and Chong Il-gwon, and by August 1949 he was a regimental commander.

After the war began, a KMAG adviser went "berserk with the idea of killing Kim," according to Muccio. The officer himself, Lt. Col. Rollins Emmerich, was not berserk: he said he would have to shoot Kim "if no one else will get rid of him." Kim was berserk: he had killed some of his own officers and men for alleged disobedience, avoided the front lines of fighting like the plague, and had beheaded fifty POWs and guerrillas (said to be just "one group" among others that had received this treatment). Kim was temporarily relieved of his command under American pressure. Later on

Seoul Police commander Chang Taek-sang. The unidentified man to his right appears to be "Tiger" Kim. Circa 1946.

Rhee made him the commander of the martial law regime in Pusan, where he distinguished himself in the squalid terror of the "conscription" campaigns, which consisted of "shanghai-ing the required number of young men off the streets." Kim told this same officer that he planned to machine-gun 3,500 political prisoners held in Pusan prisons. Emmerich told him not to—unless the city was about to fall: "Col. Kim was told that if the enemy did arrive to the outskirts of [Pusan] he would be permitted to open the gates of the prison and shoot prisoners with machine guns." Emmerich later persuaded Koreans not to execute 4,500 political prisoners in

Kim Il Sung (center) walks away from a meeting, early in the Korean War. *U.S. National Archives*

Taegu, but within weeks most of them were killed. President Rhee soon promoted Kim to deputy provost marshal, and later sent him to assist in running the occupation of Pyongyang in the fall of 1950. Although he was clearly, on this evidence, a war criminal in Korea if not necessarily in the Philippines, Tiger Kim was part of Rhee's bestiary of close and trusted confidants.[33]

what.

NORTH KOREAN ATROCITIES

We instantly return to the mentality that operated during the Cold War when we anticipate the question "But how many people did the Communists kill?" A democratic conception of justice is not dignified by assuring ourselves that even if Syngman Rhee's forces killed 200,000 political suspects, the Communists killed more. But readers will ask this question, accustomed as they are to contemporary media images of North Korea as a worst-case example of Communist rule. Often these images correspond to reality: DPRK leaders have on their hands the blood of at least 600,000 of their citizens who perished in the famines of the late 1990s. If unprecedented floods began this tragedy, the inaction or complicity of a regime that has always penetrated even the most remote hamlets indicates either reprehensible dereliction or conscious and inexcusable cruelty and inhumanity. Since the mid-1970s Amnesty International has documented the existence of political prisons and forced labor camps holding somewhere between 100,000 and 200,000 people. From the early years down to the present, the regime has staged exemplary public executions, particularly of political offenders. When the Communists recovered their territory after the Chinese intervened in the war, even Kim Il Sung had to condemn the scale of political retribution against perceived collaborators with the South. We know very little about this terrible episode, however, because the North Koreans have never evinced the slightest interest in reexamining their past in any open, democratic, or serious investigative manner. One is therefore right to presume that they have everything to hide.

Having said all that, the North and South Korea of today are vastly different than they were sixty years ago. We do not have evidence that the North Koreans ever killed their enemies in such large numbers. The land reform campaigns were much less bloody than those in the Soviet Union, China, or Vietnam; the leadership was content either to let landlords flee to the South, or to move them to non-native counties if they were willing to farm the land. From the start of the war there were reports that the North Koreans executed former ROK officials, KNP officers, leaders of rightist youth groups, and former Korean employees of the United States. The early executions often resulted from released leftist prisoners settling scores, but a DPRK Interior Ministry document stated that the KNP included many colonial police who fled the

North, sons of Northern landlords who had joined the Northwest Youth Corps, sons of landlords and capitalists in the South, and people who were relatively high up in the colonial regime. It thus declared that their crimes "cannot be forgiven."[34] Although the document said nothing about executing such people, one can imagine that this provided the basis for the executions, after a kangaroo "people's court."

North Korean battlefield executions of captured American soldiers inflamed American opinion well beyond anything the South Koreans might have been doing. This practice first surfaced in early July, and in the wake of the Inchon landing it got worse: several groups of thirty to forty executed American POWs were found, and one group of eighty-seven was retrieved just as their hands were being tied. Such behavior underpinned MacArthur's and Willoughby's frequent demands that North Korean leaders be tried for war crimes. Internal materials, however, show that SCAP had found orders from KPA leaders demanding that such practices stop, and that therefore war crimes trials would not be appropriate.[35] According to POWs, these executions appear to have occurred when it became onerous or impossible to take American prisoners to the North, and they were done in the traditional battlefield "humane" manner: one bullet behind the ear. Treatment of ROKA POWs was considerably worse, but there is little evidence on this.

Internal North Korean materials themselves show that many POWs were killed—because KPA officers sought to stop the killings. On July 25, the high command said,

> Wrong treatment of men surrendering by certain units on our side has been inviting great losses in the thought campaign. For example, certain units shot the men who were surrendering instead of capturing them. Therefore the following orders should be strictly observed. (1) Every surrendering man should be taken prisoner. (2) Shooting is strictly prohibited.

On August 16 a KPA officer said, "Some of us are still slaughtering enemy troops that come to surrender ... the responsibility of teaching the soldiers to take POWs and treat them kindly rests on the political section of each unit."[36]

American POWs who were liberated after the Inchon landing reported generally good treatment by their captors (given existing conditions), good discipline by KPA troops, and some executions. The UN Commission on the Unification and Reconstruction of Korea (UNCURK) later stated that in spite of many reports of political executions and atrocities against rightists, "few cases came to the notice" of their survey team that visited Kangwon province in early November, interviewing ROK and American officials and speaking to local people. But G-2 intelligence sources found that thousands of political prisoners were moved out of Seoul to the North, including many KNP officers, rightist youth leaders, and others who were thought later to have been eliminated.[37]

In the crisis of the Inchon landing several major massacres of political prisoners occurred. During the Northern occupation Seoul's West Gate prison held seven thousand to nine thousand people, most of them imprisoned in the last month of the occupation; they consisted mostly of ROK police, army, and rightist youths. On September 17–21, 1950, all these prisoners were moved to the North by rail, except for those who could not walk, who were shot. American sources counted 200 in graves, and estimated the total killed at 1,000; Reginald Thompson saw "the corpses of hundreds slaughtered in the last days by the Communists in a frenzy of hate and lust." In Mokpo 500 were slaughtered, another 500 were killed in Wonsan when the North Koreans withdrew, and various mass graves, presumably containing those executed by the North Koreans, were found by advancing troops. When Pyongyang was occupied, American sources reported finding thousands of corpses in a wide trench near the main prison, and 700 people were said to have been executed as the North Koreans left Hamhung.[38] But other allied forces in the North reported little evidence of atrocities by the retreating Communists. A November 30 UN Command document stated that "no reports of any [enemy] atrocities have been received from the areas recently taken by UN troops."[39]

A detailed UNCURK file documents with photographs and interviews of survivors the massacre of political prisoners in Chonju and Taejon, carried out by KWP cadres and local political agents. Most of the victims were made to dig a large pit, then shot and tossed into it; the majority were ROK policemen and youth group members. Another incident of a mass killing was properly and fully investigated, but with equivocal results. A KMAG adviser reported that in the last week of September 700 civilians had been "burned alive, shot or bayoneted by [the] Commies before leaving Yangpyong," in Kangwon province not far from the 38th parallel; pictures of the victims were taken, and witnesses said most of the dead were members of the police and rightist youth groups. But when an UNCURK team investigated this massacre they found about forty civilian bodies, and a nearly equal number of executed North Korean soldiers, still in uniform. An investigation by Vice-Consul Philip Rowe turned up only nine bodies. Local people said the rest had been carried off by the victims' families. Rowe was willing to believe this, but he was nonetheless unable to verify the KMAG account. He did not mention the murdered KPA soldiers.[40]

The evidence of North Korean atrocities in the South is nonetheless damning. For what it is worth, captured documents continued to show that high-level officials warned against executing people. Handwritten minutes of a KWP meeting on December 7, 1950, apparently at a high level, said, "do not execute the reactionaries for [their] wanton vengeance. Let legal authorities carry out the purge plan."[41] It wouldn't be much solace for the victims and their families.

Based on American and South Korean inquiries, the total massacred by North Koreans or their allies in the South was placed at 20,000 to 30,000.[42] I do not know how the figure was arrived at. UNCURK reports suggest a significantly lower figure; furthermore, the UNCURK investigations were balanced, whereas the Americans and South Koreans never acknowledged ROK atrocities. Americans who took part in planning for postvictory war crimes trials claimed that the North Koreans and the Chinese had killed a total of 29,915 civilians and POWs; it is likely that this figure includes some of the atrocities committed in southern Korea in the summer of 1950, of which the authorship is in dispute."³ We are left with the conundrum that the DPRK, widely thought to be the worst of Communist states, conducted itself better than did the American ally in Seoul. To kill 30,000 and not 100,000, though, offers no comfort.

MEASURES TAKEN: THE OCCUPATION OF THE NORTH

United Nations forces occupied the North under a governing American policy document (NSC 81/1) that instructed MacArthur to forbid reprisals against the officials and the population of the Democratic People's Republic of Korea (DPRK) "except in accordance with international law." On September 30, the day before ROKA units crossed over to the North, Acheson said the 38th parallel no longer counted: {Korea will be used as a stage to prove what Western Democracy can do to help the underprivileged countries of the world."⁴ The ROK saw itself then, as it does today, as the only legitimate and legal government in Korea, and in 1950 sought to incorporate northern Korea under its aegis on the basis of the 1948 constitution. The United Nations, however, had made no commitment to extending the ROK mandate into the North (either in 1948 or in 1950), and the British and French were positively opposed to the idea—even suggesting that ROK weakness and corruption, and the possibility that it might "provoke a widespread terror," raised questions about whether it should be allowed to reoccupy *the South*.⁴⁵

The State Department's plans for the occupation of the North called for the "supreme authority" to be the United Nations, not the Republic of Korea; failing that, it would set up a trusteeship or an American military government. The department categorically rejected the ROK claim to a mandate over the North and instead called for new UN-supervised elections. (The South wanted elections for only a hundred northern seats in the ROK National Assembly.) There may also have been secret American plans to remove Rhee: M. Preston Goodfellow cabled him on October 3, saying, "Some very strong influences are at work trying to find a way to put some one in the presidency other than your good self."[46] On October 12 the UN resolved to restrict ROK authority to the South for an interim period. In the meantime, the existing North Korean provincial administration would be utilized, with no reprisals against individuals merely for having served in middle or low-level positions in the DPRK government, political parties, or the military. DPRK land reform and other social reforms would be honored; an extensive "re-education and re-orientation program" would show Koreans in the North the virtues of a democratic way of life.[47]

In the event, however, the ostensible government in the North had nothing to do with United Nations trusteeships or State Department civil affairs plans: it was the Southern system imposed on the other half of the country. The extant "national security law" of the ROK, defining North Korea as an "anti-state entity" and punishing any hint of sympathy or support for it among its own citizens, provided the legal framework for administering justice to citizens of North Korea—under international auspices but by no means under anything that would resemble the rule of (any) law. North Korea was the only Communist country to have its territory occupied by anti-Communist armies since World War II. There this particular episode is alive and well, burned into the brain of several generations, and still governs North Korean interpretations of the South's intentions even today.

At the time, Rhee made his intentions known to an American reporter on his way back to Seoul:

> I can handle the Communists. The Reds can bury their guns and burn their uniforms, but we know how to find them. With bulldozers we will dig huge excavations and trenches, and fill them with Communists. Then cover them over. And they will really be underground.[48]

State Department officials sought some mechanism for supervision of the political aspects of the occupation, "to insure that a 'bloodbath' would not result. In other words...the Korean forces should be kept under control."[49] In fact the occupation forces in the North were under no one's control. The effective politics of the occupation consisted of the National Police and the rightist youth corps that shadowed it; ROK occupation forces were mostly on their own and unsupervised for much of October and November.[50] Washington's idea that there should be only a minimum of ROK personnel in the North was "already outmoded by events," Everett Drumwright told his State Department superiors in mid-October. Some two thousand police were already across the parallel, but he thought some local responsibility might result if police who originally came from the North could be utilized. (Thousands of police who had served the Japanese in northern Korea had fled south at the liberation, and Rhee had always seen them as the vanguard of his plans for a "northern expedition.") By October 20 An Ho-sang (Rhee's first minister of education) had his youth corps conducting "political indoctrination" across the border.[51] Paek Son-yop, commander of the ROKA 1st Division when the war started, force-marched his troops in a race to occupy his home city of Pyongyang before anyone else, and got there first "by a bare margin of minutes," Thompson wrote, "his round brown face glowing with pleasure and triumph."[52]

The British government quickly obtained evidence that the

ROK as a matter of official policy sought to "hunt out and destroy communists and collaborators"; the facts confirmed "what is now becoming pretty notorious, namely that the restored civil administration in Korea bids fair to become an international scandal of a major kind." The Foreign Office urged that immediate representations be made in Washington, because this was "a war for men's minds" in which the political counted almost as much as the military. Ambassador Oliver Franks accordingly brought up the matter with Dean Rusk on October 30, getting this response: "Rusk agrees that there have regrettably been many cases of atrocities" by the ROK authorities, and promised to have American military officers seek to control the situation.[53] The social base of the Northern regime was broad, enrolling the majority poor peasantry, so potentially almost any Northerner could be a target of reprisals. Furthermore, the South's definition of "collaboration" was incontinent, spilling over from enemy soldiers to civilians, even to old women caught washing the clothes of People's Army soldiers—like one found among knots of "emaciated, dirty, miserably clothed" people tied in ropes and being herded through the streets.[54] Internal American documents show full awareness of ROK atrocities: KMAG officers said the entire North might be put off limits to ROK authorities if they continued the violence, and in one documented instance, in the town of Sunchon, the Americans replaced marauding South Korean forces with American 1st Cavalry elements.[55]

Once the Chinese came into the war and the retreat from the North began, newspapers all over the world reported eyewitness accounts of ROK executions of people under detention. United Press International estimated that eight hundred people were executed from December 11 to 16 and buried in mass graves; these included "many women, some children," executed because they were family members of Reds. American and British soldiers witnessed "truckloads [of] old men[,] women[,] youths[,] several children lined before graves and shot down." On December 20 a British soldier saw about forty "emaciated and very subdued Koreans" being

Women guerrillas captured in North Korea, fall 1950. *U.S. National Archives*

shot by ROK military police, their hands tied behind their backs and rifle butts cracked on their heads if they protested. The incident was a blow to his morale, he said, because three fusiliers had just returned from North Korean captivity and had reported good treatment. British soldiers witnessed men, women, and children "dragged from the prisons of Seoul, marched to the fields ... and shot carelessly and callously in droves and shoveled into trenches."[56]

President Rhee defended the killings, saying "we have to take measures," and arguing that "all [death] sentences [were] passed after due process of law." Ambassador Muccio backed him up. He was well aware of ROK intentions by October 20 at the latest, cabling that ROK officials would give death sentences to anyone who "rejoined enemy organizations or otherwise cooperated with the enemy," the "legal basis" being the ROK National Security Law and an unspecified "special decree" promulgated *in Japan* in 1950 for emergency situations. This decree may indicate SCAP involvement in the executions; in any case Americans were clearly implicated in political murders in the North.

Secret American instructions to political affairs officers and counterintelligence personnel attached to the X Corps ordered them to "liquidate the North Korean Worker's Party and North Korean intelligence agencies," and to forbid any political organizations that might constitute "a security threat to X Corps." "The destruction of the North Korean Worker's Party and the government" was to be accomplished by the arrest and internment of the following categories of people: all police, all security service personnel, all officials of government, and all current and former members of the Workers' Party in both North and South. The compilation of "black lists" would follow, the purpose of which was unstated. These orders are repeated in other X Corps documents, with the added authorization that agents were to suspend all types of civilian communications, impound all radio transmitters, and even destroy "[carrier] pigeon lofts and their contents."[57] The Korean Workers' Party was a mass party that included as much as 14 percent of the entire population on its rolls; such instructions implied the arrest and internment of upward of one third of North Korean adults. Perhaps for this reason the Americans found that virtually all DPRK officials, down to local government, had fled before the onrushing troops.[58]

During firefights with guerrillas in October 1950, a memorandum from an army intelligence officer named McCaffrey to Maj. Gen. Clark Ruffner suggested that, if necessary, the Americans could organize "assassination squads to carry out death sentences passed by ROK Government in 'absentia' trials to guerrilla lead-

"It's roundup time in Korea." *Associated Press*

ers," and went on to say, "if necessary clear the areas of civilians in which the guerrillas operate," and "inflame the local population against the guerrillas by every propaganda device possible." In the aftermath of the Chinese intervention, a staff conference with Generals Ridgway, Almond, and Coulter, and others in attendance, brought up the issue of the "enemy in civilian clothing." Someone at this conference said, "We cannot execute them but they can be shot before they become prisoners." To which General Coulter replied, "We just turn them over to the ROK's and they take care of them."[59] American Counter-Intelligence Corps teams, working with Korean police and youth groups, rounded up individuals found on KWP membership lists. A war diary of the 441st CIC team shows how that unit actively sought out members of the KWP and, presumably, turned them over to South Korean justice.[60] In Pyongyang many atrocities occurred as the city changed hands in early December. Another eyewitness in Pyongyang (an American) recalled:

We drove into a schoolyard. Sitting on the ground were well over 1000 North Korean POWs. They sat in rows of about fifty with their hands clasped behind their heads. In front of the mob, South Korean officers sat at field tables. It looked like a kangaroo court in session.... To one side several North Koreans hung like rag dolls from stout posts driven into the ground. These men had been executed and left to hang in the sun. The message to the prisoners sitting on the ground was obvious.[61]

ROK authorities removed tens of thousands of young men of military age from Pyongyang and nearby towns when they retreated, forming them into a "National Defense Corps," and in the terrible winter of 1950–51, somewhere between fifty thousand and ninety thousand of them died of neglect while in ROK hands. Meanwhile, Americans perpetrated their own political murders around this time: one GI admitted to slitting the throats of eight civilians near Pyongyang, but nothing was done about it. Finally someone was punished, however, when after the second loss of Seoul two GIs were sentenced to twenty years' hard labor for having raped a Korean woman and killed a man associated with her— an ROK policeman. Unfortunately, that episode did not create a pattern for subsequent military discipline; similar incidents occurred later in the war, and to this day many rapes of Koreans by American soldiers stationed in Korea go unpunished and troop contingents all too often remain suffused with racism toward Koreans.[62]

The major atrocity always alleged by DPRK authorities was said to have occurred in the southwestern town of Sinchon, where hundreds of women and children were kept for some days in a shed without food and water, as Americans and Koreans sought information on their absconded male relatives; when they cried for water, sewage from latrines was dumped on them. Later they were doused with gasoline and roasted alive. In November 1987, together with a

Civilians guarded by South Korean right-wing youth group members, North Korea, circa October 1950. *U.S. National Archives*

Thames Television crew, I visited the charnel house and the tombs, examined original photos and newspaper stories, and spent the day with a survivor; we came away convinced that a terrible atrocity had taken place, although the evidence on its authorship was impossible to document. (Thames Television spent hours measuring the bricks from the walls of the charnel house, first in the 1951 North Korean newsreel film, then in the 1987 footage.)

Then the South Korean dissident writer Hwang Sok-yong published his novel *The Guest*, which, based on his own investigations and interviews with survivors and witnesses, related that refugee Christians from the South had returned to Sinchon during the UN occupation and presided over this appalling massacre. They and assorted right-wing youth groups murdered upward of 35,000 people in the county, about a quarter of the total population, including real or alleged Communists and others suspected of ties to the North Korean enemy. They murdered "the entire male population in

Yangjangni," a village in Shinchon. The North Koreans preferred to blame this bestiality on Americans, following their core assumption that nothing transpires in South Korea without American orders. Hwang also mentions "unspeakable atrocities" by Communists in the same area, but the only ones he mentions are executions carried out military style, and marauding guerrillas who killed "anyone who got in their way."[63]

It is highly unlikely that the North will again occupy the South, whereas it is increasingly likely that the ROK's authority will someday be extended to North Korea. When that happens, this 1950 experience will serve as a stark warning of the worst that might happen, even today, as a result of this intense, fratricidal civil conflict. This awful history is still a live memory in North Korea, because it has to be: those upon whom the crowbar of history has descended (to use Alexander Solzhenitsyn's metaphor) do not forget. Such violence is instead the most durable kind of mnemonic. Koreans inhabit a culture of particularly long memory, because of the respect they evince for the dead and the yet-unborn: one's ancestral inheritance and one's progeny, links in a procession of past and present. Therefore we can predict that the North Koreans will continue to do everything they can to avoid a collapse and absorption into the ROK.

GHOSTS OF WAR

Victims of past atrocities and injustices carry with them memories they can never quite escape, expiate, or explain to others—even those who suffer a similar fate. Instead they animate dreams, spirits, and ghosts. Here, to take just one example, is the reminiscence of a man named Pak Tong-sol, who was eight years old when he witnessed the murder of his family in Naju (a town near Kwangju) in July 1950:

> At the time, at daybreak, my family members were caught by
> the police.... They took us to a valley where they made all
> the men kneel down. After a brief speech, the police shot all
> of them including my father and uncle. Afterwards, the po-
> lice ordered the women and children to leave, but they only
> cried instead of moving. Then the police shot them too. A
> bullet penetrated my shoulder and came out through my
> armpit.... After my mother was killed, my younger sister,
> was three-year-old [*sic*], began to cry. The police beheaded
> her for this.[64]

Heonik Kwon has explored this phenomenon brilliantly in his
Ghosts of War in Vietnam, where a lively dialogue with and about
ghosts inhabits the village, social life, and broader moral and political issues. They mingle together with familial and ancestral practices and become constitutive of village lore, collective memory,
and historical meaning itself. These specters also deliver people
from the terrible political fractures of right and left, good and evil,
that defined the wars in Vietnam and Korea.[65]

Korean and Vietnamese culture are by no means identical or in-
terchangeable, but they are close enough such that Heonik Kwon's
work can provide a facsimile of the experience of millions of Korean civilians: those whose kin were massacred, or who died en
masse from air attacks, or who had families bifurcated by the
North-South impasse, thus to live out their lives with no knowledge of those on the other side of the DMZ. All of the mass suffering during the war reflected not just the dead kin, but "a ritual
crisis" that shattered the society.[66] Like Antigone, Koreans had to
choose between a state-ordered truth and the eminently more important truth burned into their bones. Past and present have their
deepest connection in Korea through ancestors, around which families have performed rituals for millennia. History and memory so
intertwine with lost relatives that for most people history, experience, loss, family, and ritual observance bleed together to create so-

cial memory. Koreans are secular and eclectic about religion, including those who have become Christians in recent decades; the afterlife that they want preeminently resides in the "great chain of being" linking distant ancestors, grandparents, the nuclear and extended family, and the progeny of all of them, until kingdom come.

Mass violence kills the beloved, but leaves nothing for the bereaved. Without the corporeal dead body a proper burial is impossible; without burial in a sacred place (the family tombs), the death cannot be assimilated to memory, and ritual is not possible; something like six thousand Americans are still missing from the Korean War, and no doubt the majority just vaporized in some high-combustion fashion—and how many Koreans did the same? Thus the evaporated dead cannot be honored, and their ghosts wander and cannot be satisfied (at the site of Korean War massacres local residents say that "ghost fire" or *honbul,* flares up from the ground[67]). Most excruciating of all is the death of young children who, in a Confucian universe, are never supposed to die before their parents. The very meaning of life is traduced, for the dead and for the living survivors, and social memory has to be recomposed in the aftermath of catastrophe. There are entire towns in Korea that perform the *chesa* (ancestral remembrance) rituals all on the same day, because that is the day a massacre happened or a town was blotted out. Here bifurcated ideology gives way to human truths. It is not an accident that a poignant reunion of opposites came during a prolonged period of reconciliation between North and South.

FORENSIC TRUTHS AND POLITICAL LIES

The Korean Truth Commission on Civilian Massacres was organized in September 2000. Its charge was to investigate massacres of civilians by all sides before and during the Korean War. Subsequently the Korean Truth and Reconciliation Commission (KTRC) was founded on December 1, 2005, to continue the massacre investigations, to look into independence movement resisters who were deemed leftist and thus excluded from the pantheon of national heroes, and to examine human rights abuses, terrorist acts, and politically fabricated trials and executions (of which it found several under the Park regime). Nearly 11,000 cases of wrongful death or massacre were brought to the commission; 9,461 of these were cases of civilian massacre. By the end of 2008 3,269 of these had been investigated. Exhumations at some 154 burial grounds turned up hundreds of bodies (460 in Namyangju, 400 in Kurye, 240 in the cobalt mines at Kyongsan, 256 at Uljin, on and on). Dozens of children, many under the age of ten, were also found, presumably victims of family exterminations. Ultimately it appears that after the war began in June, South Korean authorities and auxiliary right-wing youth squads executed around 100,000 people and dumped them into trenches and mines, or simply threw them into the sea.

The commission took just as much care with executions carried out by North Koreans or Southern leftists. In Kimjae, for example, North Koreans and local left wingers massacred twenty-three Christians accused of right-wing activity, a landlord named Chong Pan-sok and his family, and the landlord's son-in-law, who was in the police. After the Inchon landing the North Koreans and their allies killed hundreds in Seoul, Taejon, Chongju, and other towns, totaling more than 1,100, usually imprisoned police and members of rightist youth groups. However much it may discomfit American sensibilities, the record shows that Communist atrocities constituted about one sixth of the total number of cases, and tended to be more discriminating—eight landlords shot here, fourteen policemen shot there. Regardless of the authorship of atrocities, once the commission decided that cases involved wrongful death, reconciliation meant the publication of comprehensive reports followed by "official state apology, correction of the family registry... memorial services, correcting historical records... restoration of damages, [and] peace and human rights education."[68]

The restorative truths told by the survivors and living victims of the Korean conflict are fruits of the popular struggle for democracy in Korea; this surge of civil society is also a surge of suppressed information, and would never have been possible during the long decades of dictatorship. Suppressed memory is history's way of preserving and sheltering a past that possesses immanent energy in the present; the minute conditions change, that suppressed history pours forth. Thus, in the past twenty years Koreans have produced hundreds of histories, memoirs, oral accounts, documentaries, and novels that trace back to the years immediately after liberation.

This Korean outpouring is also, however, akin to what writers such as Ambrose Bierce did for Americans in the aftermath of their civil conflict, penning poignant stories that captured the terrible truths of fratricidal war. Survivors such as Chon Chun-ja did something wonderful for Art Hunter, too: by coming forward and telling their stories, they made it possible for him to begin purging himself of a terrible guilt. The personal truths of the victims and survivors should become a restorative truth, a requiem for the "forgotten war" that might finally achieve the peaceful reconciliation that the two Koreas have been denied since Dean Rusk first etched a line at the 38th parallel in August 1945.

CHAPTER EIGHT

A "FORGOTTEN WAR" THAT REMADE THE UNITED STATES AND THE COLD WAR

June 25 removed many things from the realm of theory. Korea seemed to—and did—confirm NSC 68.

—DEAN ACHESON

The Korean conflict was the occasion for transforming the United States into a very different country than it had ever been before: one with hundreds of permanent military bases abroad, a large standing army and a permanent national security state at home. Americans assume that the Vietnam War is far more important, and it is, in that it created within the massive baby boom generation decades-long anxieties and a neuralgic war of movement regarding such a host of issues (the limits of American power, the proper uses of force, the coincidence of the war with major social change in the 1960s) that most of them remained alive in recent presidential elections—George W. Bush, Bill and Hillary Clinton, John Kerry and John McCain, for example, are still at odds over what happened back then; Barack Obama was the first president to campaign on a post-'60s platform—and he won (a harbinger, finally, of a new era?). If the Vietnam War seared an entire generation, beyond that it had little effect on American foreign policy or intervention abroad (which was resurgent within a few years under Reagan), and had a minuscule impact on the domestic American economy (primarily the surge of inflation caused by Lyndon Johnson burying expenses for the war in other parts of the federal budget). Korea, however, had an enormous refractory effect back upon the United States. It didn't brand a generation, and it may be forgotten or unknown to the general public, but it was the occasion for transforming the United States into a country that the founding fathers would barely recognize. Is this phenomenon well known? It has been to some scholars for a generation.[1] Otherwise it isn't.

The Korean War was fought for mutually unknown and incommensurable (if not incomprehensible) goals by the two most important sides, North Korea and the United States. The North Koreans attacked the South because of fears that Japan's industrial economy and its former position in Korea were being revived by recent changes in American policy, because native Koreans in the South who had long collaborated with Japanese colonizers were the Korean midwives of this strategy (and now would finally get what they deserved), and because the North's position relative to the South would likely weaken over time. Kim Il Sung weighed the possibility that the United States might intervene in defense of the South, but probably downplayed its significance because he felt he had gotten joint backing for his invasion from both Stalin and Mao. What he could not have known was that his invasion solved a number of critical problems for the Truman administration, and did wonders in building the American Cold War position on a world scale.

KENNAN AND ACHESON

Korea was a critical presence in American policy at the dawn of the Cold War. As we have seen, the Truman administration identified its stake in Korea in the same "fifteen weeks" in which the containment doctrine and the Marshall Plan were hammered out. Dean Acheson, then undersecretary of state, and George Marshall, the new secretary of state, reoriented American policy away from the Pentagon's idea that the Korean peninsula had no strategic significance, toward seeing its value in the context of rebuilding the Japanese economy and applying the containment doctrine to South Korea—in George Kennan's original, limited meaning of using economic and military aid and the resources of the United Nations to prop up nations threatened by communism. It was at this time, in early 1947, that Washington finally got control of Korea policy from the Pentagon and the occupation; the effect was essentially to ratify the de facto containment policies against the Korean left wing that the occupation had been following since September 1945. George Marshall, as we saw, told Acheson in late January to draft a plan to connect a separate South Korea with Japan's economy, and a few months later Secretary of the Army William Draper said that Japanese influence would again develop in Korea, "since Korea and Japan form a natural area for trade and commerce."[2] Around the same time Acheson remarked in secret Senate testimony that the United States had drawn the line in Korea, and sought funding for a major program to turn back communism there on the model of "Truman Doctrine" aid to Greece and Turkey.

Acheson was the prime mover in 1947 and again when the United States intervened to defend South Korea in June 1950. He understood containment to be primarily a political and economic problem, of positioning self-supporting, viable regimes around the Soviet periphery; he thought the truncated Korean economy could still serve Japan's recovery, as part of what he called a "great crescent" from Tokyo to Alexandria, linking Japan with Korea, Taiwan, Southeast Asia, and ultimately the oil of the Persian Gulf. However, Congress and the Pentagon balked at a major commitment to Korea ($600 million was the State Department's figure, compared to the $225 million for Greece and Turkey that Congress approved in June 1947), and so Acheson and his advisers took the problem to the United Nations, thus to reposition and contain Korea through collective security mechanisms. But the UN imprimatur also gave the United States an important stake in the continuing existence of South Korea. This, in turn, was the worst nightmare of the top leaders in North Korea, all of whom saw a revival of Korea's links to the Japanese economy as a mortal threat.

So Kim Il Sung attacked in June 1950, hoping to unify Korea, and quickly dispatched the Southern army and government. That led the United States to intervene to reestablish the Republic of Korea, essentially under a containment doctrine commitment that was three years old by then. That goal was nearly accomplished in late September, three months into the war, but in the meantime

Truman and Acheson had decided to roll back the Northern regime as part of a general offensive against communism, exemplified by NSC 68 in April 1950. The defeat of American and allied forces in North Korea by Chinese and Korean peasant armies in the early winter of 1950 caused the worst crisis in U.S. foreign relations between 1945 and the Cuban Missile Crisis, led Truman to declare a national emergency, and essentially "demolished" the Truman administration (as Acheson put it)—Truman could have run again in 1952, but like Lyndon Johnson confronted by another impending defeat in 1968, he chose not to do so. China had no stomach for unifying Korea at great cost to itself, however, and so within a few months the fighting stabilized roughly along what is now the DMZ.

The Korean War was the crisis that, in Acheson's subsequent words, "came along and saved us"; by that he meant that it enabled the final approval of NSC 68 and passage through Congress of a quadrupling of American defense spending. More than that, it was this war and not World War II that occasioned the enormous foreign military base structure and the domestic military-industrial complex to service it and which has come to define the sinews of American global power ever since. Less obviously, the failure of the Korean rollback created a centrist coalition behind containment that lasted down to the end of the Cold War. This consensus deeply shaped how the Vietnam War was fought (no invasion of the North), evolved into the stalemate in the 1980s between those who wanted to contain Nicaragua's Sandinista regime and those who wanted to overthrow it, and governed the 1991 decision to throw Saddam Hussein's army out of Kuwait, but not to march on Baghdad. Tellingly, in the early 1950s it was public advocates of rollback or "liberation" such as Dulles and Richard Nixon who privately told the National Security Council that rollback was impossible against anything that the Communist side took seriously; general war might well be the result otherwise.

These two Korean wars—the victory for Kennan-style containment, and the defeat of Acheson's rollback—reestablished the two

Korean states and created a tense but essentially stable deterrent situation on the peninsula that has lasted ever since; the DMZ, Panmunjom, two huge Korean armies, and other artifacts of this war (even the United Nations Command) are still standing today as museums of this distant conflict. Both Koreas became garrison states and the North remains perhaps the most amazing garrison state in the world, with more than a million people under arms and young men and women both serving long terms in the military. The South suffered through three decades of military dictatorship while building a strong economy, and after a political breakthrough in the 1990s is both a flourishing democracy and the tenth-largest industrial economy. There are many other effects that this hot war had on the two Koreas, but the impact of the war on the United States was determining as well.

A MILITARY-INDUSTRIAL COMPLEX

The indelible meaning of the Korean War for Americans was the new and unprecedented American military-industrial complex that arose in the 1950s. Until that time Americans never supported a large standing army and the military was a negligible factor in American history and culture, apart from its performance in wars. The Constitution itself "was constructed in fear of a powerful military establishment," C. Wright Mills wrote, the constituent states had their own independent militias, and only the navy seemed consonant with American conceptions of the uses of national military force. Americans loved victorious generals such as Washington, Jackson, Taylor, Grant, and Eisenhower, enough to make them presidents. But after each victory the military blended back into the woodwork of American life. After reaching 50,000 during the war with Mexico in the 1840s, the army dropped to about 10,000 soldiers, 90 percent of them arrayed against Indians in the trans-Mississippi West at seventy-nine posts and trailside forts. The military ballooned into millions of citizen-soldiers during the civil war and the two world wars, but always the army withered within months and years of victory—to a 25,000-soldier constabulary in the late nineteenth century (at a time when France had half a million soldiers, Germany had 419,000, and Russia had 766,000), a neglected force of 135,000 between the world wars, and a rapid shrinkage immediately after 1945. A permanent gain followed each war, but until 1941 the American military remained modest in size compared to other great powers, poorly funded, not very influential, and indeed not really a respected profession. Military spending was less than 1 percent of GNP throughout the nineteenth century and well into the twentieth.[3]

The army was reorganized under the McKinley-Roosevelt secretary of war Elihu Root, raising its strength to 100,000, and in 1912 the War Department created a Colonial Army for the Philippines, Hawaii, and the Canal Zone that, although often understaffed, lasted until World War II and created a "cadre of semipermanent colonials" (in Brian Linn's words) with much Pacific experience. Officers and soldiers quickly settled into the unhurried, idyllic life of the Pacific Army; U.S. forces in the Philippines were almost entirely unprepared for the Japanese attack that came a few hours after Pearl Harbor. Then came instantaneous national mobilization to more than eleven million people in uniform, but again after the war Truman shrank the military: the army had 554,000 soldiers by 1948, and the air force watched most of its contracts get canceled (aircraft industry sales dropped from $16 billion in 1944 to $1.2 billion in 1947). In 1945 the navy, favored under Roosevelt for four terms, had 3.4 million officers and men and nearly 1,000 ships of all kinds; fifteen months later it had 491,663 men and just over 300 ships, and its 1945 budget of $50 billion had slipped to $6 billion. The draft ended in that same year (but got reinstated after the Communist coup in Czechoslovakia). Defense spending fell to $13 billion a year, or about $175 billion in current dollars.[4]

As Harry Truman presided over a vast demobilization of the military and the wartime industrial complex, it was as if the country were returning to the normalcy of a small standing army and hemispheric isolation. The Truman Doctrine and the Marshall Plan ended that idle dream in 1947, but Truman and his advisers still did not have the money to fund a far-flung global effort; the defense budget was steady-state in the late 1940s, hovering around $13 billion. Until 1950 the containment doctrine also approximated what its author, George F. Kennan, wanted it to be: a limited, focused, sober effort relying mostly on diplomatic and economic measures to revive Western European and Japanese industry, and to keep the Russians at bay. If the military came into the equation, Americans should send military advisory groups to threatened countries, not intervene militarily themselves.

In the aftermath of the end of the Cold War, Kennan provided a pithy expression of this limited conception: to him the containment doctrine was "primarily a diplomatic and political task, though not wholly without military implications." Once the Soviets were convinced that more expansionism would not help them, "then the moment would have come for serious talks with them about the future of Europe." After Greece and Turkey, the Marshall Plan, the Berlin blockade, and other measures, he thought that moment had arrived by 1950. However, "it was one of the great disappointments of my life to discover that neither our Government nor our Western European allies had any interest in entering into such discussions at all. What they and the others wanted from Moscow, with respect to the future of Europe, was essentially 'unconditional surrender.' They were prepared to wait for it. And this was the beginning of the 40 years of Cold War."[5] The central front had been established and fortified and the industrial recovery of Western Europe was under way, and in East Asia the "reverse course"—which Kennan was much involved in—had lifted controls on Japanese heavy industry. Soviet troops withdrew from Manchuria in and North Korea in 1948. But the Chinese revolution's stunning victories over Nationalist forces made it unlikely that a Cold War stability would descend on East Asia, akin to that in Europe.

Kennan's 1947 strategy—five advanced industrial structures exist in the world, we have four, Moscow has one, containment means keeping things that way—might have sufficed to achieve the critical goal of reviving Western and Japanese industry. NSC 68 defined a new global strategy, but it was really NSC 48 that cast the die in the Pacific: the United States would now do something utterly unimagined at the end of World War II: it would prepare to intervene militarily against anticolonial movements in East Asia— first Korea, then Vietnam, with the Chinese revolution as the towering backdrop. The complexities of this turning point have been analyzed and documented by historians, but they remain largely unplumbed, even today, among experts on foreign affairs, political scientists, journalists, and pundits, because their work places far too much weight on realpolitik and the bipolar rivalry with Moscow, and relegates the two biggest wars of the period to the shadows of global concerns.

The Chinese revolution also had a dramatic effect on American partisan politics, fueling the "who lost China" attacks by Republicans, but again Kennan took careful and sober measure of its meaning: as Mao came to power in 1949, Kennan convened a group of East Asian experts at the State Department. After listening for a while, he told them, "China doesn't matter very much. It's not very important. It's never going to be powerful." China had no integrated industrial base, which Kennan thought basic to any serious capacity for warfare, merely an industrial fringe stitched along its coasts by the imperial powers; thus China should not be included in his containment strategy. Japan did have such a base, and was therefore the key to postwar American policy in East Asia.[6] The power that revolutionary nationalism could deploy in the colonies or semicolonies of East Asia was but dimly appreciated in Washington at the time, and that certainly included Kennan. Instead his attention fastened on the only formidable industrial nation in the region, Japan, and what could be done to revive it and its economic influence in East Asia.

Over nearly two years a bunch of papers were developed in the State Department, feeding into a long analysis known as National Security Council document 48/2, "Policy for Asia," approved by President Truman at the end of 1949. This document is best known for its declassification with the Pentagon Papers in 1971, since NSC 48 called for shipping military aid to the French in Indochina for the first time (aid that began arriving before the Korean War started in June 1950). But its most important substance was in the political economy that it imagined for East Asia. Ever since the publication of the "open door notes" in 1900 amid an imperial scramble for Chinese real estate, Washington's ultimate goal had always been unimpeded access to the East Asian region; it wanted native governments strong enough to maintain independence but not strong enough to throw off Western influence. The emergence of anti-colonial regimes in Korea, China, and Vietnam negated that goal, and so American planners forged a second-best world that divided Asia for a generation.

In earlier papers that informed the final draft of NSC 48, American officials enumerated several principles that they thought should regulate economic exchange in a unified East Asian region (including China): "the establishment of conditions favorable to the export of technology and capital and to a liberal trade policy throughout the world," "reciprocal exchange and mutual advantage," "production and trade which truly reflect comparative advantage," and opposition to what they called "general industrialization"—something that could be achieved "only at a high cost as a result of sacrificing production in fields of comparative advantage." NSC 48 planners anticipated nationalist objections in the grand manner of the nineteenth-century Rothschilds:

The complexity of international trade makes it well to bear in mind that such ephemeral matters as national pride and ambition can inhibit or prevent the necessary degree of international cooperation, or the development of a favorable atmosphere and conditions to promote economic expansion.[7]

Yet "general industrialization" is just what Japan had long pursued, and what South Korea wanted, too—a nationalist strategy to build a comprehensive industrial base that contrasted sharply with the Southeast Asian countries (who tend to be "niche" economies like the smaller states in Europe).

Dean Acheson knew next to nothing about military power. For him and other American statesmen, the defeat of Japan and Germany and the struggle with communism were but one part, and the secondary part, of an American project to revive the world economy from the devastation of the global depression and world war. Acheson was an internationalist in his bones, looking to Europe and especially Britain for support and guidance, and seeking multilateral solutions to postwar problems. At first the problem of restoring the world economy seemed to be solved with the Bretton Woods mechanisms elaborated in 1944 (the World Bank and the International Monetary Fund); when by 1947 they had not worked to revive the advanced industrial states, the Marshall Plan arrived in Europe and the "reverse course" in Japan, removing controls on heavy industries in the defeated powers. When by 1950 the allied economies were still not growing sufficiently, NSC 68, written mostly by Paul Nitze but guided by the thinking of Acheson (by then President Truman's secretary of state), hit upon military Keynesianism as a device that did, finally, prime the pump of the advanced industrial economies (and especially Japan). The Korean War was the crisis that finally got the Japanese and West German economies growing strongly, and vastly stimulated the U.S. economy. American defense industries hardly knew that Kim Il Sung

would come along and save them either, but he inadvertently rescued a bunch of big-ticket projects—especially on the west coast. In Southern California these included "strategic bombers, supercarriers, and . . . a previously cancelled Convair contract to develop an intercontinental rocket for the Air Force," in Mike Davis's words. By 1952 the aircraft industry was booming again. Los Angeles County had 160,000 people employed in aircraft production. In the mid-fifties defense and aerospace accounted directly or indirectly for 55 percent of employment in the county, and almost as much in San Diego (where nearly 80 percent of all manufacturing was related to national defense). Fully ten thousand Southern California factories serviced the aerospace industry by the 1970s; California was always the land of classic high-tech, "late" industries, but airpower had myriad spin-offs and forward linkages to commercial aviation (just getting off the ground in the 1950s), rocketry, satellites, electronics and electronic warfare, light metal production (aluminum, magnesium), computer software, and ultimately the Silicon Valley boom of the 1990s.[8]

The military was never a significant factor in peacetime American national life before NSC 68 announced the answer to how much "preparedness" the country needed, thus closing a long American debate: and in mainstream Washington, it has never returned. By 1951 the United States was spending $650 billion on defense in current dollars, and finally reached that maximum point again in the early part of this new century—a sum greater than the combined defense budgets of the next eighteen ranking military powers in 2009.

THE ARCHIPELAGO OF EMPIRE

This new empire had to take on a military cast: first of all because by 1950 the problem was defined militarily (unlike Kennan's emphasis on economic aid, military advice, and the UN). Second, the United

States had nothing remotely resembling an imperial civil service. Before the 1950s the Foreign Service was a microcosm of the Ivy League and the Eastern establishment, operating outside the sight lines of most Americans and without a whole lot to do. It produced exemplary individuals like George Kennan, but it never had a strong constituency at home. It is well known that McCarthy's assault on officers in the China service ruined American expertise on East Asia for a generation, but Nixon's attack on Alger Hiss (a dyed-in-the-wool internationalist) may have had worse consequences: anyone in pinstripes became suspect—people seen as internal foreigners—and the State Department was fatally weakened. In the 1960s came the academic specialists—McGeorge Bundy, Walt Rostow, Henry Kissinger, Zbigniew Brzezinski—svengalis who would tutor the president in the occult science of foreign affairs. They also made war upon the State Department, appropriating its responsibilities while ignoring it, thus diluting its influence even more. The State Department often seems to be a foreign office with no clear constituency, but the permanent military installations around the world persist and perdure; they have an eternal writ all of their own.

In the second half of the twentieth century an entirely new phenomenon emerged in American history, namely, the permanent stationing of soldiers in a myriad of foreign bases across the face of the planet, connected to an enormous domestic complex of defense industries. For the first time in modern history the leading power maintained an extensive network of bases on the territories of its allies and economic competitors—Japan, Germany, Britain, Italy, South Korea, all the industrial powers save France and Russia—marking a radical break with the European balance of power and the operation of realpolitik, and a radical departure in American history: an archipelago of empire.[9]

The postwar order took shape through positive policy and through the establishment of distinct outer limits, the transgression of which was rare or even inconceivable, provoking immediate crisis—the orientation of West Berlin toward the Soviet bloc, for example. That's what the bases were put there for, to defend our allies but also to limit their choices—a light hold on the jugular, which might sound too strong until Americans ask themselves, what would we think of foreign bases on our soil? The typical experience of this hegemony, however, was a mundane, benign, and mostly unremarked daily life of subtle constraint, in which the United States kept allied states on defense, resource, and, for many years, financial dependencies. The aggressors in World War II, Japan and Germany, were tied down by American bases, and they remain so: in the seventh decade after the war we still don't know what either nation would look like if it were truly independent. We aren't going to find out anytime soon, either.

The Korean War was thus the occasion for recasting containment as an open-ended, global proposition. A mere decade later President Eisenhower could say, "We have been compelled to create a permanent armaments industry of vast proportions," employing 3.5 million people in the defense establishment and spending more than "the net income of all United States corporations." That was from his famous critique of the military-industrial complex in his Farewell Address; less remembered is Ike's final news conference, where he remarked that the armaments industry was so pervasive that it effected "almost an insidious penetration of our own minds," making Americans think that the only thing the country does is produce weapons and missiles.[10] When Western communism collapsed, it appeared for a few years that a serious reduction in the permanent military might occur, but "rogue states" kept it going and then the "war on terror" provided another amorphous, open-ended global commitment.

KENNAN OR ACHESON?

What our history since 1950 teaches, it seems to me, is the following: first, Kennan's limited form of containment worked, because after 1948 or 1949 there was nothing to contain; Russia was not going to attack Western Europe or Japan, and so the central front in Europe was stable and the four industrial bases held by the non-Communist side in the Cold War remained invulnerable, enabling them to develop beyond the wildest dreams of American planners in the 1940s. Second, Acheson's NSC 68 move toward globalism, requiring a huge defense budget and standing army, failed. It failed to win the wars in Korea and Vietnam, and it turned the United States into a country entirely remote from what the founding fathers had in mind, where every foreign threat, however small or unlikely, became magnified and the fundamental relationship of this country to the world was changed forever. That the United States would fight two major wars in Korea and Vietnam could never have been imagined in 1945, when both were still (correctly) seen as problems related to their long histories of colonialism; that the United States would not be able to win either war would have seemed preposterous. For all these reasons, it would have been better to stick with George Frost Kennan's sober strategies.

At the same time, Acheson's political economy—the "great crescent"—was a masterstroke. The Korean War decisively interrupted American plans to restitch American and Japanese economic relations with other parts of East Asia; indeed the repositioning of Japan as a major industrial producer in response to a raging anti-imperial revolution on the Asian mainland is the key to explaining most of East and Southeast Asian history for three decades, until the Indochina War finally ended in 1975. This forced a number of temporary compromises to Acheson's vision that lasted far longer than anyone expected, as East Asia remained divided for decades. But once Japanese economic influence flowed back into South Korea and Taiwan in the early 1960s, along with a generous showering of American aid, these two economies were the most rapidly growing ones in the world for the next twenty-five years. At the same time all three states were deeply penetrated by American power and interests, yielding profound lateral weakness. They were both strong and weak, and not by accident, because the external shaping had its origins in the workings of an American-led world economy. But the Asian divisions began dramatically to erode after the Indochina War ended, as People's China was slowly brought into the world economy. Now, with the growing integration of the economies of the region, Cold War impediments have nearly disappeared. In that sense, the East Asian region has returned to the "first principles" that Americans thought appropriate before the Chinese revolution and the Korean War demolished their plans.

CHAPTER NINE

REQUIEM:
HISTORY IN THE TEMPER
OF RECONCILIATION

Nothing amazes more than the mutability of human beings. Within one generation both the old *yangban* elite and the militarists who served Japan and then imposed an analogous dictatorship on their own people had lost their power. (Aristocratic families, of course, always have their own special type of affirmative action for their children, but their ties to the land and to the state were fundamentally severed.) Likewise, Japan changed, seemingly in the wink of an eye, from an anti-American militarist dictatorship to a friendly ally with a well-rooted democracy. Neither Japan in the 1930s nor South Korea in the 1970s or '80s were totalitarian; if you kept quiet and didn't cause problems for the leadership, you could go about your business. The decades-long struggle of young people and workers (many of them women) to democratize Korea and build a remarkably strong civil society has its relevance here only in the wonders that democracy does for history.

One major fruit of this struggle was the Korean Truth and Reconciliation Commission, pursuing a comprehensive and penetrating inquiry into the truth, defined as it was in the South African experience, in the interests of healing and restoration, in the interests of peace and reconciliation. Healing not just the people but the nation—the restorative and therapeutic value of victims and perpetrators telling and knowing the truth. The revelations of the Nogun village massacre, for example, established all those meanings of truth for the courageous survivors who have pressed their case against all odds for years—like Chon Chun Ja, a twelve-year-old girl at the time who witnessed American soldiers "play[ing] with our lives like boys playing with flies."[1] For Americans, the forensic truths establish lies at all levels of their government, perpetrated for half a century, but they also (in the commission's words) "reduce the number of lies that can be circulated unchallenged in public discourse."

This ferment in Korea also prompted a fundamental revaluation of the Korean War, now widely seen as a civil war that had its origins in the 1930s if not earlier, but was made inevitable by the thoughtless decision, taken the day after the obliteration of Nagasaki, to etch a frontier along a line no one had ever noticed before in Korea's continuous history: the 38th parallel. What American scholars learned from declassified American archives thirty years ago is now the subject of continual historical research in South Korea. Scholars have begun to come to grips with the whirlwind of Communist and anti-Communist violence, the colonial backgrounds of the leaders on both sides, and the civil war, and have poured out book after book on North Korea, studies that are generally far better—and much less biased—than the American literature on the North. The previously forbidden subject of South Korea's left-wing people's committees has also gotten attention since the mid-1980s with much new information coming available. Historians from the southwestern Cholla provinces, in which the left was strongest and which suffered the severest repression in the postwar period, have been particularly active. This work comes from a multitude of historians, and novelistic chroniclers of postwar history such as Choe Myong-hui. (Ms. Choe comes from Namwon, a hotbed of rebellion in 1945–50, and the headquarters of the U.S.-ROK guerrilla suppression command in 1949–50. When South Korean forces retook the area, they massacred so many people that the living honor the dead in mass ancestor worship, on the anniversary day of specific massacres.) This basic difference between the consensus on the Korean War among elite Americans and a new generation of Korean scholars and leaders is at the root of a growing estrangement between Seoul and Washington.

The Korean tide of suppressed memory and contemporary

reckoning with the past has established important truths for people who, after the dictatorships ended, have pressed their case against all odds for years. For scholars, the strong democracy and civil society that emerged from the bottom up in the South, in the teeth of astonishing repression and with very little support from agencies of government in the United States, validates a method of going back to the beginning and taking no received wisdom for granted. I remember how, as a young man working in the U.S. archives, I came across internal records of the suppression of peasant rebels in the fall of 1946, the breaking of strong labor unions in the cities, the American-directed suppression of the Cheju and Yosu rebellions and the many guerrillas that operated from Mount Chiri in the southwest in the period 1948–55 (finally extinguished in the joint U.S.-ROK counterinsurgent program known as Operation Rat-Killer), and wondered how all this could have disappeared without

South Korean guerrillas in front of the Chonju police headquarters. They were captured by a joint Korean-American suppression force during Operation Rat-Killer. *U.S. National Archives*

an apparent trace. Then one day I read Kim Chi Ha's poem "Chiri-san" (Mount Chiri),[2] and came to believe that I did not know the half of it:

> *A cry*
> > *a banner*
> *Before burning eyes, the glare of the white*
> *uniforms has vanished.*
>
> *The rusted scythes, ages-long poverty,*
> *the weeping embrace and the fleeting promise to return:*
> *all are gone,*
> *yet still cry out in my heart.*

THE UNITED STATES: NO REQUIEM

American historians have consistently revised their views on the Korean War: called a "police action" in the 1950s, it became the "limited war" in the 1960s, a civil war or "forgotten war" or "unknown war" in the 1970s and '80s, and in the 1990s new archives in Moscow were used to argue that it was exactly the war Truman said it was at the time: Kremlin aggression, which he rightly resisted. For the majority of Americans the war is forgotten and buried. But what is the epitaph on the American tombstone? It is not singular; the tombstone has two messages: for the Truman Cold War liberal, Korea was a success, the "limited war." For the MacArthur conservative, Korea was a failure: the first defeat in American history, more properly a stalemate, in any case it proved that there was "no substitute for victory." The problem for MacArthur's epitaph is that if MacArthur saw no substitute for victory, he likewise saw no limit on victory: each victory begged another war. The problem for the Truman liberal is that the limited war got rather unlimited in late 1950.

So we need another verdict: a split decision—the first Korean War, the war for the south in the summer of 1950, was a success. The second war, the war for the north, was a failure. Secretary of State Dean Acheson produced this schizophrenic epitaph: the decision to defend South Korea was the finest hour of the Truman presidency; the decision to march to the Yalu occasioned "an incalculable defeat to U.S. foreign policy and destroyed the Truman administration"; this was "the worst defeat...since Bull Run." However, Acheson assumed that the latter happened not to him but to his bête noire: he squares the circle by blaming it all on MacArthur, and liberal historiography has squared the circle in the same way. The Korean War happened during the height of the McCarthy period, and it was the handiwork of Dean Acheson and Harry Truman; McCarthy attacked both, and so the experience of the war disappeared in the shaping of the Cold War consensus: Truman and Acheson were the good guys. Cold War debate was almost always between the middle and the right, the consensus anchored by the McCarthys on one end and the Achesons or Hubert Humphreys on the other. Furthermore, the Korean War is no icon for the conservative or the liberal, it merely symbolized an absence, mostly a forgetting, but also a never-knowing. The American split verdict on the Korean War, coming closely on the heels of a failed war to liberate the North, was an agreement to disagree, a stitched-together mending of a torn national psyche—you remember one verdict, and forget or condemn the other; each verdict implies a corresponding amnesia. The result is a kind of hegemony of forgetting, in which almost everything to do with the war is buried history in the United States.

As the Korean War ground on it became deeply unpopular and vastly demoralizing for the American home front. Not only were American boys defeated in 1950–51 and stalemated for the next two years by rough peasant armies, but the cream of World War II generals could do nothing about it. Heroes all, their names alone conjure their glory: Almond, Clark, Dean, LeMay, MacArthur,

Ridgway, Stratemeyer, Van Fleet, Walker. Take just three lesser-known officers: Brig. Gen. Edward Craig, assistant division commander of the 1st Marine Division in Korea, had commanded the 9th Marine Regiment in the battles of Bougainville and Guam, for which he received the Bronze Star and Navy Cross for gallantry. Maj. Gen. Hobart R. Gray had fought in both world wars and also chased Pancho Villa along the Mexican border; commander of the 1st Cavalry Division in Korea, he had been Patton's chief of staff. Meanwhile, the leader of the 5th Marine Regiment in Korea, Lt. Col. Raymond Murray, battled through Guadalcanal, Tarawa, and Saipan, winning the Navy Cross and two Silver Stars.[3] One could hardly ask for a more experienced officer class—and yet the war was never won.

The Korean War is also marked by physical sites of forgetting and burial in the United States. The American versions are mundane—a stretch of interstate highway dedicated to war veterans—and appalling: the Republic of Korea listed next to Luxembourg among UN participants in Washington's Korean War Memorial, and nowhere else. Still, this memorial is a tasteful, enigmatic display that represents on the faces of the stone soldiers the mysteries and unresolved tensions of the Korean War. In a recent article about old and new monuments on the National Mall, it failed to appear—even on the map showing all the others.[4] Maya Lin's Vietnam masterpiece is what we still need for Korea. Her artful rendering, Vincent Scully wrote, "is hopeful, personal…but profoundly communal, too. We, the living, commune with the dead, are with them, love them. They have their country still. That is why this monument so broke the hearts of veterans of this war—who felt that their country had cast them out forever." Here is "America's greatest such monument," Scully said. Why? Because it expresses "the single, incontrovertible truth of war: that it kills a lot of people."

Meanwhile another Korean War memorial opened in Seoul in 1994. It was planned and developed during the Roh Tae Woo administration (Paek Son-yop was a key planner), and is a symbol in stone of the conservative ROK perspective, at least after the passing of four decades, that the North can now be "forgiven" for its invasion, and join the embrace of the successful and wealthier South: in a featured statue, a much larger ROK soldier comforts a small and weak DPRK brother.[5] The North Korean perspective on this war, of course, was virtually absent in American commentary at the time and has been ever since. Indeed, in our media North Korea has no perspective and no interests worthy of respect; it just functions as a universal and all-purpose menace. It goes without saying that its leaders haven't begun to face up to the crimes North Koreans committed in the war; as in the South, it will require an entirely different leadership to make it happen. But someday the Hermit Kingdom will open and so will its archives, and finally a full and many-sided account of the Korean War will be possible.

KOREA AND IRAQ AS MNEMONICS

The longevity and insolubility of the Korean conflict make it the best example in the world of how easy it is to get into a war, and how hard it is to get out. American troops arrived in southern Korea in September 1945, and thirty thousand of them are still there today, long after the Cold War ended and the Soviet Union collapsed. More daunting, war could come again, and very quickly— indeed a new, perhaps more catastrophic Korean War almost did come again in June 1994, as the result of American worry about North Korea's nuclear facilities. In the immediate aftermath of the apparent victory in the Iraq War, in the late spring of 2003, high American officials again spoke openly of trying to topple the North Korean regime violently. In other words, our war with North Korea continues apace: after 9/11 Donald Rumsfeld suggested preemptive nuclear strikes on rogue states,[6] and when it appeared that the invasion of Iraq would move quickly to victory, he demanded revisions in the basic war plan for Korea (called Operations Plan 5030) and also sought money from Congress for new bunker-busting nukes. The strategy, according to insiders who have read the plan, was "to topple Kim's regime by destabilizing its military forces," so they would overthrow him and thus accomplish "regime change." The plan was pushed "by many of the same administration hardliners who advocated regime change in Iraq." Unnamed senior Bush administration officials considered elements of this new plan "so aggressive that they could provoke a war."[7]

In the new century Americans have once again replicated their Korean experience—this time in Iraq. Without forethought, due consideration, or self-knowledge, the United States barged into a political, social, and cultural thicket without knowing what it was doing, and now it finds that it cannot get out. A great civilization arose and flourished at the intersection of the Tigris and the Euphrates rivers, but American leaders know almost nothing about it. Somehow they thought that they could invade a sovereign country, crush Saddam Hussein's army, and find the road to Baghdad strewn with flowers. Shortly after the occupation began in 2003, a *New York Times* reporter asked a professor at Baghdad University how he thought things were going: the scholar's first comment was "You Americans know nothing about my country."

The same might be said of the Americans who first occupied Korea in September 1945. After the death of President Franklin Delano Roosevelt (and with that, the effective death of his trusteeship plans for a unified Korea), the State Department pushed ahead with a full military occupation of Korea, or a part of it—no matter what happened, they wanted a "preponderant role" on the peninsula because they feared thousands of guerrillas in Manchuria who might combine with Soviet forces, should the Red Army fight the Japanese in Korea. Why were they concerned about Korea in the first place, a country that had never attracted serious American attentions before? Korea was thought to be important to the postwar security of Japan (the enemy that the United States was still fighting). So Kim Il Sung and his allies were the problem then, and they remain the problem today—with no solution to the problem in sight.

In the trite phrases of Washington policymakers, this would be called "lacking an exit strategy." In fact the United States has had no exit strategy anywhere since 1945, except in places where we were kicked out (Vietnam) or asked to leave (the Philippines): American troops still occupy Japan, Korea, and Germany, in the seventh decade after the end of World War II. Policymakers—almost always civilians with little or no military experience (Acheson is the archetype)—get Americans into wars but cannot get them out, and soon the Pentagon takes over, establishes bases, and the entire enterprise becomes a perpetual-motion machine fueled by a defense budget that dwarfs all others in the world.

If our contemporary occupation of Iraq follows suit, the country will be divided, civil war will erupt (beyond what has transpired already), and millions will die but nothing will be solved; and in the 2060s, thirty thousand American troops will still be there, holding the line against the evil enemy (whoever he might be), with a new war possible at any moment. We have been locked in a dangerous, unending, but ultimately futile and failed embrace with North Korea since Dean Rusk consulted a map around midnight on the day after we obliterated Nagasaki with an atomic bomb, and etched a border no one had ever noticed before, at the 38th parallel. When will we ever learn?

THE TEMPER OF RECONCILIATION

To take everything with a sunny, fact-based equability (were the *ianfu* forced or not?), to get angry at nothing (was Curtis LeMay a pyromaniac or not?), to indulge the empirical at the expense of judgment (did we really burn down *every* North Korean town?), to offer silly equivalencies (North Korea and the Nazis), and to con-

234 · *The Korean War*

fuse objectivity with justice, a spurious on-the-one-hand and then on-the-other, negating the human necessity to make choices and render judgments: Is this right? Judgments might be "points of view." Or they might be called wisdom. Objectivity might really mean empathy, and ultimately magnanimity—especially toward those who have suffered most at history's hands.

Similar ideas inhabit Nietzsche's essay "The Uses and Disadvantages of History," where, as we saw, he begins with cattle munching grass in a field. We envy them because they appear to be happy, cavorting in the grass, sleeping and eating and making little cows just as they please. "Why not tell us about your happiness?" a passerby asks. The beast wants to answer but can't—" 'I always forget what I was going to say'—but then he forgot this answer, too, and stayed silent: so that the human being was left wondering." The cattle experience only the moment, without melancholy or boredom. A child playing in the same field is, likewise, blissfully blind to past and future. But the passerby wonders why a chain linking past and present always clings to him, no matter how much he tries to avoid it. A moment returns as a ghost, and we experience what the cows cannot: the "it was," the past, which beats incessantly upon our minds and gives pain, conflict, suffering—and meaning. Our powers of thought and evaluation give us our human difference: the individual as "a thing that lives by negating, consuming and contradicting itself" (like, say, Prime Minister Abe Shinzo).

Memory has its opposite: forgetting, which Nietzsche thought "essential to action of any kind." The unhistorical and the historical are necessary in equal measure to human health, because forgetting is a gatekeeper of conscience—how immoral the world would look without forgetting, he wrote in *Beyond Good and Evil*. To act in the present is to live unhistorically, and it is also to *repress*. In a passage that Freud learned much from, Nietzsche wrote of the plastic power of people to suppress truth, to heal wounds, to go on, to transform, to re-create broken molds. The former sex slaves who have insisted on Japanese accountability and contrition are exactly broken human vessels, re-created into strong mettle through painful struggle. To find ways to acknowledge past crimes, to grasp how they happened, and to reconcile with the victims is another path toward self-respect and strength.

These are the qualities and attributes of human thought, anxiety, memory, amnesia, strength. They do not express Korean or Japanese or American difference. In fact, South Korean leaders have come very far toward a useful understanding of history's value. Korea surely suffered one of the worst twentieth-century histories of any nation, and remains divided in the new century. Yet when Kim Dae Jung was elected in 1997, a charismatic politician rather than a historian or scholar, he inaugurated a sweeping effort at reconciliation with the North *and* with the rebellious southwest of his native land, which had lived very uncomfortably from the 1890s into the 1990s with the Japanese, the Americans, and successive Korean military dictators. At his inauguration he pardoned two previous militarists, Chun Doo Hwan and Roh Tae Woo, who had been sentenced to death or life imprisonment in 1996. As scholars such as Na Kan-chae of Chonnam University have argued, the trials of Chun and Roh and Kim's election in 1997 represented a distinct victory for the people of Kwangju and South Cholla, even if they came many years later and after great suffering.

One of Kim's projects was "A History That Opens the Future," dedicated to fresh and honest examination of any number of difficult issues in modern Korean history, and between Korea and its neighbors. After his term in office and his successor's, it is fair to say that South Korea is finally one unified nation, all orthodox and heterodox "points of view" are aired, and enormous progress was made in reconciling with Pyongyang. Most people have transformed their image of the North, from evil Communist devils to brothers and cousins led by nutty uncles. In an important speech in April 2007, Kim's successor, Roh Moo Hyun, criticized Japanese leaders for seeking to justify the actions of their forebears in the 1930s and

'40s, instead of finding common understanding with their neighbors: "true reconciliation, whether domestic or international, is possible only on a foundation of historical truth."[8]

When the Korean War began, about three hundred people died in the town of Kurim, near the southwestern coast. Kurim is a village of ancient familial continuity, whose history traces back a millennium, with four clans; today it has about six hundred households. In the conflicts after liberation, villagers attacked each other with pitchforks and hoes ("hoe squads"), a common occurrence throughout the region. Some villagers supported guerrillas in the hills, who also foraged indiscriminately for what they needed. When the war broke out some villagers killed some policemen and right wingers. When South Korean forces recaptured Kurim in October, the police killed ninety alleged Communist sympathizers. Guerrilla war continued in the region throughout 1950, but after the war stabilized in 1951 a local ROKA sergeant executed thirteen more villagers in a nearby valley. Choi Jae-sang was twelve when the police told his older sister to take her clothes off; when she refused they shot her in the head in front of her parents. This village civil war left just about every family with a grievance and desire for revenge; for decades opposing families did not speak to each other. But it became a symbol of reconciliation throughout South Korea when, in 2006, village elders published a 530-page history of Kurim, listing the war dead without naming the killers, and sponsored joint memorial services. It turned out the elders had collectively decided, after the war ended, not to reveal who killed whom, or to pursue revenge.[9]

The purpose of the various South Korean inquiries has not been to sow blame or refight Cold War battles, but to seek reconciliation between North and South and to establish an understanding and an orientation that produces *verstehen* of one's former enemy—not sympathy, perhaps not even empathy, but an understanding of the principles that guide one's adversary, even if one finds those principles abhorrent or deeply wounding to one's own knowledge of what happened historically with this same enemy. After all, to blame one side (as most Americans do) for all the blood and agony of the past century since Japan seized Korea is to fit an extraordinarily complex, merciless, and implacably brutal history through the eye of an ideological needle. But through techniques of requiem under a fair system of justice—investigation, trial, testimony, adjudication, apology, purge, reparations—people can finally reconcile, propitiate, and put their ghosts to rest. Once the enemy's core principles are understood without blinking, once we view our history with this adversary from all sides, appeals can be made to the adversary's worldview. And, of course, full recognition of what one side (the South) did might lead to a better understanding of all the grievances husbanded by the other side. But perhaps the greatest gain is self-knowledge, for if you do not know yourself and what others think of you, rightly or wrongly, it is difficult to navigate a complicated world.

So we come again, finally, to the human being as opposed to the cow: modern individuals must "squander an incredible amount of energy . . . merely to fight their way through the perversity in themselves," Nietzsche wrote. Cows don't have to worry about that, but we do—and so do leaders such as Abe Shinzo and a succession of American presidents. Our only recourse is "the scalpel of truth" and to use it ruthlessly "to regulate and punish" in the ultimate interest of justice, magnanimity, and reconciliation. South Korea is the only East Asian nation to have done this—to examine its own history and its conflicts with other countries fully, carefully, and without blinkers.

Imagine now what the enemy thinks. Their leaders fought Japanese militarists long and hard in the wilds of frozen Manchuria for a decade, a pitiless and unforgiving struggle indeed, but one that set them apart from all but a handful of other Koreans in 1945 and, in their eyes, bequeathed their right to rule. The sole reigning sign of truth and justice was that those who sacrificed everything against the Japanese imperialists would inherit the motherland—and those

An underground factory in North Korea. *U.S. National Archives*

who stood with that Japanese enemy would get what they deserved. The north wind was stronger after five years had passed, with blooded soldiers, and so they did what the weaker side also wanted to do, which was to use the new, massed army that Koreans lacked during decades of colonial oblivion to attack and obliterate the other side. It would have happened, and almost did happen, in a matter of weeks. But lo, the invasion unwittingly played into the hands of the United States, which for its own very different reasons joined the battle—and snatched Korean defeat from the jaws of victory.

The United States intervened first for the defense, and then for the offense: the worst happened, their territory was occupied by an American army. But China determined to defend its borders and support its comrades in arms. Soon the battle devolved into inconclusive warfare along the central front, negotiations opened, and two years later an armistice was signed—except that the unhindered machinery of incendiary bombing was visited on the North for three years, yielding a wasteland and a surviving mole people who had learned to love the shelter of caves, mountains, tunnels, and redoubts, a subterranean world that became the basis for reconstructing the country and a memento for building a fierce hatred through the ranks of the population. The leaders who survived draw a straight line from 1932, when their struggle began, through this terrible war, down to the present. Their truth is not cold, antiquarian, ineffectual knowledge, but "a regulating and punishing judge,"[10] a burned-in conviction that their overriding goal is to persist until victory is finally won, and if the whole of the state needs to be subordinated to this task, so be it.

Thus we arrive at our absurd predicament, where the party of memory remains concentrated on its main task, perfecting a world-historical garrison state that will do its bidding and hold off the enemy, and the party of forgetting and never-knowing pays sporadic attention only when it must, when the North seizes a spy ship or cuts down a poplar tree or blows off an A-bomb or sends a rocket into the heavens. Then the media waters part, we behold the evil enemy in Pyongyang—drums beat, sabers rattle—but nothing really happens, and the waters close over until the next time. We don't approve of them but pay little attention and pat ourselves on the back, while they mimic Plato's *Republic* or monolithic Catholicism or Stalin's cadres: they engineer the souls of their people from on high, starting at the beginning just as their neo-Confucian forebears did, when a human being is all innocence and wonder, and continuing until they have at least the image if not the reality of perfect agreement and coherence, a "monolithicism" (their term) seeking a one-for-all great integral that will smite the enemy. They think they know good and evil in their bones, but we aren't so sure.

North Korea's National Defense Commission in 2009.

Notice how the inertia of deterrence (all sides are thoroughly deterred in Korea and have been since 1953) yields an ever-increasing capability for mayhem not just on one side, but on all sides. A new Korean War could break out tomorrow morning, and Americans would still be in their original state of overwhelming might and unfathomable cluelessness; armies ignorant of each other would clash again, and the outcome would again yield its central truth: there is no military solution in Korea (and there never was).

In 2009 the North Korean government was run by a National Defense Commission whose twelve members could constitute a short list of honored Korean War veterans. They are the keepers of the past, and the prisoners of it. This party of memory has braced itself against the pressures of past, present, and future since 1945, up against the greatest military power in world history. Americans think they know this story, of a vain, feckless, profligate, cruel, and dangerous leadership, symbolized by Kim Jong Il, but they are very wide of the mark. As for the leaders of that "indispensable power," they know not the nature of this war nor the qualities of their enemy. This is not a matter of forgetting; it is a never-knowing, a species of unwilled ignorance and willed incuriosity, which causes them time and again to underestimate the adversary—and thereby confer priceless advantage upon him. Finally, there is the evil, grinning image of the war itself, reaper of millions of lives and all for naught, because it continues, it is the odds-on survivor, it never ends. It returns in myriad forms—memory, trauma, ghosts, repression, the quotidian coiled tensions along the DMZ—to taunt the living, as the only "perfect tense" to survive Korea's tragedies since the national division.

The Pacific War began in 1931 and ended in 1945, just as the Korean War began in 1945 and has never ended, even if the fighting stopped in 1953. Nor has the North Korean–Japanese war that began in 1931–32 ever ended; South Korea normalized its relations with Japan in 1965, but through many failed negotiations Pyongyang and Tokyo have never normalized or reconciled—and thus there has been no "closure" to either war from the North Korean standpoint; neither has come to an appropriate resolution. These are not the American demarcations for these wars, of course, but many histories in Japan and Korea conventionally begin these two conflicts in 1931 and 1945, and the history-obsessed North Koreans trace a straight line from the present back to that long-lost first day of March in 1932. Those who suffer terrible wars have a finer sense of when they begin and when they end.

If Americans have trouble reflecting on this "forgotten war" as a conflict primarily fought among Koreans, for Korean goals, they should hearken to the great chroniclers of their own civil war. International involvement was important—and particularly U.S. involvement—but the essential dynamic was internal to the

Strolling through a rebuilding Pyongyang in 1957. *Courtesy of the artist, Chris Marker, and Peter Blum Gallery, New York*

peninsula, to this ancient nation that has known a continuous existence within well-recognized boundaries since the time of Mohammed. Korea remains divided so long after the Berlin Wall fell because this war cut so deeply into the body politic and the Korean soul.

Eventually the Korean War will be understood as one of the most destructive and one of the most important wars of the twentieth century. Perhaps as many as 3 million Koreans died, at least half of them civilians (Japan lost 2.3 million people in the Pacific War). This war raging off Japan's coast gave its recovery and industrialization a dynamic boost, which some have likened to "Japan's Marshall Plan." In the aftermath of war two Korean states competed toe-to-toe in economic development, turning both of them into modern industrial nations. Finally, it was this war and not World War II which established a far-flung American base structure abroad and a national security state at home, as defense spending nearly quadrupled in the last six months of 1950, and turned the United States into the policeman of the world.

Acknowledgments

I would like to thank Jonathan Jao of Random House for suggesting the idea of this book to me, for his sharp and careful editing, and for shepherding the manuscript through the various stages of preparation and publication. John McGhee provided deft and meticulous copy editing, for which I am most grateful. Jessica Waters and Dennis Ambrose of Random House were also courteous, highly skilled, and most helpful. Two of my Ph.D. students at the University of Chicago, Su-kyoung Hwang and Grace Chae, taught me much through their work on the Korean War. Many, many others have aided my scholarship since I published my first book on this war in 1981, but I want to particularly thank Marilyn Young, the late James B. Palais, and Wada Haruki. Finally, my gratitude to Meredith, Ben, Ian, and Jackie for their love and support.

Notes

Archive Glossary

FO British Foreign Office

FR Foreign Relations of the United States

HST Harry S Truman Presidential Library

MA Douglas MacArthur Archives (Norfolk)

NA National Archives

NDSM *Nodong Sinmun* (Worker's Daily), Pyongyang

NRC National Records Center

PRO Public Record Office (London)

RG Record Group

USFIK U.S. Forces in Korea

Introduction

1. Hastings (1987), 105.

Chapter 1: The Course of the War

1. Tim Weiner, "Robert S. McNamara, Architect of a Futile War, Is Dead at 93," *New York Times* (July 7, 2009), A1, A9–10.
2. Michael Shin's forthcoming book is the best analysis of this phenomenon.
3. Several veterans have told me that they thought fragging was more common in Korea than in Vietnam. I have no way of judging this matter.

4. William Mathews Papers, box 90, "Korea with the John Foster Dulles Mission," June 14–29, 1950.
5. Acheson Seminars, Princeton University, Feb. 13–14, 1954. (These seminars were designed to help Acheson write his memoirs.)
6. For documentation see Cumings (1990), ch. 14.
7. I discuss this episode at greater length in *War and Television: Korea, Vietnam and the Persian Gulf War* (New York: Verso, 1992).
8. Noble (1975), 20, 32, 105, 118–19.
9. Acheson Seminars, transcript of Feb. 13–14, 1954. Kennan quoted from remarks he wrote down in a notebook in late June 1950. Gen. Omar Bradley also noted Acheson's domination of the decision process, in Bradley (1983), 536. Kennan supported Acheson's decisions in a memo written on June 26, saying that "we should react vigorously in S. Korea" and "repulse" the attack. If the United States failed to defend the ROK, he thought, Iran and Berlin would then come under threat. (Princeton University, George Kennan Papers, box 24, Kennan to Acheson, June 26, 1950.) For Acheson's discussion of the decisions, see Acheson (1969), 405–7.
10. Truman Presidential Library (HST), Presidential Secretary's File (PSF), CIA file, box 250, CIA daily report, July 8, 1950.
11. Thames Television interview, Athens, Georgia, September 1986. See also Thomas J. Schoenbaum, *Waging Peace and War* (New York: Simon and Schuster, 1988), 211.
12. Korean War veterans quoted in Tomedi (1993), 186–87, 197–205; Sawyer (1962), 124–26, 130, 134, 141, 153.
13. Princeton University, Dulles Papers, John Allison oral history, April 20, 1969; ibid., William Sebald oral history, July 1965. Sebald quotes from his diary "words to that effect" from MacArthur; see also Casey (2008), 28, 68.
14. *New York Times,* July 14, 1950.
15. *New York Times,* July 19, 1950.
16. *New York Times,* Aug. 21, 1950. See Christopher Simpson's searing account of the bloody Nazi suppression of guerrillas in the Ukraine, which he considered "without equal in history." Christopher Simpson, *Blowback: America's Recruitment of Nazis and Its Effects on the Cold War* (New York: Weidenfeld and Nicolson, 1988), 13–26.
17. Letter to *The New York Times,* July 16, 1950. Taylor noted that these precepts have not always been followed by Western armies.
18. *New York Times,* Aug. 5, 1950; British Foreign Office, FO317, piece no. 84065, Sawbridge to FO, Aug. 17, 1950; Carlisle Barracks, Matthew Ridgway Papers, box 16, Willoughby to Ridgway, Aug. 7, 1950.
19. National Records Center (NRC), Record Group (RG) 338, Korean

Military Advisor Group (KMAG) file, box 5418, "KMAG Journal," entries for July 24, Aug. 8, 1950; handwritten "G-3 Journal," July 1950; Appleman (1961), 478; *New York Times*, Aug. 17, 1950; NRC, RG349, box 465, CIC report of Aug. 17, 1950.

20. MacArthur Archives (MA), RG6, box 80, ATIS issue no. 28, March 11, 1951, translating a notebook that is identified as belonging to Choe Pae-yun, an intelligence officer, and quoting Pak Ki-song. It was captured on Feb. 4, 1951. The other document is in Carlisle Barracks, William V. Quinn Papers, box 3, periodic intelligence report no. 120, no date but probably January 1951.

21. James (1993), xi, 140–44, 178, 195.

22. Michael Walzer, *Just and Unjust Wars: A Moral Argument with Historical Illustrations* (New York: Basic Books, 1977), 117–23.

23. Zhang (1995), 44.

24. Ibid., 63, 71–84.

25. Quoted in Knox (1985), 390.

26. National Archives (NA), Office of Chinese Affairs file, box 4211, Hong Kong to State, Oct. 26, 1950; FO317, piece no. 83271, FO minute on Mukden to FO, Nov. 23, 1950. Nieh Jung-chen was close to Chou En-lai, having worked in Berlin in 1924 under Chou's direction; he entered Whampoa in 1925, again helping Chou to recruit Communists, including Lin Piao. Nieh played "a key role" in getting Russian weapons to troops readying for battle in staging areas in Korea. Under Lin Piao's overall command, Li T'ien-yu led crack Thirteenth Army troops into Korea between October 14 and 20; interestingly, Li had commanded a 100,000-soldier column in fierce battles with the Nationalists in the crisis period of May 1947 in Manchuria, when large numbers of Koreans had joined the battle. (See William W. Whitson, *The Chinese High Command: A History of Communist Military Politics*, with Chen-hsia Huang [New York: Praeger, 1973], 93–95, 307, 338–39.)

27. William R. Corson, *The Armies of Ignorance: The Rise of the American Intelligence Empire* (New York: Dial Press, 1977), 205.

28. Knox (1985), 469, 604; Thompson (1951), 147.

29. MA, RG6, box 9, MacArthur to Army, Nov. 6, 1950; MacArthur to JCS, Dec. 4, 1950. Gascoigne thought Willoughby probably sought "to cook figures" on how many Chinese were in the North, noting that the total mushroomed overnight from 17,000 to 200,000 (FO317, piece no. 84119, Gascoigne to FO, Nov. 24, 1950); see also HST, PSF, CIA file, box 248, daily reports for Nov. 27–Dec. 16, 1950; Carlisle Barracks, Gen. Edward Almond Papers, "Korean War, Historical Commentary," Almond letters to H. E. Eastwood, Dec. 27, 1950, and W. W.

Gretakis, Dec. 27, 1950. Hungnam was shielded for several days while allied troops were evacuated.

30. Thompson (1951), 247, 265.
31. For extensive documentation on the violence and terror of the air war see Cumings (1990), ch. 21.
32. NA, Diplomatic Branch, 995.00 file, box 6175, George Barrett dispatch of Feb. 8, 1951; also Acheson to Pusan Embassy, Feb. 17, 1951.
33. The best account of POWs in the Korean War is Biderman and Meyers (1983); see also Foot (1990), 109–21, 197–98. General Dean wrote that his captors studied Marxist-Leninist doctrine the way they might have the old Confucian classics, and seemed entirely genuine in their belief that they were building a better life. See Dean (1954), 192 and passim.
34. Figures differ considerably from one source to another; compare for example the Hutchinson encyclopedia (http://encyclopedia .farlex.com/Korean+War+casualties), with www.britannica.com/EB checked/topic-art/616264/67418; I think the former is closer to the mark than the latter, and thus used its figures in the text.
35. Truman immediately likened Korea to the civil war in Greece, SCAP issued an early press release saying that the United States was "actively intervening in the Korean civil war," and correspondents frequently said the same. This caused the State Department's Public Affairs office to send out instructions to every official stressing that "labels can be terrifically important," and the name "civil war" should never be used. See Casey (2008), 41.

CHAPTER 2: THE PARTY OF MEMORY

1. Jon Herkovitz, "Japan's PM Haunted by Family's Wartime Past," Oct. 20, 2008. I am grateful to Jun Yoo for sending me this report. See also Kosuke Takahashi, "Taro Aso with a Silver Spoon" (Sept. 23, 2008), www.atimes.com/atimes/Japan/J124Dh02.html.
2. Tamogami Toshio, "Was Japan an Aggressor Nation?" www.japan focus.org.
3. Quoted in a thorough report by Larry Niksch, "Japanese Military's 'Comfort Women System,' " *Congressional Research Service* (April 3, 2007), 6 (emphasis added).
4. Niksch, ibid., 10; Tessa Morris-Suzuki, "Comfort Women: It's Time for the Truth (in the Ordinary, Everyday Sense of the Word)," March 22, 2007, Australia Peace and Security Network (APSnet).
5. Soh (2008), 3, 12, 15, 91–92, 103, 125, 138–40, 183, 186.
6. Ibid., 193, 211–16. See also a new book on Korean soldiers in the Japanese army by Tak Fujitani, forthcoming from the University of Chicago Press.

7. See, for example, Saundra Pollock Sturdevant and Brenda Stoltzfus, *Let the Good Times Roll: Prostitution and the U.S. Military in Asia* (New York: New Press, 1992).

8. Morris-Suzuki, "Comfort Women."

9. Han Hong-koo's brilliant historical exegesis, based on rare materials in Korean, Chinese, and Japanese, is the best English-language source on the origins of the North Korean leadership. See Han, *Wounded Nationalism: The Minsaengdan Incident and Kim Il Sung in Eastern Manchuria* (Seattle: University of Washington Press, forthcoming). In subsequent paragraphs on the U.S. occupation, all information is documented in Cumings (1981).

10. Yamamuro (2006), 259.

11. The Korean title is *In'gan Munje*, which might be translated as "human problems" or "the problem of humanity." It first appeared serially in *Tonga Ilbo* in 1934, and was translated into English by Samuel Perry and published as *From Wonso Pond* (New York: Feminist Press, 2009), hereafter Kang (1934). Kang died at the age of thirty-nine in 1944, and ROK dictators banned her work for three decades.

12. Bertolt Brecht, "The Measures Taken," in John Willett and Ralph Manheim, eds., *The Measures Taken and Other Lehrstücke* (New York: Arcade Publishing, 2001), 9, 34.

13. NA, Office of the Chief of Military History, "Military Studies on Manchuria" (1951), consisting of interviews by American officers of former Japanese counterinsurgency commanders. The officers gave this as the reason why "Kim Il Sung and Choe Hyon went to the Soviet Union about February and returned to Manchuria about May or June." Wada Haruki coined the term "guerrilla state."

14. Ibid.; for a longer discussion of Japanese methods, with documents, see Lee (1966).

15. Ibid., both.

16. Han (1999), 8, 13.

17. Kim's arrest by Chinese comrades was long shrouded in mystery, but various sources now attest to it, and Han Hong-koo's scholarship has lifted the veil on many of these early 1930s events.

18. Han (1999), 324–26; Suh (1988), 37–38.

19. Kim Se-jin, *The Politics of Military Revolution in Korea* (Chapel Hill: University of North Carolina Press, 1973), 48–57.

20. Charles K. Armstrong, *The North Korean Revolution, 1945–1950* (Ithaca, N.Y.: Cornell University Press, 2003), 31; NA, Office of the Chief of Military History, "Military Studies on Manchuria" (1951).

21. Suh (1988), 37–38.

22. Kim's Feb. 8, 1948, address, in *Choguk ŭi t'ongil tongnip kwa minjuhwa rŭl*

wihuyo (For the unification, independence, and democratization of the homeland) (Pyongyang, 1949), 73–87.

23. See, for example, Nicholas Eberstadt, *The End of North Korea* (Washington, D.C.: American Enterprise Institute, 1999), 1.

24. My wife, Meredith Woo, produced a documentary on the displaced Koreans called *Koryo Saram,* and has interviewed many survivors.

25. In recent years scholars reading several of the relevant languages, such as Wada Haruki, Charles Armstrong, Han Hong-koo, and Andrei Lankov, have excavated Kim's history as an anti-Japanese guerrilla from 1931 to 1945.

26. Lankov (2002), 7–8, 59.

27. I found the documents on this and reported them in Cumings (1990).

Chapter 3: The Party of Forgetting

1. "On the Uses and Disadvantages of History for Life," in Nietzsche (1983), 60–61.

2. Quoted in Friedlander (1979), 182.

3. Rosenberg (1995), xiii; also Jameson (1981), 9; Foucault (1972), 8–13; Friedlander (1979), 79.

4. Nietzsche (1967), 57–58, 61 (emphasis in original); Winter (2006), 271.

5. Martha Gellhorn, *The Face of War* (New York: Atlantic Monthly Press, 1988), 274–75.

6. Nietzsche (1983), 78, 84.

7. Public Record Office (PRO), London, FO file 317, piece no. 83008, Stokes to Bevin, Dec. 2, 1950.

8. Adam B. Ulam, *Expansion and Coexistence: Soviet Foreign Policy, 1917–1973,* 2nd ed. (New York: Praeger, 1974), 520.

9. Thucydides, *History of the Peloponnesian War,* trans. Rex Warner (New York: Penguin Books, 1954), 147.

10. Fussell (1975), 155.

11. Casey (2008), 219, 221–22. One of the only querulous films on the war, Sam Fuller's *Steel Helmet* (1950), instantly became a subject of political attack.

12. Reginald Thompson found beauty in Korea, but he too clearly enjoyed being in Japan much more. See Thompson (1951), 272.

13. www.amazon.com/Ten-Best-Books-Korean-War/Im/R44H26DIA NVO9.

14. Robert Kaplan, for example, was most impressed with General Paek in his article "When North Korea Falls," *The Atlantic* (Oct. 2006), 64–73. From the 1950s to the 1980s the World Anti-Communist League brought together anti-Communists in Seoul, Taipei, and other threat-

ened right-wing regimes, with Japanese and American ultra-rightists (like Sasakawa Ryoichi, who gave much money to the league). MacArthur's G-2 chief General Willoughby also appears to have aided the World Anti-Communist League when it was headquartered in Seoul, obtaining funds from the right-wing extremist Billy James Hargis Crusade. See the letters from Jose Hernandez, secretary-general of the WACL, to Willoughby, Willoughby Papers, box 12. This league had South Korea and Taiwan as its founding countries, and along the way accumulated an appalling assortment of Eastern European émigré war criminals, superannuated prewar fascists, anti-Semites, and aficionados of Latin American death squads. Gen. John Singlaub, another hero of *The Coldest Winter* (52), organized the American branch of the World Anti-Communist League in the 1980s, working closely with CAUSA International, an organization founded by Reverend Sun Myung Moon. See the extensive information in Scott Anderson and Jon Lee Anderson, *Inside the League* (New York: Dodd, Mead, 1986), 55, 120, 150–51, 238.

When I worked on the Thames Television documentary *Korea: The Unknown War,* I learned that Reed Irvine of Accuracy in Media had called up a Boston public television producer, Austin Hoyt (who was working with Thames and directed the PBS version of the film), and intimated that if our project did not interview certain people, he would charge it with bias. The first person mentioned was Gen. Richard Stilwell, a CIA operative in Korea during the war, whom Hoyt agreed to interview, telling me that they would have done him anyway. Stilwell then recommended we interview James Hausman, who then recommended his good friend Paek Son-yop.

15. Hendrik Hertzberg, "The Fifth War," *New Yorker* (Nov. 30, 2009), 23.
16. Martin (2004), 63.
17. Ibid., 65; Lowe (1997), 59–60. I discuss all this over a full chapter in *Origins,* vol. II.
18. Horwitz (1997), 31, 82, 119, 149, 156, 207, 230, 270, 272.
19. Horwitz estimates that 6 million Americans served in the war (1).
20. Gregory Henderson, "Korea, 1950," in Cotton and Neary (1989), 175–76. See also Henderson (1968).
21. Ha Jin (2004), 13, 35, 51, 57, 89, 159. (*General Dean's Story* is one American account that does locate Ha Jin's Korea in its vision.)
22. Ibid., 150–52, 174–75, 186.

CHAPTER 4: CULTURE OF REPRESSION

1. Knightly (1975), 338. This is a superb account of Korean War reportage.

2. See Knox (1985), 6, 67, 116, and passim.
3. Dean (1954), 163.
4. *New York Times,* Sept. 1,3, 1950.
5. *New York Times* editorial, July 27, 1950; *New York Times* editorial, July 5, 1950. The CIA at this time also listed Kim as an imposter who stole the name of a heroic guerrilla who died in Manchuria about 1940.
6. Thompson (1951), 39, 79.
7. Knox (1985), 117–18, 157, 288, 295, 359.
8. Knightly (1975), 344–54; Foot (1990), 67. For a full discussion of censorship, which began by fits and starts in December 1950 and became fully institutionalized later in 1951, see Casey (2008), 8–9, 170–71, and passim. "Stories that tend to discredit the ROK forces" were from then on forbidden.
9. Knightly (1975), 347.
10. See Princeton University, Allen Dulles Papers, box 57, Ascoli to Dulles, April 8, 1952. See also Jon Halliday and Bruce Cumings, *Korea: The Unknown War* (New York: Pantheon Books, 1988), 72. The quotation on the CIA as a liberal refuge is from Corson, *Armies of Ignorance,* 27. Although he could not in the end prove it, Stanley Bachrach was convinced that the CIA funded the "Committee of One Million," another arm of the China Lobby. (See his *The Committee of One Million: "China Lobby" Politics* [New York: Columbia University Press, 1976], 55.)
11. David Oshinski quotes the "sock full" line in *A Conspiracy So Immense: The World of Joe McCarthy* (New York: Free Press, 1983), 111; the Soviet comment from *Izvestia* is in *New York Times,* March 27, 1950; "Communists and queers" and "egg-sucking liberals," ibid., April 21, 1950.
12. Capehart is quoted in Hodgson (1976), 34 (emphasis added). In 1951 a constituent wrote to Senator Tom Connally, "The people of Texas are tired of this British Appeasement, that is being loaded on this country by the British, and the Britisher whose Title is Secretary of State [*sic*]." Elmer Adams to Connally, May 21, 1951, Tom Connally Papers, box 45.
13. Or what one did not look like: Thomas F. Murphy, federal prosecutor in the Hiss case, said, "The Communist does not look like the popular conception of a Communist. He does not have uncropped hair, he does not wear horn-rimmed glasses nor carry the Daily Worker. He doesn't have baggy trousers." (*New York Times,* March 13, 1950.)
14. The investigations of Grajdanzev and others are in MA, Willoughby Papers, box 18, "Leftist Infiltration into SCAP," Jan. 15, 1947, and

thereafter; Willoughby supplied his 1947 studies to Benjamin Mandel of the McCarran Subcommittee after Mandel solicited them, and also stated that he had given them to McCarthy (box 23, Mandel to Willoughby, Feb. 19, 1954). See also Willoughby to W. E. Woods of HUAC, May 1, 1950, Willoughby Papers, box 10.

15. *New York Times,* March 14, 22, 27, and 31, 1950. For an excellent account of the Lattimore case see Stanley I. Kutler, *The American Inquisition: Justice and Injustice in the Cold War* (New York: Hill and Wang, 1982), 183–214.

16. *New York Times,* April 4, 1950.

17. *New York Times,* May 16, 1950.

18. "Transcript of Round Table Discussion on American Policy toward China," State Department, Oct. 6–8, 1949, declassified in Carrolton Press, CRC 1977, item 316B. Someone, apparently a State Department official, placed a big question mark on the original transcript, next to Lattimore's point about collaborators in the Rhee regime. The transcript quotes Taylor as saying "cold prosperity sphere," obviously a transcriber's error, which I corrected in the quotation. On Lattimore's support for the U.S. role in the Korean War, see *New York Times,* Aug. 1, 1950.

19. *New York Times* editorials, April 5 and 19, 1950. Other responsible officials who held this "shocking view" were, for example, most of the high Army Department officials in 1948–49, who were ready to write off the ROK even if it meant a Communist takeover; Gen. Lawton Collins told the 1951 Senate MacArthur Hearings, in testimony deleted at the time, that Korea "has no particular military significance," and if the Soviets were fully to occupy the peninsula, Japan would be in little greater jeopardy than it already was from Vladivostok and the Shantung Peninsula.

20. McAuliffe (1978), 147.

21. Hodgson (1976), 89, 97.

22. Letter to the *New York Times,* July 10, 1950.

23. Interview with a Korean American who still wishes to remain nameless. This person also alleges that at least one mildly liberal, anti-Rhee Korean professor on the west coast lost his position after an FBI investigation, narrowly avoided deportation to Korea, and was stateless and prevented from getting a passport for many years. Several of the deported Koreans were connected with the leftist Korean newspaper published in Los Angeles, *Korean Independence.*

24. *U.S. News,* Sept. 29, 1950.

25. Oshinsky (1983), 180.

26. On Hoover, Willoughby, Whitney, and Smith helping McCarthy, see

Thomas C. Reeves, *The Life and Times of Joe McCarthy* (New York: Stein and Day, 1982), 318, 502; for the 1953 episode, see Willoughby Papers, box 23, John W. Jackson letters, written on Justice Department stationery to Willoughby and to Ho Shih-lai, both dated Oct. 16, 1953. The faked files (on Lattimore, John Service, and others) are discussed in Robert Newman, "Clandestine Chinese Nationalist Efforts to Punish Their American Detractors," *Diplomatic History* 7:3 (Summer 1983) 205–22.

27. Karl Wittfogel, *Oriental Despotism* (New Haven: Yale University Press, 1957).

28. Leon Trotsky, *Stalin* (New York: Stein and Day, 2nd ed., 1967), 1–2, 358. See also Stephen Cohen, *Bukharin and the Bolshevik Revolution* (New York: Vintage Books, 1979), 291, for Bukharin's depiction of Stalin as "a Genghis Khan"; also Isaac Deutscher, *Stalin: A Political Biography* (London: Oxford University Press, 1949), 472: Stalin was "primitive, oriental, but unfailingly shrewd."

29. Poppe's defection is discussed in more detail in Christopher Simpson, *Blowback.*

30. Perry Anderson, *Lineages of the Absolutist State* (London: Verso, 1974), 462–549.

31. See, for example, Chong-sik Lee, "Stalinism in the East: Communism in North Korea," in Robert Scalapino, ed., *The Communist Revolution in Asia* (Englewood Cliffs, N.J.: Prentice-Hall, 1969).

32. Kim Jong Il tries to get American attention "by appearing to be barmy—a gambit aided by the fact that he almost certainly is." Coll, "No Nukes," *New Yorker* (April 20, 2009), "Talk of the Town."

33. Daniel Sneider, "Let Them Eat Rockets," *New York Times* Op-Ed, April 8, 2009.

34. Martin (2004), 259.

35. Jameson (1981), 295–96, 298; see also Kantorowicz (1957), 4–14. For an excellent analysis of the nature of the North Korean regime see Heonik Kwon, "North Korea's Politics of Longing," *Japan Focus* (April 2009).

36. Quoted in Theodore Von Laue, *Why Lenin, Why Stalin, Why Gorbachev* (New York: HarperCollins, 1997), 182. See also 155.

CHAPTER 5: 38 DEGREES OF SEPARATION: A FORGOTTEN OCCUPATION

1. Akizuki Tatsuichiro, *Nagasaki 1945,* trans. Nagata Keiichi (New York: Quarter Books, 1981), 24–25, 31, 155.

2. Central Intelligence Agency, "Korea," SR-2, summer 1947, and "The Current Situation in Korea," ORE 15–48, March 18, 1948.

3. Sawyer (1962), 80–82.

4. Lowe (1997), 44.

5. The quotations and events in this section are drawn from military government reports from the time, cited in my *Origins of the Korean War,* vol. I (Princeton, N.J.: Princeton University Press, 1981), 298–304.

6. U.S. 6th Infantry Division Headquarters (Dec. 31, 1946), in XXIV Corps Historical File, NA.

7. Cumings (1981), 364.

8. Here I draw material from ch. 4, 161–86, in Soon Won Park, *Colonial Industrialization and Labor in Korea: The Onoda Cement Factory* (Cambridge, Mass.: Harvard East Asian Monographs, 1999).

9. Seong Nae Kim, "Lamentations of the Dead: The Historical Imagery of Violence on Cheju Island, South Korea," *Journal of Ritual Studies* 3:2 (Summer 1989), 253. See also John Merrill, "The Cheju-do Rebellion," *Journal of Korean Studies* 2 (1980), which gives a figure of 30,000 (194–95).

10. NA, USFIK 11071 file, box 62/96, transcript of Hodge monologue to visiting congressmen, Oct. 4, 1947; RG332, XXIV Corps Historical file, box 20, "Report of Special Investigation—Cheju-Do Political Situation," March 11, 1948, conducted by Lt. Col. Lawrence A. Nelson. Nelson was on Cheju from Nov. 12, 1947, to Feb. 28, 1948.

11. USFIK, G-2 Weekly Summary no. 116, Nov. 23–30, 1947; *Seoul Times,* June 15 and 18, 1950. These issues reported the results of a survey by a team of journalists from Seoul.

12. Seong Nae Kim, "The Cheju April Third Incident and Women: Trauma and Solidarity of Pain," paper presented at the Jeju 4.3 Conference, Harvard University, April 24–26, 2003.

13. *Seoul Times,* June 18, Aug. 6, Aug. 11, 1948; USFIK G-2 Intelligence Summary no. 144, June 11–18, 1948; NA, Office of the Chief of Military History, "History of the U.S. Army Forces in Korea" (HUSAFIK), vol. II, part 2, "Police and National Events, 1947–48." In a report to the National Assembly on the origins of the insurgency, Defense Minister Yi Pom-sok traced it to "the propaganda and plots of the so-called People's Republic which sprang up right after Liberation," which were "still in existence" on Cheju. (NA, 895.00 file, box 7127, Drumwright to State, enclosing Yi Pom-sok's December 1948 report.) But the usual Rhee line was to blame it on the North Koreans.

14. USFIK G-2 Intelligence Summaries nos.134–142, April 2–June 4, 1948; *Seoul Times,* April 7 and 8, 1948; HUSAFIK, "Police and National Events, 1947–48."

15. Carlisle Barracks, Rothwell Brown Papers, Brown to Hodge, "Report of Activities on Cheju-Do Island [*sic*] from 22 May 1948, to 30 June 1948."

16. Pyongyang, *Nodong Sinmun* (Worker's Daily, NDSM), Feb. 11, 1950. Cheju leftists and Communists never had effective relations with the North Koreans, and even today the remnant survivors of the Cheju insurgents in Osaka remain independent of the North, publishing accounts of the rebellion without taking a pro–Kim Il Sung line.

17. NA, RG94, Central Intelligence, entry 427, box no. 18343, 441st CIC detachment, report from Cheju of June 18, 1948.

18. NA, USFIK 11071 file, box 33, "Opinion on the Settlement of the Cheju Situation," July 23, 1948, by Ko Pyong-uk, KNP superintendent.

19. Rothwell Brown Papers, Brown to Hodge, "Report of Activities on Cheju-Do Island [*sic*] from 22 May 1948, to 30 June 1948"; *Seoul Times,* June 5 and 7, 1948. I have found no evidence of the return of Japanese officers, but that does not mean it did not happen.

20. *Seoul Times,* Aug. 6 and 11, 1948; G-2 Intelligence Summary no. 146, June 25–July 2, 1948; NA, RG338, KMAG file, box 5412, Roberts, "Weekly activities," Nov. 8, Nov. 15, Dec. 6, 1948. Roberts also said that rebels were burning villages, but it seems to have been the official authorities who did most of the burning.

21. USFIK, G-2 Intelligence Summary no. 154, Aug. 21–27, no. 159, Sept. 24–Oct. 1, no. 163, Oct. 22–29, 1948; NA, RG94, Central Intelligence, entry 427, box no. 18343, 441st CIC detachment monthly report, Oct. 21, 1948; 895.00 file, box no. 7127, Drumwright to State, Jan. 7 and 10, 1949.

22. NA, 895.00 file, box no. 7127, Drumwright to State, March 14, 1949; Muccio to State, April 18, 1949.

23. FO, F0317, piece no. 76258, Holt to Bevin, March 22, 1949.

24. NA, 895.00 file, box no. 7127, Drumwright to State, May 17, 1949; Muccio to State, May 13, 1949.

25. "The Background of the Present War in Korea," *Far Eastern Economic Review* (Aug. 31, 1950), 233–37; this account is by an anonymous but knowledgeable American who served in the occupation. See also Koh Kwang-il, "In Quest of National Unity," *Hapdong t'ongshin,* June 27, 1949, 149, quoted in *Sun'gan t'ongshin,* no. 34 (Sept. 1949), 1. Also NA, RG349, FEC G-2 Theater Intelligence, box 466, May 23, 1950, G-2 report on Cheju, which has the governor's figures. He put the preinsurgency island population at 400,000, which I think is high. For a detailed North Korean account, see Yi Sung-yop, "The Struggle of the Southern Guerrillas for Unification of the Homeland," *Kulloja* (The Worker), Jan. 1950, 18.

26. NA, 895.00 file, box 7127, account of a survey of Cheju by Capt. Harold Fischgrund of KMAG, in Drumwright to Muccio, Nov. 28,

1949. Fischgrund thought all members of the NWY should be removed from the island, but of course they were not.

27. NA, 795.00 file, box 4299, Drumwright to State, June 21, 1950; box 4268, Drumwright to Allison, Aug. 29, 1950, enclosing a survey, "Conditions on Cheju Island." See also *Korean Survey* (March 1954), 6–7. The Americans put Yi's death in June, but in awarding him a posthumous medal the North Koreans said he died in a guerrilla skirmish on the mainland in August 1949. See NDSM, Feb. 11, 1950.

28. Seong Nae Kim, "Lamentations of the Dead," 251–85.

29. "History of the Rebellion," USFIK 11017 file, box 77/96, packet of documents in "Operation Yousi [*sic*]."

30. "Operation Yousi," ibid., "G-3 to C/S," Oct. 20, 1948; "W.L. Roberts to CG, USAFIK," Oct. 20, 1948; "Capt. Hatcher to G-3," Oct. 21, 1948; "History of the Rebellion," USFIK 11071 file, box 77/96, KMAG HQ to Gen. Song Ho-song, Oct. 21, 1948. The message is unsigned, but was presumably from Roberts. This file contains numerous original messages from Korean military and police units to and from USAFIK headquarters; also many daily intelligence reports. On the American C-47s see 740.0019 file, box C-215, Muccio to State, May 3, 1949. KMAG was at that time called PMAG, since it was still "provisional."

31. Interview with Thames Television, Feb. 1987.

32. Hoover Institution, M. Preston Goodfellow Papers, box 1, draft of letter to Rhee, no date but late 1948.

33. NA, 895.00 file, box 7127, Drumwright to State, Feb. 11 and 21, 1949. In March 1949 Drumwright urged two vice-consuls to solicit political information from American missionaries:

> Emphasize, at all times, that the Mission is fully aware that the Missionaries' work is fully understood to be non-political. Intimate, however, that their integration into the local scene and their business throughout the countryside both make it inevitable (especially with their command of the Korean language) that considerable "political" information come [*sic*] to their attention even without conscious effort. In the work of the U.S. Government to fight Communism and keep the Korean Government strong, it must know what is going on outside of Seoul, and just this miscellaneous Missionary information is invaluable.

See NA, 895.00 file, box 7127, Drumwright directive included in Drumwright to State, March 17, 1949. See also ECA official Edgar A. J. Johnson's testimony to Congress on June 13, 1950, to the effect that the ROKA had killed five thousand guerrillas in the past year, and that it was "prepared to meet any challenge by North Korean forces" (quoted in *New York Times*, July 6, 1950).

34. "Military Studies on Manchuria."

35. Hugh Deane Papers, "Notes on Korea," March 20, 1948.
36. *New York Times,* March 6 and 15, 1950.
37. Paul Preston, Letter to the Editor, *Times Literary Supplement* (May 1, 2009), 6.
38. NA, 895.00 file, box 7127, Muccio to State, May 13, 1949; Drumwright to State, June 13, 1949.
39. NDSM, Feb. 6, 1950. Mount Songak is in the middle of Kaesong, and the 38th parallel cuts across it. When I visited Kaesong in 1987, this mountain was still pockmarked by the scars of artillery shells.
40. UN Archives, BOX DAG-1/2.1.2, box 3, account of briefing on June 15, 1949.
41. MacArthur Archives, RG9, box 43, Roberts to Department of the Army, Aug. 1, Aug. 9, 1949; *New York Times,* Aug. 5, 1949; NDSM, Feb. 6, 1950.
42. NA, 895.00 file, box 946, Muccio, memos of conversation on Aug. 13 and 16, 1949.
43. State Department official Niles Bond told Australian officials that Muccio and Roberts "were constantly warning the Koreans that such a step [an attack northward] would result in the stoppage of American aid, the withdrawal of the Military Mission," and other measures. See Washington to Canberra, memorandum 953, Aug. 17, 1949; also British Foreign Office (FO 317), Piece #76259, Holt to FO, Sept. 2, 1949.
44. Cumings (1990), 572–73, 582–85.
45. See documents II through VI translated and reprinted in *Cold War International History Project Bulletin,* no. 5 (Spring 1995), 6–9.
46. I have never seen such a high number. He may be including ethnic Koreans in China. Zhang (1995), 44–45.
47. Anyone who thinks they know exactly what happened in June 1950 is insufficiently well read in the documentation; there is still much more to be learned from Soviet, Chinese, and North and South Korean archives—and from the U.S. National Security Agency, which still has not declassified crucial signals intelligence on the Korean War.
48. Columbia University, Wellington Koo Papers, box 217, Koo Diaries, entry for Jan. 4, 1950. Goodfellow arrived in Seoul on September 27, 1949 (895.00 file, box 7127, Muccio to State, Oct. 7, 1949). He went back in December 1949, which is the recent visit referred to in the quotation.

CHAPTER 6: "THE MOST DISPROPORTIONATE RESULT": THE AIR WAR

1. Truman left office in 1952 with a 35 percent approval rating, but when he hit 23 percent earlier it was the lowest in recorded polling history, and it barely recovered thereafter. See Peter Baker, "Bush's Unpopularity Nears Historic Depths," *Washington Post,* republished in *Ann*

Arbor News (July 25, 2007), A8; also Casey (2008), 215, 292, 365. Bush subsequently went below Truman's margin in 2008.

2. Friedrich (2006), 14–17, 50, 52, 61–62, 71, 76. See also Eden (2004), 66, 78, and James (1993), 4.

3. Quoted in Friedrich (2006), 82, 485.

4. Princeton University, J. F. Dulles Papers, Curtis LeMay oral history, April 28, 1966. South Korean cities were bombed only when North Koreans or Chinese occupied them, and the destruction was much less than in the North. On the bombing as a war crime, see Walzer (1992), 155–56.

5. Crane (2000), 32–33, 66–68, 122–25, 133; Knox (1985), 552.

6. Lovett in Truman Library, Connelly Papers, "Notes on Cabinet Meetings," Sept. 12, 1952.

7. Hermann Knell, *To Destroy a City: Strategic Bombing and Its Human Consequences in World War II* (Cambridge, Mass.: Da Capo Press, 2003), 25, 334.

8. Crane (2000), 133.

9. Friedrich (2006), 85–87, 110, 151.

10. Hermann Lautensach, *Korea: A Geography Based on the Author's Travels and Literature*, trans. Katherine and Eckart Dege (Berlin: Springer-Verlag, 1945, 1988), 202.

11. Crane (2000), 160–64.

12. Cumings (1990), 750–51; Rhodes (1995), 448–51.

13. Samuel Cohen was a childhood friend of Herman Kahn; see Fred Kaplan, *The Wizards of Armageddon* (New York: Simon and Schuster, 1983), 220. On Oppenheimer and Project Vista, see Cumings (1990), 751–52; also David C. Elliot, "Project Vista and Nuclear Weapons in Europe," *International Security* 2:1 (Summer 1986), 163–83.

14. Cumings (1990), 752.

15. Dean (1954), 274.

16. Thames Television, transcript from the fifth seminar for *Korea: The Unknown War* (November 1986); Thames interview with Tibor Meray (also 1986).

17. Friedrich (2006), 75, 89; Knell (2003), 266; Crane (2000), 126; Foot (1990), 208; Crane (2000), 168–71.

18. Karig et al. (1952), 111–12.

19. Crane (2000), 168–71.

20. Knell (2003), 329.

CHAPTER 7: THE FLOODING OF MEMORY

1. Ernest J. Hopkins, ed., *The Civil War Stories of Ambrose Bierce* (Lincoln: University of Nebraska Press, 1970), 48. Here I draw partially on my

"Occurrence at Nogun-ri Bridge: An Inquiry into the History and Memory of a Civil War," *Critical Asian Studies* 33:4 (2001), 509–26.

2. Hanley et al. (2001), 236–37. I worked with this Associated Press team from time to time, and believe their investigative work deserved a Pulitzer Prize. But their book came out just as 9/11 happened, and got buried.

3. *New York Times,* Sept. 30, 1999.

4. Doug Struck, "U.S., South Korea Gingerly Probe the Past," *Washington Post* (Oct. 27, 1999), A-24.

5. John Osborne, "Report from the Orient—Guns Are Not Enough," *Life* (Aug. 21, 1950), 74–84.

6. Walter Karig, "Korea—Tougher Than Okinawa," *Collier's* (Sept. 23, 1950), 24–26. Gen. Lawton Collins remarked that Korea saw "a reversion to old-style fighting—more comparable to that of our own Indian frontier days than to modern war." (*New York Times,* Dec. 27, 1950.)

7. Eric Larrabee, "Korea: The Military Lesson," *Harper's* (Nov. 1950), 51–57.

8. Thompson, *Cry Korea,* 39, 44, 84, 114.

9. Quoted in Richard Falk, "The Vietnam Syndrome," *The Nation* (July 9, 2001), 22.

10. See Cumings (1981), 335–37.

11. *New York Times,* Aug. 2, 1950; Dean (1954), 49; Cumings (1990), 400.

12. "A Leader Turned Ghost," *New York Times* (July 22, 2008), A10. (Note that this AP report carried no byline.)

13. In Chongwon at least seven thousand people were murdered over a weeklong period. See Chae Sang-hun, "Unearthing War's Horrors Years Later in South Korea," *New York Times* (Dec. 3, 2007).

14. Winter (2006), 55–57.

15. South African statements quoted in Minow (1998), 55. See also her useful catalog of ways to achieve truth, justice, and reconciliation, 88.

16. London, *Daily Worker,* Aug. 9, 1950.

17. NRC, RG242, SA2009, item 6/70, KPA HQ, *Choson inmin ûn tosalja Mije wa Yi Sûng-man yokdodûl ûi yasujon manhaeng e pukssu harira* (The Korean people will avenge the beastly atrocities of the American imperialist butchers and the Syngman Rhee traitors), no date, but late 1950, 40–41. The *Haebang Ilbo* (Liberation Daily), a North Korean newspaper published in Seoul on Aug. 10, 1950, put the figure at four thousand.

18. Appleman (1961), 587–88, 599.

19. HST, PSF, "Army Intelligence—Korea," box 262, joint daily sitrep no. 6, July 2–3, 1950; HST, National Security Council (NSC) file, box 3, CIA report of July 3, 1950.

20. NA, 795.00 file, box 4267, London Embassy to State, Aug. 11, 1950; Public Record Office, London Foreign Office records, FO317, piece no. 84178, Tokyo Chancery to FO, Aug. 15, 1950; Gascoigne to FO, Aug. 15, 1950; Chancery to FO, Aug. 17, 1950. (J. Underwood must have been from the well-established Underwood missionary family in Korea.) Another British report said that when reporters photographed brutal beatings of prisoners by ROK police, American and ROK authorities prohibited publication of the photos (Chancery to FO, Sept. 13, 1950).

21. Col. Donald Nichols, *How Many Times Can I Die?* (Brooksville, Fla.: Brownsville Printing Co., 1981), cited in Korea Web Weekly, www .kimsoft.com. Nichols wrote, "The worst part about this whole affair was that I learned later that not all people killed were communists."

22. *The Crime of Korea* (1950), Armed Forces Screen Report, issue #125. No place of production, but such films were prepared in the Pentagon for public distribution.

23. *New York Times* (Sept. 30, 1999), A16. On police massacres of civilians more generally after the war broke out, see Chae Sang-hun, "Unearthing War's Horrors Years Later in South Korea," *New York Times* (Dec. 3, 2007).

24. Choe Sang-Hun, "South Korean Commission Details Civilian Massacres Early in Korean War," *New York Times* (Nov. 27, 2009), A5, A8.

25. Tokyo Australian mission to British Foreign Office, July 10, 1950 (courtesy Gavan McCormack); *New York Times,* July 1, 1950.

26. NRC, RG349, box 465, CIC report, Aug. 17, 1950. This report also said that, according to ROK officials, "approximately 80 percent of the South Korean population would offer no resistance to North Korean forces."

27. MA, RG6, box 60, G-2 report of July 22, 1950; NDSM, July 6, 1950; NA, State Department Office of Intelligence Research file, report no. 5299.17, July 16–17, 1950.

28. Cumings (1981), 172, 175, 504–5; Noble (1975), 26–27, 152, 253n; Sawyer (1962), 15.

29. Blair (1987), 141.

30. *Haebang ilbo,* July 29, 1950 (copies of which are available in the National Records Center, Record Group 242); *New York Times,* July 22, 1950. The diary is translated in MA, RG6, box 78, Allied Translator and Interpreter Service, issue no. 2, Oct. 5, 1950.

31. *New York Times,* July 14, 1950; interview with Keyes Beech, Thames Television, Feb. 1987; State Department, Office of Intelligence Research file, report no. 5299.22, July 21–22, 1950; also *New York Times,* July 26, 1950.

32. *New York Times,* Aug. 1 and 3, 1950; Appleman (1961), 206–7.

33. *New York Times,* July 11,1950; FO, FO317, piece no. 84178, Sawbridge to FO, July 25, 1950; *Manchester Guardian,* July 13, 1950; NRC, RG338, KMAG file, box 5418, report of Aug. 2, 1950. Most of the information and quotations about Kim are in Muccio's report, 795.00 file, box 4267, " 'Tiger' Kim vs. the Press," May 12, 1951. Muccio wrongly placed Kim in Pusan when the war began, and got the date of his removal wrong (saying it was July 7, 1950, when it was definitely after August 2). See also NA, USFIK 11071 file, box 65/96, Yosu rebellion packet; also "The Yosu Operation, Amphibious Stage," by Howard W. Darrow. At Yosu, Kim refused to follow the orders of two American advisers who told him not to try to land the 5th Regiment at Yosu; he tried to do so anyway, and failed. On the beheading incident, see NA, RG338, KMAG file, box 5418, entries for July 26 and Aug. 2, 1950. On Rhee and Tiger Kim, see Ridgway Papers, box 20, draft of a message Muccio planned to present to Rhee, May 3, 1951, chiding Rhee for relying on Tiger Kim and others, rather than the established agencies. On Kim and Emmerich in Pusan, see Charles J. Hanley and Jae-Soon Chang, "Korea Mass Executions," Associated Press (July 7, 2008), based on American documents found and declassified by the *Pusan Ilbo.*

34. See, for example, HST, PSF, CIA file, box 248, daily report for July 8, 1950; the North Korean document is in NA, RG242, SA2009, item 6/72, *Haksûp Chaeryojip.*

35. NA, 795.00 file, box 4269, MacArthur to Army, Sept. 1, 1950; this report mentioned but two incidents: one on July 10, where two Americans were found, and one on Aug. 17, where forty-one were killed. On the post-Inchon killings see *New York Times,* Sept. 30, 1950.

36. MA, RG6, box 78, ATIS issue no. 2, Oct. 5, 1950, document signed by Kim Chaek; issue no. 9, Nov. 27, 1950, document of Aug. 16, 1950. On July 26, the 715th KPA detachment also issued orders to stop incidents in which soldiers stole people's property and used it for themselves. See NA, RG242, SA2010, item 3/81, secret military order of July 26, 1950.

37. UNCURK, "Report on a Visit to Chunchon, Capital of Kangwon Province, Republic of Korea," Nov. 30, 1950; I am indebted to Gavan McCormack for this reference. See also *New York Times,* Sept. 29, 1950. On the movement northward, see MA, RG6, box 14, G-2 report of Oct. 16, 1950; RG349, CIC, Nov. 6, 1950 report. The latter said that hundreds and sometimes thousands of South Korean civilians moved north with the retreating KPA.

38. 795.00 file, box 4299, Drumwright to State, Oct. 13, 1950; box 4269, Emmons to Johnson, Nov. 13, 1950; Thompson (1951), 92; *New York Times,* Oct. 20, 1950.

39. NA, RG319, G-3 Operations file, box 122, UNC operations report for Nov. 16–30, 1950.

40. NA, RG338, KMAG file, box 5418, KMAG journal, entry for Oct. 3, 1950; Harold Noble Papers, Philip Rowe account of Oct. 11, 1950.

41. Handwritten minutes of a KWP meeting, apparently at a high level, Dec. 7, 1950, translated in MA, RG6, box 80, ATIS issue no. 29, March 17, 1951.

42. HST, PSF, NSC file, box 3, CIA report of Oct. 4, 1950; *New York Times,* Oct. 6 and 14, 1950.

43. War Crimes Division, Judge Advocate Section, *Extract of Interim Historical Report* (Korean Communication Zone, AP234, Cumulative to 30 June 1953), quoted in MacDonald (1986), 8, note 41.

44. Here I draw on Cumings (1990), and on Callum MacDonald, " 'So Terrible a Liberation'—The UN Occupation of North Korea," *Bulletin of Concerned Asian Scholars* 23:2 (April–June 1991), 3–19. Professor MacDonald cited NSC 81/1 in " 'So Terrible a Liberation,' " 6; also Truman Presidential Library, Matthew Connelly Papers, box 1, Acheson remarks in cabinet meeting minutes for Sept. 29, 1950.

45. FO, FO317, piece no. 84100, John M. Chang to Acheson, Sept. 21, 1950, relayed to the FO by the State Department; see also *Foreign Relations of the United States* (FR) (1950), 3: 1154–58, minutes of preliminary meetings for the September Foreign Ministers' Conference, Aug. 30, 1950.

46. A sixteen-page diary on American plans for military government in the North is available in Hoover Institution, Alfred Connor Bowman Papers (Bowman was then chief of the army's Military Government Division). American officers sought specifically to keep ROK officials out of this administration. See also M. Preston Goodfellow Papers, box 1, Goodfellow to Rhee, Oct. 3, 1950.

47. FO, FO317, piece no. 84072, Washington Embassy to FO, Nov. 10, 1950, enclosing State Department paper on the occupation. The State Department's John Allison told the British that Ben Limb's claim that the ROK government was "the only legitimate government of all Korea" was "in direct conflict with the position taken by the U.S. Government" and by the UN, both of which saw the ROK as having jurisdiction only in those areas where UNCOK observed elections. 795.00 file, box 4268, Allison to Austin, Sept. 27, 1950. On the UN resolution, see London *Times,* Nov. 16, 1950.

48. Rhee quoted by Hugh Baillie (the president of United Press International), in Baillie, *High Tension* (London: Harper, 1960), 267–68, as cited in MacDonald (1986), 8, note 51.

49. 795.00 file, box 4268, Durward V. Sandifer to John Hickerson, Aug. 31, 1950, top secret.

50. A State Department study dated Dec. 27, 1950, said that the ROK occupation included "the extension of the Tai Han Youth corps, the use of ROK CIC detachments, the use of ROK military police and railway guards, and some use of ROK police, particularly in the northeastern area." See MacDonald (1986), 10. This does not appear to include people whom the KNP specially recruited for the occupation.

51. NA, 795.00 file, box 4268, Acheson to Muccio, Oct. 12, 1950. Acheson wanted Muccio to assure that the KNP would operate under UN command. See also box 4299, Drumwright to State, Oct. 14, 1950; *New York Times,* Oct. 20, 1950.

52. *Manchester Guardian,* Dec. 4, 1950.

53. Ibid., handwritten FO notes on FK1015/303, U.S. Embassy press translations for Nov. 1, 1950; piece no. 84125, FO memo by R. Murray, Oct. 26, 1950; piece no. 84102, Franks memo of discussion with Rusk, Oct. 30, 1950; Heron in London *Times,* Oct. 25, 1950.

54. FO, FO317, piece no. 84073, Korea to FO, Nov. 23, 1950.

55. NA, RG338, KMAG file, box 5418, KMAG journal, entries for Nov. 5, 24, 25, and 30, 1950.

56. Thompson (1951), 274; NA, 795.00 file, box 4270, carrying UPI and AP dispatches dated Dec. 16, 17, and 18, 1950; FO317, piece no. 92847, original letter from Private Duncan, Jan. 4, 1951; Adams to FO, Jan. 8, 1951; UNCURK reports cited in Truman Presidential Library, PSF, CIA file, box 248, daily summary, Dec. 19, 1950. See also London *Times,* Dec. 18, 21, and 22, 1950.

57. Almond Papers, General Files, X Corps, "Appendix 3 Counterintelligence," Nov. 25, 1950; William V. Quinn Papers, box 3, X Corps periodic intelligence report dated Nov. 11, 1950. (Quinn was the X Corps G-2 chief.) Emphasis added.

58. FO, FO317, piece no. 84073, Tokyo to FO, Nov. 21, 1950.

59. Carlisle Military Barracks, William V. Quinn Papers, box 3, X Corps HQ, McCaffrey to Ruffner, Oct. 30, 1950; Ridgway Papers, box 20, highlights of a staff conference, with Ridgway and Almond present, Jan. 8, 1951.

60. MacDonald (1986), 13.

61. Ibid., 11.

62. Department of State documents, cited in ibid., 17, note 136, and other information cited on 18–19.

63. Hwang Sok-yong, *The Guest*, trans. Kyung-ja Chun and Maya West (New York: Seven Stories Press, 2007), 79–103, 203–6.

64. TRCK, www.jinsil.go.kr/english, Feb. 23, 2009.

65. Kwon (2008), 166; Cho (2008), 16.

66. In the words of Drew Faust, president of Harvard, foreword to Kwon (2006), xii.

67. Choe Myong-hui used this as the title of her monumental documentary of the murderous political trials of her hometown, Namwon. See *Honbul* (Fire Spirit), 3 vols. (Seoul, 1985–92).

68. Dr. Steven Kim, Truth and Reconciliation Commission, "Major Achievements and Further Agendas," December 2008, courtesy of *Japan Focus;* also Charles J. Hanley and Jae-Soon Chang, "Children Executed in 1950 South Korean Killings," Associated Press, Dec. 6, 2008.

CHAPTER 8: A "FORGOTTEN WAR" THAT REMADE THE UNITED STATES AND THE COLD WAR

1. Odd Arne Westad, *The Global Cold War: Third World Interventions and the Making of Our Times* (Cambridge, U.K.: Cambridge University Press, 2005), 66, 416, note 58.

2. NA, 740.0019 file, box 3827, Marshall's note to Acheson of Jan. 29, 1947, attached to Vincent to Acheson, Jan. 27, 1947; RG335, Secretary of the Army File, box 56, Draper to Royall, Oct. 1, 1947. Here I draw on parts of Cumings, *Dominion from Sea to Sea: Pacific Ascendancy and American Power* (New Haven, Conn.: Yale University Press, 2009).

3. C. Wright Mills, *The Power Elite* (New York: Oxford University Press, 1956), 175–76; Marcus Cunliffe, *Soldiers and Civilians: The Martial Spirit in America, 1775–1865* (Boston: Little, Brown, 1968), ch. 1; E. J. Hobsbawm, *The Age of Empire, 1875–1914* (New York: Pantheon Books, 1987), 351; Sherry (1995), 5.

4. Russell F. Weigley, *History of the United States Army* (New York: Macmillan, 1967), 475, 486, 568; Gerald T. White, *Billions for Defense: Government Financing by the Defense Plant Corporation During World War II* (University: University of Alabama Press, 1980), 1–2; Davis, "The Next Little Dollar: The Private Governments of San Diego," in Mike Davis, Kelly Mayhew, and Jim Miller, *Under the Perfect Sun: The San Diego Tourists Never See* (New York: New Press, 2003), 65.

5. *New York Times*, Op-Ed, March 14, 1994.

6. Quoted in Cumings (1990), 55.

7. Cumings (1990), 171–75.

8. Davis, "The Next Little Dollar," 66–67, 78; Roger W. Lotchin, *Fortress California, 1910–1961: From Warfare to Welfare* (Urbana: University of Illinois Press, 1992), 65, 73, 184, 23; Neal R. Peirce, *The Pacific States of*

America: People, Politics, and Power in the Five Pacific Basin States (New York: W. W. Norton, 1972), 165–69.

9. In May 1966 de Gaulle said he wanted "full sovereignty [over] French territory" and so asked Washington to take American forces and bases home. See Chalmers Johnson, *The Sorrows of Empire: Militarism, Secrecy, and the End of the Republic* (New York: Henry Holt, 2004), 194.

10. Eisenhower quoted in Sherry (1995), 233–35.

CHAPTER 9: REQUIEM: HISTORY IN THE TEMPER OF RECONCILIATION

1. *New York Times,* Sept. 30, 1999, A16.

2. David R. McCann's translation, in *The Middle Hour: Selected Poems of Kim Chi Ha* (Stanfordville, N.Y.: Human Rights Publishing Group, 1980), 51.

3. Knox (1985), 82–83, 449.

4. Nicolai Ourossoff, "The Mall and Dissonant Voices of Democracy," *New York Times* (Jan. 16, 2009), C30.

5. Sheila Miyoshi Jager and Jiyul Kim, "The Korean War After the Cold War: Commemorating the Armistice Agreement," in Jager and Mitter (2007), 242.

6. Chinoy (2008), 68.

7. Bruce B. Auster and Kevin Whitelaw, "Pentagon Plan 5030, a New Blueprint for Facing Down North Korea," *U.S. News & World Report* (July 21, 2003); see also Chinoy (2008), 234.

8. President Roh Moo Hyun, "On History, Nationalism and a Northeast Asian Community," *Global Asia,* April 16, 2007.

9. Choe Sang-hun, "A Korean Village Torn Apart from Within Mends Itself," *New York Times* (Feb. 21, 2008), A4.

10. Nietzsche (1983), 88.

FURTHER READING

THE KOREAN WAR

Acheson, Dean (1969). *Present at the Creation: My Years in the State Department.* New York: W. W. Norton & Company.

Appleman, Roy (1961). *South to the Naktong, North to the Yalu.* Washington, D.C.: Office of the Chief of Military History.

Baik Bong (1973). *Kim Il Sung: Biography I—From Birth to Triumphant Return to the Homeland.* Pyongyang: Foreign Languages Press.

Biderman, Albert D., and Samuel M. Meyers, eds. (1968). *Mass Behavior in Battle and Captivity: The Communist Soldier in the Korean War.* Chicago: University of Chicago Press.

Blair, Clay (1987). *The Forgotten War: America in Korea 1950–1953.* New York: Times Books.

Bradley, Omar N., with Clay Blair (1983). *A General's Life: An Autobiography of a General of the Army.* New York: Simon and Schuster.

Casey, Stephen (2008). *Selling the Korean War: Propaganda, Politics, and Public Opinion in the United States, 1950–1953.* New York: Oxford University Press.

Chen Jian (1996). *China's Road to the Korean War.* New York: Columbia University Press.

Chinoy, Mike (2008). *Meltdown: The Inside Story of the North Korean Nuclear Crisis.* New York: St. Martin's Press.

Cho, Grace M. (2008). *Haunting the Korean Diaspora: Shame, Secrecy, and the Forgotten War.* Minneapolis: University of Minnesota Press.

Cotton, James, and Ian Neary, eds. (1989). *The Korean War in History.* Atlantic Highlands, N.J.: Humanities Press International.

Crane, Conrad C. (2000). *American Airpower Strategy in Korea, 1950–1953.* Lawrence: University Press of Kansas.

Cumings, Bruce (1981). *The Origins of the Korean War, I: Liberation and the Emergence of Separate Regimes, 1945–1947.* Princeton, N.J.: Princeton University Press.

——— (1990). *The Origins of the Korean War, II: The Roaring of the Cataract, 1947–1950.* Princeton, N.J.: Princeton University Press.

Dean, William F. (1954). *General Dean's Story,* as told to William L. Worden. New York: The Viking Press.

Foot, Rosemary (1990). *A Substitute for Victory: The Politics of Peacemaking at the Korean Armistice Talks.* Ithaca, N.Y.: Cornell University Press.

——— (1987). *The Wrong War.* Ithaca, N.Y.: Cornell University Press.

Fulton, Bruce, Ju-Chan Fulton, and Bruce Cumings (2009). *The Red Room: Stories of Trauma in Contemporary Korea.* Honolulu: University of Hawaii Press.

Gardner, Lloyd, ed. (1972). *The Korean War.* New York: New York Times Company.

Goldstein, Donald, and Harry Maihafer (2000). *The Korean War.* Washington, D.C.: Brassey's.

Goncharov, Sergei N., John W. Lewis, and Xue Litai (1993). *Uncertain Partners: Stalin, Mao, and the Korean War.* Stanford, Calif.: Stanford University Press.

Ha Jin (2004). *War Trash.* New York: Vintage Books.

Halberstam, David (2007). *The Coldest Winter: America and the Korean War.* New York: Hyperion.

Han Hong-koo (1999). "Kim Il Sung and the Guerrilla Struggle in Eastern Manchuria." Ph.D. diss., University of Washington, 1999.

Hanley, Charles J., Sang-Hun Choe, and Martha Mendoza (2001). *The Bridge at No Gun Ri: A Hidden Nightmare from the Korean War.* New York: Henry Holt and Company.

Hastings, Max (1987). *The Korean War.* London: Michael Joseph.

Henderson, Gregory (1968). *Korea: The Politics of the Vortex.* Cambridge, Mass.: Harvard University Press.

Hodgson, Godfrey (1976). *America in Our Time: From World War II to Nixon—What Happened and Why.* New York: Doubleday & Co.

Hooker, John (1989). *Korea: The Forgotten War.* North Sydney, Australia: Time-Life Books.

Horwitz, Dorothy G., ed. (1997). *We Will Not Be Strangers: Korean War Letters Between a M.A.S.H. Surgeon and His Wife,* foreword by James I. Matray. Urbana and Chicago: University of Illinois Press.

Hwang Sok-yong (2007). *The Guest,* trans. Kyung-ja Chun and Maya West. New York: Seven Stories Press.

James, D. Clayton (1993). *Refighting the Last War: Command and Crisis in Korea, 1950–1953.* New York: The Free Press.

Kang, Kyong-ae (1934, 2009). *From Wonso Pond,* trans. Samuel Perry. New York: Feminist Press.

Karig, Walter, Malcolm W. Cagle, and Frank A. Manson (1952). *Battle Report: The War in Korea.* New York: Rinehart.

Kaufman, Burton I. (1986). *The Korean War: Challenges in Crisis, Credibility, and Command.* Philadelphia: Temple University Press.

Kim Il Sung. *With the Century.* Pyongyang: Foreign Languages Press, multiple volumes.

Knightly, Phillip (1975). *The First Casualty: From the Crimea to Vietnam—The War Correspondent as Hero, Propagandist, and Myth Maker.* New York: Harcourt Brace Jovanovich.

Knox, Donald (1985). *The Korean War: Pusan to Chosin—An Oral History.* New York: Harcourt Brace Jovanovich.

Lankov, Andrei (2002). *From Stalin to Kim Il Sung: The Formation of North Korea, 1945–1960.* New Brunswick, N.J.: Rutgers University Press.

Lee, Chongsik (1966). *Counterinsurgency in Manchuria: The Japanese Experience.* Santa Monica, Calif.: The RAND Corporation.

Linn, Brian McAllister (1997). *Guardians of Empire: The U.S. Army and the Pacific, 1902–1940.* Chapel Hill: University of North Carolina Press.

Lowe, Peter (1997). *The Origins of the Korean War,* 2nd ed. New York: Longman.

MacDonald, Callum (1986). *Korea: The War Before Vietnam.* New York: Macmillan.

Martin, Bradley K. (2004). *Under the Loving Care of the Fatherly Leader: North Korea and the Kim Dynasty.* New York: Thomas Dunne Books.

Matray, James I. (1985). *The Reluctant Crusade: American Foreign Policy in Korea, 1941–1950.* Honolulu: University of Hawaii Press.

Meade, E. Grant (1951). *American Military Government in Korea.* New York: King's Crown Press.

Merrill, John (1989). *Korea: The Peninsular Origins of the War.* Wilmington: University of Delaware Press.

Noble, Harold Joyce (1975). *Embassy at War,* ed. and introduced by Frank Baldwin. Seattle: University of Washington Press.

Offner, Arnold (2002). *Another Such Victory: President Truman and the Cold War, 1945–1953.* Stanford, Calif.: Stanford University Press.

Roth, Philip (2008). *Indignation.* New York: Random House.

Salter, James (1997). *Burning the Days: Recollection.* New York: Vintage Books.

Sawyer, Major Robert K. (1962). *Military Advisors in Korea: KMAG in Peace and War.* Washington, D.C.: Office of the Chief of Military History.

Stone, I. F. (1952). *The Hidden History of the Korean War.* New York: Monthly Review Press.

Stueck, William (1995). *The Korean War: An International History.* Princeton, N.J.: Princeton University Press.

——— (1981). *The Road to Confrontation.* Chapel Hill: University of North Carolina Press.

Suh Dae-sook (1988). *Kim Il Sung: The North Korean Leader.* New York: Columbia University Press.

Tanaka, Yuki, and Marilyn B. Young, eds. (2009). *Bombing Civilians: A Twentieth-Century History.* New York: The New Press.

Thompson, Reginald (1951). *Cry Korea.* London: Macdonald & Company.

Tomedi, Rudy (1993). *No Bugles, No Drums: An Oral History of the Korean War.* New York: John Wiley & Sons.

Weintraub, Stanley (2000). *MacArthur's War: Korea and the Undoing of an American Hero.* New York: The Free Press.

Zhang, Shu Guang (1995). *Mao's Military Romanticism: China and the Korean War, 1950–1953.* Lawrence: University Press of Kansas.

History and Memory

Chirot, Daniel, and Clark McCauley (2006). *Why Not Kill Them All? The Logic and Prevention of Mass Political Murder.* Princeton, N.J.: Princeton University Press.

Eden, Lynn (2004). *Whole World on Fire: Organizations, Knowledge, and Nuclear Weapons Devastation.* Ithaca, N.Y.: Cornell University Press.

Foucault, Michel (1972). *The Archaeology of Knowledge and the Discourse on Language,* trans. A. M. Sheridan Smith. New York: Pantheon Books.

Friedlander, Saul (1979). *When Memory Comes,* trans. Helen R. Lane. Madison: University of Wisconsin Press.

Friedrich, Jörg (2006). *The Fire: The Bombing of Germany, 1940–1945,* trans. Allison Brown. New York: Columbia University Press.

Fussell, Paul (1975). *The Great War and Modern Memory.* New York: Oxford University Press.

Hopkins, Ernest J., ed. (1970). *The Civil War Stories of Ambrose Bierce.* Lincoln: University of Nebraska Press.

Jager, Sheila Miyoshi, and Rana Mitter, eds. (2007). *Ruptured Histories: War, Memory, and the Post–Cold War in Asia.* Cambridge, Mass.: Harvard University Press.

Jameson, Fredric (1981). *The Political Unconscious: Narrative as a Socially Symbolic Act.* Ithaca, N.Y.: Cornell University Press.

Kantorowicz, Ernst H. (1957). *The King's Two Bodies: A Study in Medieval Political Theology.* Princeton, N.J.: Princeton University Press.

Koselleck, Reinhart (2004). *Futures Past: On the Semantics of Historical Time,* trans. Keith Tribe. New York: Columbia University Press.

Kwon, Heonik (2006). *After the Massacre: Commemoration and Consolation in Ha My and My Lai.* Berkeley: University of California Press.

——— (2008). *Ghosts of War in Vietnam.* New York: Cambridge University Press.

Maier, Charles S. (1997). *The Unmasterable Past: History, Holocaust, and German National Identity.* Cambridge, Mass.: Harvard University Press.

McAuliffe, Mary Sperling (1978). *Crisis on the Left: Cold War Politics and American Liberals, 1947–1954.* Amherst: University of Massachusetts Press.

Minow, Martha (1998). *Between Vengeance and Forgiveness: Facing History After Genocide and Mass Violence.* Boston: Beacon Press.

Nietzsche, Friedrich (1966). *Beyond Good and Evil: Prelude to a Philosophy of the Future,* trans. Walter Kaufmann. New York: Vintage Books.

——— (1974). *The Gay Science,* trans. Walter Kaufmann. New York: Vintage Books.

——— (1967). *On the Genealogy of Morals,* trans. Walter Kaufmann. New York: Vintage Books.

——— (1983). *Untimely Meditations,* trans. R. J. Hollingdale. New York: Cambridge University Press.

Oshinsky, David M. (1983). *A Conspiracy So Immense: The World of Joe McCarthy.* New York: The Free Press.

Rosenberg, Tina (1995). *The Haunted Land: Facing Europe's Ghosts After Communism.* New York: Vintage Books.

Sherry, Michael S. (1995). *In the Shadow of War: The United States Since the 1930s.* New Haven: Yale University Press.

Soh, C. Sarah (2008). *Sexual Violence and Postcolonial Memory in Korea and Japan.* Chicago: University of Chicago Press.

Walzer, Michael (1992). *Just and Unjust Wars: A Moral Argument with Historical Illustrations,* 2nd ed. New York: Basic Books.

Wilshire, Bruce (2006). *Get 'Em All! Kill 'Em!: Genocide, Terrorism, Righteous Communities.* New York: Lexington Books.

Winter, Jay (2006). *Remembering War: The Great War Between Memory and History in the Twentieth Century.* New Haven, Conn.: Yale University Press.

———— (1995). *Sites of Memory, Sites of Mourning: The Great War in European Cultural History.* New York: Cambridge University Press.

Yamamuro Shin'ichi (2006). *Manchuria Under Japanese Domination,* trans. Joshua A. Fogel. Philadelphia: University of Pennsylvania Press.

INDEX

resistance, 46; and impact of Korean War, 209, 216–17; and importance of army, 56–57; and Inchon, 19; Japanese hunt for, 53–54; Kim Jong Il compared with, 97, 98; and "king's two bodies" concept, 98; and KPA, 56–57; and last major North Korean offensive, 19; in Manchuria, 44, 45, 51–55, 141; media stories about, 77, 81, 97; and North Korean push south, 17; and POW camps, 76; reputation of, 53; rumors about, 46, 77, 81; and Sino-Korean relations, 52–53; Soviet/Stalin relations with, 57–58, 71, 144, 208; as starting Korean War, 64; stereotyping of, 97, 99; and UN forces in North Korea, 22–23; and U.S. "exit strategy," 233; and U.S. views of Korean War, 6; war plans/goals of, 21, 208

Kim Jong Il, 45, 97, 98, 232, 241
Kim Paek-il, 132, 183, 184, 185
Kim Sok, 115, 116
Kim Sok-won, 44, 53–54, 140–42
"king's two bodies" concept, 98
Kishi Nobosuke, 39, 43, 44
KNP. *See* National Police, Korean
Korea/Koreans: anti-colonialism in, 215; anti-Japanese feelings in, 8, 43–47; aristocracy in, 4; brutality of, 134; civil war in, 35, 64–67, 79–80, 136, 139, 146, 226, 242–43; disunity in, 55; division of, 46–47, 103–4, 109; G.I. views of, 14, 180; history of, 3–4; image/stereotypes of, 4–5, 74; Lattimore views about, 88–91; liberation from Japanese of, 171; modernization of, 47, 105; political culture/life in, 98–99, 106–8, 171–72; postwar leaders for, 106; Rhee pleas for unification of, 6–7; social structure in, 4, 65, 137; Soviet evacuation of, 6; trusteeship for, 105–6, 109, 232; U.S. commitment to defense of, 72; U.S. lack of understanding of, 80, 232; U.S. occupation of, 106, 109–10, 111–12, 113–18; U.S. policy toward, 72, 105–6, 111–12, 208–11; U.S. visions of democracy in, 5; women in,

41–43; during World War II, 4–5. *See also* Korean War; North Korea; South Korea; *specific person or topic*
Korean Democratic Party, 182
Korean Economic Mission, 8
Korean People's Army. *See* KPA
Korean Truth and Reconciliation Commission (KTRC), 173, 178, 201–3, 225–26
Korean Truth Commission on Civilian Massacres, 201
Korean War: air war in, 29–30, 33–34, 147, 149–61; American and Korean scholars' views about, 226, 228; American defections in, 79; armistice in, 34–35, 239; beginning of, 5–16, 44–47, 64, 65, 71, 91, 143–45, 146, 238, 241; casualties in, 9, 19, 21, 35, 243; as civil war, 35, 64–67, 79–80, 226, 228, 242–43; and collapse of resistance in South, 11; ending/"exit strategy" for, 64, 233, 241; as "forgotten war," 62, 63, 64, 120, 203, 207, 228, 242; goals of, 207–8; impact on U.S. and Cold War of, 207–21; importance of, 243; and invasion of South Korea, 9, 16–17, 18–19, 142, 144, 179, 180; as "limited war," 79, 228; in literature, 67–76; as ongoing war, 231–33; origins of, 104–5, 226; physical sites marking, 230–31; as police action, 228; reevaluation of, 226–31; as solving nothing, 35; suspension of, 31–35; time frame for Americans of, 65; truce talks in, 31–35; and UN forces in North Korea, 22–31, 71; as undeclared war, 35; as "unknown war," 63, 79, 228; unpopularity of, 149, 229; U.S. entry into, 11–13, 64, 66, 238; as U.S. success or failure, 228–31; U.S. views about, 65–66; Vietnam War compared with, 5, 35, 65, 67, 207; who started the, 64, 65–66; World War II compared with, 17, 22, 35, 67, 169–70; World War II generals in, 229–30. *See also specific person or topic*
Korean War Memorial, Seoul, 230–31
Korean War Memorial, U.S., 230

Bruce Cumings is the Gustavus F. and Ann M. Swift Distinguished Service Professor in History at the University of Chicago and specializes in modern Korean history, international history, and East Asian–American relations.